Praise for *In Clive's Footsteps* by Peter Holt includes:

'Sheer Gusto . . . Holt's creditable debut in Paul Theroux and Jonathan Raban Territory'   *Daily Express*

'A true gem of a travel book'   *Western Mail*

'Holt's eye for human oddities and his sense of the past in India are razor-sharp'   *Observer*

'Highly entertaining . . . clearly delights those he meets as successfully as he does the reader'   *Times Literary Supplement*

Stars Of India

Stars
of
India

Travels in Search of Astrologers
and Fortune-Tellers

PETER HOLT

MAINSTREAM
PUBLISHING

EDINBURGH AND LONDON

For Sarah

First published in Great Britain in 1998 by
MAINSTREAM PUBLISHING COMPANY (EDINBURGH) LTD
7 Albany Street
Edinburgh EH1 3UG

This edition 1998

ISBN 1 84018 003 X

A catalogue record for this book is available from the British Library

Typeset in Palatino and Present
Printed and bound in Great Britain by Butler and Tanner Ltd, Frome

The astral sage Garga, who lived around 2,000 years ago, proclaimed, 'As the night without a light, as the sky without the sun, so is a king without an astrologer: like a blind man he erreth on the road.'

Contents

Acknowledgements

Numerous people gave me help and encouragement while I was writing this book. Most of them are mentioned in the following chapters with a few exceptions: Joshua Kopraparambil for his hospitality in Kerala, Ivan P. Cherry in Bombay, Valmik Thapar in Delhi and the Naryan family in Madras. Thank you also to historian Patrick Curry for providing me with background material, and to distinguished illusionist Simon Drake for urging me not to be taken in by so-called occult events when they could simply be very clever magic tricks.

And a special thanks to my Indian astrological 'guru', the supremely brilliant K.N. Rao who gave me so many of his contacts and so much of his time.

Introduction

I was twenty when I first visited a fortune-teller. I'd been having a tough time romantically and wanted reassurance that the girl of my dreams was about to step into my life. I booked a session with an elderly lady clairvoyant in London. She came recommended by a friend, who insisted she was marvellous and very accurate.

I can recall little of the visit except that my soothsayer was a creepy old dear who lived in a mouldy basement somewhere off Marble Arch. She rabbited on for over an hour and I remember more the smell of cats than what she told me. She certainly did nothing to lift my spirits.

After that my experiences with prediction remained confined to scanning the horoscope pages in newspapers, a habit I have come to realise is utterly ludicrous. How on earth can you divide humanity into twelve sections and then make predictions on the basis of the sun sign alone?

My fascination with more sophisticated methods of prediction was sparked off in 1988 when I visited India for the first time for a journey on the trail of my ancestor Robert Clive, founder of British India.

During that expedition my head had been full of pukka sahibs and eighteenth-century colonial dreams. But mystical India began to rub off on me and while staying in the old French colony of Pondicherry I took a day trip thirty miles south to the town of Vaithishwaran Koil to the home of a 'Nadi' reader called Mr Chellian. An Indian friend assured me that Mr Chellian had a solid reputation for accurate predictions and I was mildly curious to listen to what he could tell me about my future.

The Nadi is one of the world's most extraordinary methods of astrological prediction. I go into it at some length in this book, but briefly, it involves the astrologer reading the client's future off an ancient Sanskrit manuscript.

Mr Chellian told me some startlingly accurate things about my past and my family. And from that moment I was hooked. I wanted to discover more about methods of divination in the country which claims to have perfected the art of prediction. So a few years later, I returned to India to investigate the cosmic forces that make the subcontinent tick. This book is the result of that journey.

1

Somnath – Where Man First Walked on Earth

The early evening sun cast an amber glow across Santi Lal's face as he reflected on his life as a gambler.

'Astrology has shown me the right path,' he said. 'You see, I am a very educated graduate in commerce, but that did not mean business was the right life for me. I started a roofing nails factory in Bombay. Within three years I lost three hundred thousand rupees. Then I tried a chemicals business and I lost another twenty thousand rupees. Then medical goods and I lost that business as well.

'After all this I am thinking that commerce is not in my nature. Then I go to an astrologer. He studies my chart and he says that speculation and gambling is good for me. What have I to lose? I start gambling and immediately I make money. I would be insane not to believe in astrology.'

I had drifted into conversation with Santi Lal a few minutes after strolling into the temple complex of Somnath. This Hindu pilgrimage site lies like a citadel to the gods behind high ramparts overlooking the Arabian Sea at the southern end of the nose of Gujarat.

It was the end of a steamy day. The temple grounds were crowded with worshippers gathering to watch the sunset before the evening puja (prayers). Crouching fathers smoothed tablecloths onto the ground while their wives produced picnics from raffia baskets. Little girls in their best frocks shrieked at pigeons dive-bombing from the temple tower. Their brothers, in shorts and droopy knee-length socks, idly threw stones at scavenging stray dogs who came too close to the food. Lovers took turns to snap chocolate-box photographs of each other as the soft underbelly of the clouds around the sun changed to pink. Down on the shore, men in rolled-up trousers linked arms with their wives, the hems of their saris damp from paddling in the roaring surf. Boys dug crabs from deep holes in the sand. They played a heartless game, tying pieces of string to the creatures' legs and dragging them along the beach.

Santi Lal and I were perched on the bastion wall. It was an uncomfortable place to talk. There was a sheer drop behind us and I have never liked heights. As tiny children tried to scramble onto the parapet, anxious mothers pulled them back for fear they would tumble a hundred feet to the grey sands below.

Teenaged boys pressed awkwardly around us. They stared long and hard at me through serious, narrow eyes. I was a rare foreign visitor to the temple. When they had gained enough confidence to speak, they broke into smiles and tried to sell me packets of peanuts or make me give them cigarettes.

Santi Lal surveyed the family rituals being played out before us. 'Notice the smiles,' he said. 'Western people have the smile of the Mona Lisa which isn't really a smile at all. In India you will see healthy laughing smiles and pure hearts. The people may be biologically weak because they are not getting proper food, but they have low stress because they trust in God. Mother will always trust her son; wife will trust her husband to do well for her. In the West there is separation between woman and man. But in India we believe that marriage is made in heaven, not by man.'

Santi Lal was in his fifties. He was a short man with white hair who brought expression to his words by rolling his eyes. He was dressed in blue shirt and grey trousers. A regular visitor to Somnath, he was the curious spiritual blend that one comes to expect in India. For six months each year he lived in ashrams at Hindu temples around the country. The rest of the time he stayed in Bombay, earning a living by gambling at the racetrack and speculating on the stock market.

'One-day cricket matches are good too.'

'Cricket?'

'Oh yes, the planets have a big influence on cricket. Perhaps that is why us Indians are so good at it.' He wiped a palm across his greying beard. 'Last week I bet that England would beat Pakistan. I won a thousand rupees. God and his stars never get it wrong. I will celebrate my win with prayers in the temple this evening.'

I asked him if he really believed that share prices were governed by the stars. He shrugged. 'Well, there seems to be some connection between Mars and Saturn whenever there is a bull on the market. And

Jupiter is in retrograde at the moment, so there's not much point in putting on big money. Wait for Mars and Rahu.[1] That will send prices up.'

'So you've made good money from this system?'

'Sometimes. But the trouble is, the stockbrokers are all studying the same planetary movements, so everyone is thinking the same way.'

'Stockbrokers in London or on Wall Street would think you're all completely mad.'

'People in the West are too straightforward, everything is too scientific. A few mysteries never hurt anyone.'

Somnath seemed like a good place to start my journey. According to Hindu mythology, the temple is the oldest place in creation. It is literally the place where man first walked on earth. A visit to Somnath is essential for development of the soul and Hindus believe that it should be the first pilgrimage destination of their lives.

Santi Lal explained the story. Daksha Prajapti, a priest in the court of Brahma, the Hindu lord of creation, had twenty-seven[2] daughters. The girls were all married to Soma, the Moon God. The most beautiful daughter was Rohini, and her charms so bowled over Soma that he gave her all his attention to the exclusion of the others. The jealous sisters complained to their father, who threatened to punish his son-in-law if he did not mend his ways. Soma ignored the warning, so Daksha cursed him with the words: 'Thou shalt wane.'

Soma developed leprosy and, day by day, he began to lose his light. In an effort to overcome the disease, he performed various sacrifices, but still he grew increasingly yellow. Eventually his wives took pity on him and told Daksha that the punishment was too severe. Daksha was unable to lift the curse, but he could mitigate it. So now, although the moon still disappears every two weeks, it gradually recovers its original silvery sheen within the next fortnight.

....

[1] Rahu is the Indian name for the shadow planet known in Western astrology as the north lunar node or the Dragon's Head. The south node, or Dragon's Tail, is called Ketu. Traditionally, Indian astrologers regard Rahu and Ketu as of the utmost importance. Otherwise they use only the visible planets, ignoring Neptune, discovered only in the last century, and Pluto, first sighted in 1930. They are discounted on the grounds that they are both too far from Earth to have any significant effect.

....

[2] Symbolising the twenty-seven constellations and the twenty-seven days of the sidereal circumambulation of the moon.

But Daksha imposed a condition. He insisted that Soma repent by leaving the heavens and taking a bath in the sea. Soma was so relieved to have been let off the hook that he built a temple of gold at what is now Somnath. He dedicated Somnath to the most powerful of the Hindu gods, Lord Shiva, and created Brahmin priests, the first men on earth, to tend the shrine. The story became legend; and the ancient rishis (holy men) of India were to claim that, of all the heavenly bodies, it is the moon that exercises the greatest influence over the evolution of mankind.

More earthly historians believe that the Somnath temple dates from around the first century when it was acclaimed as the richest place of worship in the world. Thanks to centuries of looting and destruction by Moslem invaders, the complex was rebuilt five times. After being sacked yet again in 1706, the temple lay in ruins until 1950 when the entire site was reconstructed.

There are no gold walls at Somnath now, but in keeping with the legend, the façade appears golden at sunset. As Santi Lal talked, the dying sun, the father of the stars and the giver of life to all things, spilled orange on to the mellowed stones. I remarked how sensible the Hindus were to have a site of creation. 'I wonder why the Christian church has never promoted a place as the actual Garden of Eden.'

'Yes, that's something I've never been able to understand,' Santi Lal agreed.

If the power of the planets remains a mystery, so also does the origin of astrology. The Hindus claim it was they who started it all; or rather their gods. The Hindus say that astrology originated with Brahma, the creator, who taught it to Surya, the Sun god. From Surya, the knowledge was passed down, through a line of divine teachers, to a sage called Bhrigu, the first human being to learn astrology. Even today in India you will find astrologers using a manual called the *Bhrigu Samhita*. (Samhita means 'collection' in Sanskrit.) It is not known whether or not this is Bhrigu's original text.

The official line taken in history books is rather different. They record that the Chaldeans, one of the Mesopotamian peoples, were the first to tap into the force of the cosmos around 3000 BC. Their findings were then collated by the Greek, Ptolemy, whose four-volume *Tetrabiblos* was for centuries the most influential astrological textbook. Aha, say the Hindus, what else would you expect to read in *western* history books? Of course, western historians want to credit the West for the origins of astrology. But why does the West not admit that the ancient holy men of India were practising astral divination long before the Chaldeans?[1]

The Indians point to one of their most sacred texts, an astrological treatise by the sage Parasara which they claim was written pre-3000 BC – a much revised version is still the most widely used astrological handbook in India today. (Beware! Parasara claims that the gods sent him a message warning that sceptics who dismiss astrology as nonsense without trying to understand it, will go to hell and will be reborn blind.)

The Indians also remind us that the ancients had a word for astrology, or rather, two words: *jyotisha sastra*, meaning literally in Sanskrit 'the science of light'; an astrologer is a *jyotish*. This can either be taken as the light emitting from the stars, or, metaphorically, as the light thrown on the dark recesses of the future.

The Indians have a hard task convincing the rest of the world that they were the first civilisation to realise that the planets affect our lives. Apart from the Parasara text, the alleged date of which is regarded with great scepticism by western historians, there is virtually no documented astrological evidence. The country's ancient history was based on the oral tradition and little was written down.

Not surprising, argue the Indians.

The pioneering Hindu astrologers of ancient times were mostly illiterate. They practised quietly in remote rural villages and handed down their findings by word of mouth. Their discoveries eventually filtered through to the West where they were picked up by the Chaldeans.

Perhaps we will never know the true answer – although Indian historians are now trying to prove against enormous odds that Indian colonists settled in Egypt around 7000 BC – but I like to think that the study of the planets began in India. Certainly, the fervour with which her people tackle the stars indicates that the country's astrological roots are very deep indeed.

Where else but in India will you find so many experts in prediction?

....

[1] The Indians are perhaps justified in believing that western textbooks are biased against them. A Life Science Library book on mathematics admits that ancient Hindu mathematicians invented both the written symbols for numbers which we use today and the decimal system. You would think that this was rather an important discovery in the field of mathematics. Life Science Library seem to think otherwise. They give the Indians a mere four lines in a book a hundred and eighty pages long.

Santi Lal was the first Indian I had talked to at length about astrology since arriving on the subcontinent via Bombay a few days earlier. And here he was, his face a picture of serenity, telling me that because an astrologer had suggested he would make a good gambler – an occupation not normally associated with a happy, spiritual life – he had done exactly that and was now reaping the rewards. Nor was his faith in the stars the fly-blown meandering of a neurotic, desperate for control over his destiny. Far from it. I was to discover that Santi Lal's unswerving belief in the power of the planets was the norm in India.

Virtually everyone I spoke to over the next five months of travelling admitted they had been to an astrologer, palmist or clairvoyant at least once in their lives. Many people said they visited a soothsayer of some description once a week or more.

I was to meet experts in divination of all backgrounds, from village fortune-tellers to venerated seers who offer predictions to senior government officials. Everywhere I went I heard of new astrologers and assorted mystics with whom I 'must' meet if my researches were to be complete; and I discovered that most Indian cities boasted 'astro research centres'. They usually turned out to be nothing more than a local soothsayer in partnership with a jobbing printer, probably a relative, churning out unintelligible pamphlets purporting to be on the occult sciences.

Then there were the clients. I met stuffy businessmen at airports who at first dismissed astrology as rubbish, but when pushed further admitted that yes, they had occasionally visited astrologers, 'but only for fun'. I wonder how many travellers at a European or American airport would know where to find an astrologer. Even Roman Catholics, still quaking from the Pope's latest directive that reading horoscopes will send you straight to hell, confessed cautiously that they would only get married, move house, start a business, choose a school for their children, buy a new motorbike, bullock etc if the stars were favourable.[1]

I was to discover that day-to-day life in India is almost totally influenced by the planets. For Hindus believe that God created the ever-changing cosmos as an indication of his will for us; that astrology aids spiritual growth because through the horoscope you can see a creator controlling the universe.

----

[1] In his catechism published in 1992, Pope John Paul II declared in a major overhaul of the Roman Catholic Church that reading horoscopes, along with drug-taking and gambling, was a mortal sin that condemned an individual to everlasting punishment and 'total alienation from God'.

That is the crux of it – a belief in God, a need for His guidance.

Hindu astrology has so much more appeal than the western variety. In India, your astrologer will give you a precise reading based on events that have happened, or will happen, in your life. Many western astrologers offer little more than a character analysis. Thus the Indian version tends to be more exciting and revealing than the psychological rambling of the West.

Until the end of the last century, Hindu and western astrology were very similar. But in the 1890s an English astrologer, Alan Leo, revolutionised the interpretation of the planets. Leo was an original 'New Age' man. His slogan was 'character is destiny' and he began to steer astrology away from an emphasis on events. Event-based astrology had long been a problem in the Christian world because it appeared to impinge on free will. Western astrologers who tried to maintain that the stars were an indication of God's will, did not endear themselves to the Church or, ultimately, the establishment.

Leo thought he was doing astrology a service by getting away from this. Also, since he was no longer predicting a person's future fortune, he was not breaking the laws that had discriminated against astrologers since the Middle Ages. He was doing no more than tell a person what his character was like and what would happen to him as a consequence of his character. The planets took on different meanings, so in the new framework of Leo's astrology, Mars, for example, represented your willpower, instead of accidents, Saturn became your karma, rather than representing the father, and Venus was your need for love and affection instead of men or women.

Before 1890, western astrologers considered that a person's ascendant, or rising sign, was the most precise indication of their character and destiny. After all, the ascendant changes sign every two hours, as opposed to the Moon which changes every two and a half days and the Sun which changes once a month. Leo and his followers discarded tradition in favour of practical science. They decided that the Sun was the most important influence on the basis that the light of the Moon reflects off the Sun and the other planets are so far away that we can hardly see them. Sun signs, they declared, would form the roots of the new astrology. This meddling did not impress the astrologers of India who continue to use the traditional system. They say it is far superior in accuracy and they regard a person's Sun sign as relatively unimportant compared with the ascendant.

The light at Somnath was fading fast. The blue sky had turned to grey and the setting sun played hide-and-seek with the clouds, picking out sparkling ridges across the sea. It slowly dipped into the horizon and blazed like a furnace for a few moments before disappearing. To the east the moon hung high above the temple as if watching over an old friend.

As darkness fell we left the walls and joined the stream of worshippers walking towards the temple. Everyone seemed to be gaping at me, the lone white man well off the normal western tourist trail. It takes a week or two for me to become hardened to the stares in India. Santi Lal sensed my unease. He put his arm around my shoulders as if we had known each other for ever and guided me up the steps for the evening puja. It was a comforting gesture.

Inside, the stone carvings of the temple flickered in the light of oil lamps. The building echoed with noise as pilgrims ritually clanged the temple bell. A man sat in a corner squeezing out doleful notes from a tiny harmonium. His eyes were clamped shut and he tossed his head in deep devotion. People jostled to pay their respects at the Hindu effigies.

We stopped by a large marble image of Lord Shiva's bull, the means by which, according to legend, he travels through the heavens. The flower garlands wrapped around its horns gave off a heavy perfume. Santi Lal touched the statue. He kissed the head and mouthed a prayer. He turned round, squeezed my hand and gently steered me towards the bull. He indicated that I should do the same. I didn't know what to do so I gave the statue a clumsy pat.

Santi Lal whispered to me: 'All knowledge comes from Shiva and his wife Parvati, including the knowledge of astrology. Any predictions made are messages from them.'

His words struck me with an extraordinary sensation of peace. I felt that I was meant to start my journey in Somnath, that I was meant to be in India. I looked at the throng of worshippers and felt love for people I had never met. The enthusiasm of the temple had infected me. I was in the clutches of India's magic.

Fears of a few days earlier seemed to vanish – I had arrived in the country with great apprehension. I had no contacts in the world of Indian-fortune telling and little more than faith that I would meet people by word of mouth. Nor had I chosen the best time to come to India. It was August, the tailend of the hot season, and I was struggling against high humidity and temperatures of over thirty-five degrees centigrade. Indiaphile friends back in England had warned me about the fiery climate when I announced I was starting my journey in the summer. I had ignored their advice, muttering something along the lines of wanting to experience the 'heat' of *Heat and Dust*. I was beginning to regret my decision; the steamy air squeezed all energy out of me.

Santi Lal said his prayers (and presumably thanked Shiva for his cricket win). We left the temple and said our goodbyes after sipping tea at one of the makeshift chai stalls outside the gates.

I walked past a jumble of souvenir shops lit by fluorescent tubes back to my hotel. It was a dusty lodging with lime-green paint and the faint whiff of drains. Insouciant staff hung about by the reception desk watching Hindi movies on a black-and-white TV. Even with the windows thrown wide open, my room was unbearably stuffy. I slept fitfully in a heat that diluted the blood.

Apart from an atavistic desire to see where the world began, my reason for visiting Somnath was to find and interview a temple priest-astrologer. In the last century most Brahmin priests also had a basic knowledge of astrology and I hoped that if any temple in India boasted an in-house soothsayer, it would be a great spiritual centre like Somnath. This turned out to be wishful thinking.

I met the temple manager, Mr Vaishnav, completely by chance as I breakfasted on chapattis at one of the lean-to restaurants in the main street. He was snatching a quick coffee on his way to work. I introduced myself as a writer from England and he suggested that we go and talk in his office.

Mr Vaishnav's room was in the corner of flaking cloisters a hundred yards from the temple. The only decoration was a crumpled school map of India pinned to a wall. It fluttered lightly from the breeze created by ceiling fans. There was a single desk in the middle of the room, dull brown and faded by sunlight.

As soon as Mr Vaishnav had sat down, a rush of people clamoured around him. They wielded bundles of files, full of papers to be signed by the boss. Someone brought in a telephone and plugged it into a socket by the window. There was only one phone in the whole building. It was moved around from office to office as it was needed.

Mr Vaishnav had been in his job for less than a week. He had just retired as director of an Ahmedabad textile company when the trustees of Somnath offered him the post of temple manager.

'The trustees said they wanted a man like me who has been used to managing people,' he said. 'I wanted a nice retirement job where I could meditate and do yoga. When I finish work I go and sit in the temple alone.

'It is the perfect life for me. My wife is dead, my five dogs are dead, so there wasn't much for me back home. I was inspired by Christian missionaries I met in Ahmedabad and I thought I really must put something back into society.' Mr Vaishnav paused and laughed. 'That's it. I'm a Hindu inspired by Christians. I suppose that's what you call One World.'

In his flawlessly pressed grey slacks and white shirt, Mr Vaishnav looked more like a factory manager than the keeper of a temple. But he radiated enthusiasm and was keen to knock some sense into the place.

'This is a good temple, but so much development is needed,' he sighed.

The staff were stuck in their ways. They had allowed Somnath to go to seed. But twentieth-century Hindus expected decent facilities.

'In the old days the people used to do pilgrimages with hardness,' Mr Vaishnav said. 'You were supposed to suffer. People travelled long distances on foot or by cart. But today they want to be comfortable. They arrive in air-conditioned cars and they need good guesthouses.' He pursed his lips and grimaced. 'And frankly, the temple guesthouse is not very good.'

I remarked that last night I had tried to find a bed there. I had been put off by a receptionist who implied with a grimace that the rooms were dirty, there was no water and, unless I was down to my last rupee, I'd be better off on the beach.

'Oh dear, oh dear. That is exactly what I mean. I would like to make the guesthouse like a three-star hotel with foreign food for the foreigners.'

'I shouldn't worry about that too much. I'm sure most foreigners like Indian food.'

'Well, whatever the case, there's a lot of work to be done.'

A boy brought us tea and biscuits. I steered Mr Vaishnav on to the subject of astrology. He informed me with a sorrowful look that there were no more astrologers at Somnath. It would have been a different story a hundred years ago when it was part of the temple priests' duties to draw up horoscopes. Today's priests wouldn't even understand the planets.

'In the old days the priests were learned men. They passed their knowledge on to their sons who automatically became priests after them. But today their sons don't want the low monthly wages.' Mr Vaishnav sniffed with mild disgust. 'They'd rather become electrical engineers or computer programmers.'

He noticed my disappointment.

'Even if you have not found one of your fortune-tellers here, at least you have come to Somnath. It will bring you good luck. It is the best place you could have started your journey.'

After talking for a few more minutes, he showed me out into the main street. It was horribly hot outside after his fan-cooled office. Flies buzzed around our heads. I looked at the temple. A faded red flag on top of the tower sagged in the still air. The sun shone white on the walls.

'Do you really believe,' I asked Mr Vaishnav, 'that the world began here?'

'Yes, of course. Our holy books, the Vedas,[1] say that creation of all human beings began at Somnath.'

'That doesn't sound very scientific.'

'Huh! That's the trouble with westerners. Science has to come into everything.' He took a small towel from his pocket and wiped the sweat off his face. 'Science may have helped me run my factory in Ahmedabad, but it cannot tell me where I came from.' We shook hands and he smiled. 'I think you will be pleased you came here. Somnath is a good place for beginnings.'

After Somnath, I had planned to go to Dwarka, a small coastal town a hundred and twenty miles to the north and another highly revered Hindu site said to have been the capital of the god Krishna.

But I changed my mind after a chance meeting with a sadhu (a wandering holy man[2]) outside my hotel.

He asked me the sort of questions that foreigners become accustomed to in India. Where was I from? What was I doing? Did I like Indian food? I explained my purpose and moaned to him that I hadn't been able to find a temple astrologer. He gave me a look that said Hinduism ain't what it used to be.

The sadhu was quite short. Strands of straggly, shoulder-length hair all but covered his face. He had buck teeth, deep brown eyes and resembled a banjo player in a hillbilly band. After nine months at the temple he was about to return to his home town of Tanjore in the south. He had roamed India for four years pursuing his spiritual mission. 'Where God takes me, I go,' he said.

He was embarrassed about the decline of astrology in the temples. 'Our ancestors were very orthodox, but priests don't care for the old ways anymore.' He seemed to feel guilty at being part of a generation which was leaving the occult arts behind.

....

[1] Ancient spiritual texts, the orthodox Hindu scriptures.

....

[2] The writer Jan Knappert describes a sadhu as 'a person who has succeeded in suppressing his desires, so that he has acquired true insight into the essence of reality, which is that all people and all creatures are one'.

'No astrologers at Dwarka either,' he said, adding that my best bet was to head for the big city, Ahmedabad. I would find experts in prediction there. We parted company at the bus stand. Just before I boarded the bus north, he warned me not to be conned by fake astrologers. This was a pet subject of irritation for him.

'As soon as they see you're a foreigner they'll rip you off.' And as if to demonstrate that wandering holy men can also be human beings, he declared in faultless English, 'Fucking bastards they are, too.'

Mr Patel's Lesson Jn Astrology

For the nine-hour journey to Ahmedabad I put my life in the hands of a half-shaven bus-driver with an enormous, boozy nose mapped with veins and crevices. He drove like any other bus-driver on the subcontinent – too fast with little regard for his passengers and even less for the oncoming trucks that he passed with inches to spare. He revelled in this game of chicken, slamming his palm on the horn, his bulging eyes staring unflinchingly ahead. Strands of tinsel tied to the wing mirrors flapped wildly as we hurtled over scrubby plains littered with camels, donkeys, goats and elderly Massey Ferguson tractors.

The road was dotted with wrecked vehicles – one had crashed very recently, judging by the bloodied tarmac and dazed men sitting by a stoved-in lorry. Signposts warned us that this was an 'accident prone zone'. 'Destination or death – what is your choice?' they asked us. I looked at my fellow travellers' impassive faces. They were as unconcerned by the driving as Indian bus passengers always are. I wondered if it was in any of our stars that we should die today?

In an attempt to distract myself from what looked like certain death at any moment, I buried myself in a book I had bought in Bombay the moment I arrived in India. The *Brihat Samhita* is an encyclopedia of superstitions and astrological observations. It is one of several Hindu texts that is essential reading for Indian experts in divination and was to become a sort of mystical manual for me in the weeks ahead.

The book is thought to have been the work of a sixth-century astrologer called Varaha Mihira. Mihira was a great scholar whose source of material was the sacred Vedic books known as the sastras.

The *Brihat Samhita* can also be described as one of the world's first self-help books. And as my bus careered through the Gujarat countryside, I amused myself with Mr Mihira's notes on relationships, or what he quaintly termed 'amiability'.

'A man of agreeable manners enjoys sexual pleasures fully and not so one of a morose nature for he cannot secure the love of women . . .'

'Real love makes one beloved of other, and hatred makes a person unpopular. There is great sin attached to attempts to win the favour of a person by the practise of magic or the use of drugs . . .'

'It is not manly in a person thoughtlessly to attempt to do a thing or utter a falsehood with a view to please others.'

In his chapter on sex, Mr Mihira offers advice on how a man can tell if his wife truly loves him. A loving wife 'will in the presence of her lord, show, as if by accident, her navel; she will allow her hair to fall loose as if by accident, will raise her eyebrows and will cast a side-look at her husband; she will spit aloud, laugh openly, get first into the bed, crack her joints and yawn. She will look at her husband when his look is turned from her, scratch her ears, and speak in his praise in his absence.' A man would do best to choose a 'modest' wife who 'does not first exhibit an inclination to sexual embrace, but who is nevertheless subject to sexual passion. Her hair is of good smell and she extends her arms to her lord to serve as a pillow for his head.'

An unloving wife 'will contract her eyebrows, will never feel cheerful; her lips will be dull and she will be harsh in her speech; she will wash her face after sexual enjoyment and will go to bed before her lord and rise after him'. Men should be particularly wary of a woman who 'sleeps too much, who is of an over bilious, phlegmatic or windy temperament, who perspires often, whose hair is short or grey and who indulges in low language'.

You can predict a woman's future depending on which day of the week that her first period began. If it was a Monday, 'she will become chaste'; Tuesday 'she will suffer grief'; Wednesday 'she will get sons'; Thursday 'she will live in plenty'; Friday 'she will prosper well'; Saturday 'she will meet with early death'.

Mihira does not have time for unfaithful husbands: 'A man who commits adultery shall dress himself in the skin of the ass with hairy side without, and beg his meals for six months.' He claims that men are more likely to commit adultery than women, writing: 'Hence the superiority of women over men. Whenever men refrain from sexual pleasure after the death of their wives, they do so because of their inability [to have sex]. Women boldly preserve their chastity after the death of their husbands to continue their state of widowhood.'

Mihira believes that all women are born with 'personal purity' and that any faults they develop are due to the behaviour of the men they meet. A tremendous admirer of the female form, he concludes: 'In my opinion, a pleasure like that of embracing a woman who has just attained womanhood, whose speech is short, soft, sweet and broken, whose bosoms are high and large and who herself is full of sexual passion, is not to be found even in the house of Brahma, the creator.'

The outskirts of Ahmedabad arrived. It was the usual urban muddle of shacks and workshops. Builders' yards overflowed with mountains of rotting junk – lavatory bowls, drainage pipes, tyres and wooden well-tops. The flotsam mingled uncomfortably with prosperous suburban streets lit by splurges of crimson bougainvillaea. Ahead of us, the city was gripped in a typhoon of dust.

A persuasive auto-rickshaw driver practically kidnapped me at the bus station. He took me to a new hotel which was presumably paying him commission for any guests he brought there. It was a modest establishment grandly named the Arif International. (I noticed that as part of the westernisation sweeping the country, Indians were in the habit of sticking the word 'International' on the end of almost everything.) The Arif had been open only a month and an army of workmen was still piecing together the reception area.

I was greeted by the deputy manager, a lively 60-year-old in horn-rimmed glasses called Mr Chataiwala. He was thrilled to see an Englishman. He explained that three years earlier he had travelled to Britain to stay with his son in Bromley, Kent. He proudly fingered his blue-striped shirt and announced that he had bought it in the Bromley branch of Marks and Spencer. I felt almost at home.

After completing the vast amount of paperwork that is demanded in Indian hotels, I told Mr Chataiwala that I was looking for a good astrologer. He was beside himself with excitement. He was delighted that a foreigner was taking an interest in the occult sciences. He requested me to wait in my room while he found me a guide to take me to a Hindu gentleman called Mr Patel, the best fortune-teller in Ahmedabad.

An hour later I was in the hands of Mr Chataiwala's friend, a young Moslem called Mohammed Iqbal. Mohammed was in his mid-twenties with a wispy Ayatollah beard that reached to his chest. He was training to be a social worker, but if I found it easier, I could call him by his nickname of Mr Readymadewallah, a diminutive he had earned during a career in the off-the-peg garment business.

Mohammed's brown eyes blazed bright with spirituality and kindness. After we had introduced ourselves, he gave me a welcome gift in the form of handfuls of rose petals which he produced from his pocket. He pressed them into my hands like a posy. He was dressed in white kurta and pyjamas with a little Moslem hat. He was a devout member of his faith and had recently returned from an Islamic conference in Jaipur. He prayed each day, rising at 4 a.m. 'Then I go and sit in a park and think.' He was tolerant of other religions. 'You may be Christian, Mr Peter, but to me you are my brother. God does not want to see Moslems, Hindus, Christians and Buddhists fight each other.'

He told me a story. Two blind people went to an elephant. One touched the feet and declared the elephant was a pillar. The other touched the tail and said the elephant was a rope. 'It is the same with God, we worship him in different ways,' Mohammed said. 'It doesn't matter what blind men believe in because the elephant is still the elephant. God is still God.'

We set out in an auto-rickshaw for the suburb of Maninagar. Mohammed gave me a brief rundown on the city. Sixteenth-century Ahmedabad was compared to the finest European cities like London and Rome. It is now one of India's biggest industrial centres, concentrating on calico manufacture. The majority of the four million population is Moslem and the city features six hundred mosques with some of the best examples of Islamic architecture in the country. It was also the home of Mahatma Gandhi who began his historic march against the British salt tax from here in 1930. Gandhi's ashram, lying among lawns under the shade of ashoka trees on the banks of the Sabarmati River, remains a monument to the father of modern India.

The *Brihat Samhita* contains strict guidelines for the astrologer: 'He must be of cleanly habits, noble-minded, eloquent, meek, truthful and without jealousy; his joints must be well built and of good growth and he must have no physical defects. He must be of remarkable genius and capable of solving any difficulties save in matters of direct divine interference.' The book contains several warnings: 'A pretentious astrologer whose knowledge of the science has been picked up from what has occasionally fallen on his ears ought not to be consulted.' But almost more important for the client: 'He who ridicules the words of an astrologer or sneers at the science itself, will suffer miseries in the hell of darkness.'

Not wishing to suffer the miseries of hell, I arrived with an open mind at the home of Mr Shambhuprasad M. Patel, said to be Ahmedabad's finest expert in prediction. He lived in a quiet side street in the ground floor flat of a two-storey house. The garden was shaded by banana palms. I had not made an appointment, but Mr Patel was happy to see me at short notice. He was a doll-like man in his late seventies with splintery arms and dainty wrists. He wore baggy white pyjamas. His grey hair was slicked over a delicate, slightly sunken face.

The sitting-room was painted sky blue. Mohammed and I sat on simple wooden chairs while Mr Patel squatted on a bed. His legs were splayed out at forty-five degree angles either side of him in the way that a child sits. Next to him was a tray laid out with his kit for making paan – betel nut plus chewing additives used widely in India as a mild stimulant and digestive. His kit consisted of an array of spices, scissors and prods. He had a gravelly cough and spat into a little cup. He explained that a mixture of paan and chewing tobacco helped to soothe his irritated chest.

With Mr Patel were two men. He had been giving them lessons in astrology. 'But I have taught them too well and they are becoming much better astrologers than I,' he laughed. His pupils shook their heads furiously. Their guru was far too modest.

Astrology is the realm of the educated person in India. It is a hobby for the middle-classes. Like many astrologers I was to meet, Mr Patel was a professional person who took up the art late in life with a serious purpose. The former headmaster of an Ahmedabad secondary school, he began studying the stars and planets in order to provide vocational guidance for his pupils.

'I was puzzled why some children failed exams and some passed,' Mr Patel said. 'For example, I discovered that the poorest boy doing his homework under a street light could pass his matriculation with distinction. But a rich fellow, with all the advantages in life, could fail everything. I wondered if the stars had any effect and that is how I started studying astrology.'

He claimed that astrology was far more reliable than western aptitude tests for choosing a boy or girl's career. 'I have had great success in this field and my students have thanked me very much.' Mr Patel gurgled and spat a red gob of betel juice into his cup. 'That was more than thirty-five years ago. The predictions started when I retired. One man came to me, and then another, and now my house is flooded with visitors.' He looked at Mohammed and me and laughed loudly. 'And today it is you who have flooded my house.'

We were joined by Mr Patel's wife, a severe-looking lady in an elegant sari with her grey hair swept back into a bun. She appeared from the kitchen where she had been preparing tea. She passed among us with a tray.

'What does your wife think about the house being full all the time?' I asked. Mr Patel laughed and clapped his hands like a toddler.

'Because of her magnanimity I am able to devote my time to astrology.' He threw her a wary glance. 'Otherwise she would have thrown me out years ago. She is a master of education herself, you know, an important educational name in Gujarat and has written many poems.' Mrs Patel remained silent. She allowed a slight smile before returning to the kitchen.

Mr Patel popped another paan into his mouth and ruminated quietly for a moment. His jaws revolved with a steady discipline. Then he launched into an astral discourse. He explained that, even as we spoke, the stars were influencing us all.

'It is now 5.25 p.m. At this very moment, Libra is rising. Libra is the scale, the sign of balance, which means that everyone in this room is feeling balanced mentally.' Mr Patel beamed and looked at all of us in turn to check we were happy. He went on, 'Now, today the Moon is in Pisces. Pisces is the sign of Jupiter, which is the planet of learning. And you have come to see me on a Wednesday, which is the day of Mercury, planet of communication.'

'So it's no coincidence that I've come on a Wednesday?'

'Absolutely not,' Mr Patel answered. 'I knew immediately that you had come to learn and communicate. Even if you had not introduced yourself I would have said that you are a scribe trying to learn something.' He pointed at the tape recorder I was using to take notes. 'Nor is it a surprise that you have that machine since Mercury also deals with electronics.'

He defined what it meant when a stranger arrived on the other days of the week: Thursday, Jupiter's day, is for education, finance and legal matters. 'If a stranger turns up on a Thursday,' Mr Patel said grimly, 'he is likely to bring a writ with him.' Friday, Venus's day, is a pleasure day for music and dancing. A visitor is likely to ask you to a party.[1]

Saturday, Saturn's day, is for labour, old age, fatigue and hardship. 'A day of garbage,' Mr Patel said bluntly.

'So how come that in the West, Saturday is the big night out?' I asked. Mr Patel shook his head sadly. We always got it wrong in the West.

---

[1] The *Brihat Samhita* adds that Friday is a good day for 'spermatic drugs, friendship with prostitutes and buffoonery'.

'Saturday is very bad,' he said. 'It should be a rest day. It is not right to enter into revelry on Saturdays. You should take rest and pray. If you stay up all Saturday night you will not be happy. And if Mars is in the ascendant you are likely to go out and shoot people.' Mr Patel emphasised the point by pretending to hold a machine-gun and making rat-a-tat noises.

'Is that why there is trouble at Saturday football matches back home?'

'No question about it. Much better to hold them on Sundays.' Mr Patel cleared his throat and continued: 'Sunday – the Sun being the planet of government, perhaps a government official such as a tax inspector will visit you.' Monday, the Moon's day is 'a very nice day.' 'The Moon has relations with females and emotions. So if a strange lady arrives, she could turn out to be your new girlfriend.' Tuesday is the day of Mars, the warlord. Prepare yourself for a visit from the army or police. (Tuesday is generally an inauspicious day, according to the *Brihat Samhita*.)

Until now, there had been seven of us in the room, but at this point a neighbour arrived to have his chart read. Mr Patel looked at his watch. 'According to my calculations, Scorpio has just entered the horizon. Scorpio is the sign of number eight. Count how many people are in this room.'

I counted eight people.

'This is no coincidence either. We have just come out of Libra, which means seven people, and look! This man has just turned up to make eight.' I was impressed.

We moved to my horoscope. Mr Patel said he could not give me a perfect reading because he had not been given enough time to prepare a proper chart. He stressed that he was not a professional and charged nothing for his services.

'Even if a poor man comes to me I treat him with the same respect as a millionaire. Some astrologers charge a lot of money, but I ask for nothing. Astrology should be a free public service.'

Mr Patel requested my birth details and I told him that I was born at Bognor Regis, a small seaside town on the south coast of England, on 21 January, 1956.

'And your time of birth?'

'My mother thinks it was about 10 p.m.'

This was the detail that was to cause havoc with my visits to astrologers throughout my journey. For the precise time of a person's birth is essential for a Hindu astrologer. Without it, you cannot expect a truly accurate reading. But what constitutes the time of birth? Is it the time when the baby's limbs first appear? Or is it when the child is completely born? Most astrologers I met, including Mr Patel, declared that birthtime is the exact moment when the umbilical cord is tied and the baby begins life on its own. Another school of thought says the greatest accuracy can be reached if you know the precise time of your conception. What with the heat of the moment, not to mention the embarrassment of asking your parents about it, it is rare to provide this information. There can't be many couples who are willing to have sex once and then wait for the results, but I like the idea of New-Age men timing their orgasms with a stop-watch, so their offspring can have an accurate horoscope.

Mr Patel scrutinised me disapprovingly. '"About 10 p.m." is not very accurate. Astrologers will not take you seriously if you say "about 10 p.m".'

'I'm sorry, but that's the best my mother can do. She says her head was full of chloroform and she can't remember a thing about it.'

'And your father?'

'He can't remember either.' I revealed how the circumstances of my birth had been rather chaotic. According to my mother, the doctor had arrived direct from a dinner party in a dishevelled state. The anaesthetist was wearing a rumpled dinner jacket and announced that he had been moving a grand piano. Both smelled strongly of liquor.

Mr Patel regarded me with a pitiful look. What a way for a baby to enter the world. 'In that case,' he said, '10 p.m. will have to do.'

We sat in silence while my host consulted his battered copy of the *Ephemeris*, the reference manual that gives the position of the planets at a person's birth. Then he began to tell me something about myself. Considering how little time he had been given to prepare my horoscope and the vagueness of my birthtime, he was astonishingly accurate.

'Two years ago you had a bad time,' he said. 'It had a lot to do with a girl.' I agreed that my romantic life at that time had resulted in a great deal of angst. Mr Patel went on, 'You got a bad slap.'

'I suppose that's one way of putting it.'

'It was very bad.' Mr Patel chuckled deeply. His friends joined in the laughter and there was much thigh-slapping and mirth. I was to learn that Indian astrologers have a bizarre sense of humour when it comes to personal misfortune, especially that connected with women. The subject of sex always aroused great hilarity.

'And in 1982 you had a big change in your life that made you successful?' I replied that that was the year when I had been made editor of a Fleet Street newspaper column.

'But since '89 you have been a nomad, moving from place to place.' I began writing travel books in 1989. Then he started on my health and body. He pointed to my stomach.

'I would say that you have some identification mark near your waist.' I lifted my T-shirt to reveal a small birthmark on my navel. Mr Patel reacted with nonchalance.

'Told you so.'

'That's astonishing.'

'No, that is astrology.'

He added, 'I would say also that you have ear problems and your ankles are not strong.' He was right. My right ear was recovering from an inflammation and I have endured a life of sprained feet.

'And you need to look after your stomach. It may cause you some problems quite soon.' At the time I was perfectly okay, with not a hint of the stomach upsets that plague foreigners in India. But these were prophetic words. Mr Patel told me a lot more, much of which was correct. He also referred to my future, which included a happy marriage and successful career. I returned to my hotel in a buoyant mood.

That evening, Mohammed and Mr Chataiwala joined me for dinner. We went to a restaurant called the Food Inn. Mohammed had enjoyed the afternoon with Mr Patel – 'a real gentleman not to charge money' – but generally he was scornful of astrologers.

'As a Moslem, I do not believe that astrology has anything to do with God.' But he did believe that he was psychic. 'I am convinced you will get married to an Indian girl. Probably a Catholic from Goa.'

Mr Chataiwala was also a Moslem, but unlike Mohammed he had great respect for astrology, particularly after a disaster that had befallen him a few years earlier. He was running a highly profitable business in synthetic fibres. One day an astrologer warned him that malefic planets were at work. He would go bust if he wasn't careful.

'I took no notice,' Mr Chataiwala said. 'Then two years ago my partner ran off with all the money. I was wiped out, all my money was gone. Without capital I could not start another business. That is why at the age of 60 I had to take a job as a deputy hotel manager.' Mr Chataiwala smiled sadly. 'It is not easy working under someone else, you know.'

'Didn't you take any precautions after the astrologer said you might go bankrupt?' I asked. He shrugged.

'If you were a successful businessman, Mr Peter, and an astrologer told you that you could lose it all, would you take precautions?'

'Probably not.'

Mr Chataiwala brightened. 'I am suffering, Mr Peter, but I am happy enough because happiness is not monetary. I have good food, my children are healthy, their children are healthy. I know that I have good luck. Do you believe in luck?'

'I believe in destiny.'

'That is good.'

The food arrived. Mr Chataiwala and Mohammed burped joyously as they sampled a variety of dishes, and Mr Chataiwala interrogated me about my views on the supernormal.

'What would you do, Mr Peter, if an astrologer told you that if you travel by train you will have an accident. Would you take the train?'

I laughed nervously. If an astrologer had told me this in England, I'd have probably taken no notice. But I was caught up in the Indian way of things.

'I think I'd possibly go by bus.'

'I would also go by bus.'

We turned to Mohammed. He was scooping fistfuls of rice into his mouth.

'What about you?' I asked. He swallowed and wiped his mouth with the back of his hand.

'I would go by train. I would let God take care of me.'

Mr Chataiwala ignored his friend. He went on, 'The Indian mentality is to be scared and superstitious. For example, we believe it is very unlucky if a cat crosses the road in front of us. If it happens on the way to work, you should go straight back to bed and stay there all day.' He added darkly, 'Neighbours who keep cats are not popular because they might cross your path.'

I pointed out that if a black cat crosses in front of you in England it meant quite the opposite.

'Mmm.' Mr Chataiwala reflected on this. He was not surprised. 'When I was in England everybody seemed to keep cats.'

'Black cats?' Mohammed looked up from his food.

'Not necessarily,' Mr Chataiwala returned. 'I saw all sorts of cats, including ginger ones.' Mohammed snorted. Cats, ginger or not, bothered him little.[1]

----

[1] The Hindus much prefer dogs to cats. The *Brihat Samhita* reports that a dog with 'five nails in each of its hind legs, three in the left front leg, and six in the right front leg, the tip of whose nose is red, whose eyes are like stars and whose ears are soft' will make his master very rich. NB: It is also considered excellent luck if a dog pees on you or your horse!

Superstitions have played a large part in Indian life for centuries. Although many may seem absurd, they have evolved after years of observation. I quote from a book of Indian occult practices written at the turn of the century:

If a serpent crosses the road in front of you it denotes severe calamity and death.

Never ask a Hindu where he is going. If he is going for some urgent work, he is sure to fail if asked.

Sneezing at the commencement of a job is an omen of failure.

If a bedstead is broken while a person is sleeping he will die unless he propitiates the gods.

To sleep with the head pointing north means death and disease.

No broomstick should be kept upright as it indicates an impending quarrel in the family.

To weigh corn at the time of an earthquake increases prosperity.

The recipe to make a dwarf tall: take him to the doorstep at the time of an earthquake and stretch him.

Mr Chataiwala found the last one rather amusing. 'I'm not sure an earthquake would give you much time to stretch anything,' he said.

A vicious stomach upset forced me to spend two days longer in Ahmedabad than I had intended. Mr Patel's prediction had come horribly true. After a dreadful night of wind and vomit, Mohammed took me to a gastroenterologist who diagnosed dysentery and prescribed four different kinds of pill.

Mohammed suggested my affliction could be psychological. 'Perhaps you got ill because Mr Patel said you might have stomach problems.' I put it down to some tap water I had drunk during a hot moment in Jamnager. Whatever the cause, I was confined to my hotel room for two days. I had endless visits. Mr Chataiwala invited me to dinner at his home, but I declined. His boss, the hotel manager, was keen to take me to another astrologer who was said to be very accurate. The room boys also knew astrologers they wanted to take me to. In fact, everyone wanted to talk about astrology.

My final evening in Ahmedabad ended in farce. The manager had made a booking error. Much to my annoyance, he explained I would have to move to another room because I had been double-booked with a honeymoon couple. Eventually, at 11 p.m., he told me that the couple had decided to stay elsewhere, so I could remain where I was. This was not the end of it, however. For the next two hours I had to put up with a queue of noisy friends who had come to pay their respects to the bridal couple. Their looks of discomfort, following a rush of Gujarati greetings, when the door was opened by a bilious Englishman with a yellowish tinge to his face, made the disturbances all worth while.

3

Reading Shadows

The Maharanas of Mewar, rulers of the Rajasthan city of Udaipur, believed that they were directly descended from the Sun. However presumptuous the notion may seem today, their superstitious subjects accepted this amazing feat of biology without question. Certainly, such grandiosity did the Mewars no harm: their dynasty lasted fourteen hundred years in southern Rajasthan, one of the few areas in India which escaped Moslem invasion. Even after the Kingdom of Mewar came under British control in 1818, Udaipur managed to avoid virtually all foreign cultural influences.

As one would expect from a family with an ancestor like the Sun, the Mewars believed strongly in the power of the planets. Udaipur's founder, the sixteenth-century Maharana Udai Singh, picked the site for his new capital only after long consultations with his court astrologers, and in his palace there are wall-paintings featuring astrologers advising their masters on matters such as marriage. It was obligatory for the family to pray to the sun before eating, and imitation gold suns are dotted around the palace so that worship could continue during the cloudy weather of the monsoon.

I took a taxi for the journey from Ahmedabad to Udaipur. What with my rumbling stomach and the nuptial visiting parties I had slept little the previous night. The thought of another bumpy bus journey was horrific.

Endless roadworks pitted the highway as we crossed the Tropic of Cancer from Gujarat into Rajasthan. The sunlight struggled to break through a fog of pale golden dust thrown up by regiments of men and women striking at the ground with hammers. The women were dressed in colourful, cheap saris in cheerful Rajasthani shades which contrasted with their dull work. Their daughters, cherubic cheeks puffed out from the strain, carried away rubble in shallow baskets. Little boys with stick legs sat on rock mounds lazily controlling the traffic with red and green flags.

There was a great jam of trucks at the Rajasthan border. Yelling policemen waving lathis (batons) tried in vain to sort out the chaos. The landscape became more interesting after the brown flatness of Gujarat. Emerald green bushes dotted steep hillsides, which rose up either side of the road. Feathery ashoka trees were bursting with orange flowers. Bougainvillaea in myriad tones of pink and purple hung on the sandy walls of farmhouses. A haze of yellow maize fields stretched into the distance.

The greenery increased as we reached Udaipur and I noticed a slight drop in temperature. The city is bordered by two lakes, Pichola and Sagar, whose placid blue waters are said to cool the air in the hottest season. In order to make the most of the fresh breezes, I found a guesthouse high on the bluff overlooking Lake Sagar. And so I came to my purpose in Udaipur – to find a shadow-reader. I reasoned that in the City of Sunrise I would find an expert in shadow-reading, one of the most obscure of the Indian astrological arts.

As it turned out, this was easier said than done. I spent a hot, sticky morning pounding the narrow streets asking people if they knew anyone who could read shadows. Virtually everyone I spoke to said there were no shadow-readers left in Udaipur. The locals were far more interested in trying to sell me souvenirs. Today Udaipur is one of the most tourist-infested spots in India with a trinket shop lurking behind almost every candy-coloured shutter in the old city. But I persevered and eventually I was directed to a Brahmin astrologer called Bansidhar Shastri, who lived off the main street of Moti Chotta. There was a slim chance he could help me.

I found Bansidhar sitting on a wooden bench outside a temple where he had been performing his morning puja. He was a middle-aged man with a soft face and doleful eyes. His chest was bare and a dhoti loosely covered the lower half of his loins. He looked up at me warily when I told him I was looking for a shadow-reader.

'I have not been asked about shadow-reading for many years,' he said.

Excitement crept into my voice. 'Does that mean you know how to do it?'

'Yes, I can do it.'

I sat next to him on the bench and we talked. He explained that shadow-reading evolved as a way of finding a person's birthtime in the days before birth certificates. If an orphan had no idea when he was born, the astrologer could measure his shadow, make a variety of calculations, and produce the correct answer.

'In the old days, before proper birth records, the shadow method was very important,' Bansidhar said. 'It is an ancient science, which has come down by word of mouth. But I fear it is dying. Computers can make any calculations we want these days. By the next generation shadow-reading will be dead. People will not be interested in the old arts.' Bansidhar had been an astrologer for forty years, as his father had also been. 'But not my son,' he said sadly. 'My son is a tour guide.'

Bansidhar had not read anyone's shadow for several years, and I had to persuade him to read mine. Eventually he agreed, but he explained that he could only do it at around midday when the sun was directly overhead. It was now 11 a.m. He suggested that I take tea at his house while we waited.

On the way to his home, we were accosted by an elderly man, who introduced himself as Bansidhar's cousin, Pandir Shastri. Whereas Bansidhar was a quiet, shy man, Cousin Pandir radiated a boisterous youthfulness. His face was freckled with liver spots and his ivory hair was tied into a top-knot the size of a cricket ball. Fortune-telling of all descriptions ran in the Shastri family for Pandir turned out to be a palmist. He insisted on joining us.

We descended into the tangle of Udaipur's back alleys which were designed centuries ago like a labyrinth to confuse would-be invaders. Bansidhar's house stood in the corner of a small courtyard where children played alongside tethered goats. Chickens scattered in our path as we walked through a low doorway.

We climbed a tight spiral staircase that opened into a surprisingly large, airy chamber with stained-glass windows overlooking the main street. A sequence of frescoes telling stories from Rajasthan's history ran around the whitewashed walls into which were stuck a series of hexagonal mirrors – a traditional Rajasthani way of reflecting the sunlight into a room. The only furniture was an ancient treadle sewing machine and a large metal wardrobe.

The three of us sat cross-legged on the floor on brightly coloured mats. At the far end of the room Bansidhar's wife was balanced on her haunches sifting rice over a bowl. She paused briefly to smile hello to me before wiping the sweat from her forehead and returning to her work. Pandir gazed around the room and smiled wistfully.

'I was born downstairs in this house and I like this house much more than mine. There are very good vibrations here.'

Another man had followed us up the stairs. He put his hands together in the traditional Indian manner of greeting and gave a little bow. He had heard that an English writer was in the neighbourhood and was keen to meet me.

'I am not an astrologer,' he said. 'I am a philosopher and therefore interested in anything anyone has to say.' The philosopher had a heavy black beard and beamed through maroon lips. He settled heavily on a mat at the back of the room and began jotting notes in an exercise book.

Although we were in Bansidhar's house, the talkative Cousin Pandir took it upon himself to lead the conversation, and we embarked on a spirited trail that bounced haphazardly from astrology to metaphysics.

'Life is a chain of chemical reactions,' Pandir began. 'You get some energy, you spend some energy. Which means there must be a source of energy. I believe that our energy comes from space and that each human body is at this very moment receiving different waves from different planets.'

'Very good, very well put.' The philosopher looked up from his notebook and vigorously nodded his encouragement. Pandir was his guru, he explained. He was very proud of the old man. Pandir acknowledged his pupil with a fleeting dip of his head and smoothed a straggle from his beard. He chattered on. 'I have learned to get extra energy from the planets through meditation. Do you know, for example, how you can find all the answers in your own shadow?'

'Tell me,' I said.

'Go outside early in the morning and sit on the ground with your legs crossed. Then, as the sun rises, watch how your shadow grows. Do this every day. You will discover that you are never bigger than your shadow. But eventually you will see your shadow lift up and go into the sky. Then you will get the answers to everything.' He held up a finger. 'When I place this finger in the sun it will make a shadow. If I think the shadow should be vast, the shadow will be vast. If you think the shadow should be small, the shadow will be small. So you see, this is how meditation has an effect on the external.'

Bansadhir smiled shyly at these words of wisdom, but said nothing. The philosopher scribbled furiously. Pandir opened a little tapestry bag and produced a twist of old newspaper. His bony fingers picked out a piece of chewing tobacco, which he gently wedged between his cheek and gums.

Pandir continued his lesson in life with a simple meditation technique. He told me to sit cross-legged and upright like a pyramid so that my body would attract maximum planetary power. Then he instructed me to raise my hands so they were pointing upwards and to put my thumbs against my first fingers.

'Your first finger is for good knowledge,' he said. 'Pray hard and you will be very intelligent. If you want to be rich, put your thumb against your second finger and it will bring you money. Your third finger is for fame and your little finger is for good health. Do this everyday, always remembering to pray at the same time, and you will get practical results.'

He grinned enthusiastically and a bubble of tobacco juice appeared at the corner of his mouth. 'And now to the future,' he said. He rummaged in his bag again. This time he brought out a pair of pebble glasses. He slid them on to the end of his nose and grabbed my right hand. He peered at my palm.

A month before leaving England, I had bought a book on do-it-yourself palmistry. I thought that while I was investigating the occult sciences in India, I might as well learn at least one method of divination. Palmistry seemed quite easy, simply a question of memorising the lines and their meanings. I was subsequently to learn from astrologers that the position of my stars – Sun in Aquarius, Moon in Aries and the rising sign of Virgo – made me a good candidate for learning the occult sciences. Whatever the case, I had practised my new-found art on friends in London and discovered I was surprisingly accurate. I told Pandir this. He was delighted and took on the role of teacher.

'Palmistry is very helpful to humans, I will tell you some rules,' he said. 'The active hand is the hand in which we take the pen.' He sniggered. 'Or the hand we would slap someone with. That hand tells you about your present life and the other hand is your previous life'.[1]

Bansidhar had been listening quietly. Now he broke his silence.

'My cousin is a very good palmist. He has given a speech on the radio about his skill.'

Pandir was lapping up the attention. He adopted a melodramatic, theatrical pose and solemnly studied my hand. Here was the great master about to astound me with his insight. He pointed at a brown mole on my heart line.

---

[1] There are various schools of thought about which hand to read in Hindu palmistry. Most palmists I met said a man's present life is on his right palm, a woman's on her left.

'Very unusual,' he declared. 'Western palmists say a mole on the hand is bad, but in the East we say it is very good.' I was relieved to hear it. He went on, 'So you know a little palmistry . . . what is this line?' He pointed at the line that ran from above my thumb to my wrist.

'The life line,' I said.

'Very good. But did you know that when a line starts from any place on the life line and goes downward further than the life line that it means paralysis?'

'I've never heard that.'

'Oh, but it is true. It is one of the most certain rules of palmistry.'

He paused while I digested this gloomy information.

'I can see that you will live to about 75, but I do not like the look of that downward line when you are about 40.' Pandir stared at me seriously.

'You don't mean . . ?' I think I went white. There was a hush in the room. Then Pandir giggled.

'No, no, it is only a joke. I was only studying the effect on you when you thought you might be paralysed.' He hooted merrily.

'A joke? Only a joke?' My heart thumped wildly. 'Bloody strange joke!'

From the back of the room, the philosopher seemed about to burst with laughter. He held his head in his hands, rocking from side to side. 'Oh, that is very good, very good indeed.' Even the dour Bansidhar managed a smile. I asked Pandir, 'And what did you learn from my reaction when you told me I might be paralysed?'

'That you are a nervous person.'

'Well, wouldn't anyone be nervous if they were told that?'

'Yes, you are probably right. But paralysis is a most interesting subject. Did you know that if a person is paralysed on the right-hand side of the body he can never be cured? But paralysis on the left side can be cured?' No, I did not know this. I asked if we could move to a brighter subject.

'Like ladies?' Pandir peered at my hand. The philosopher licked his lips in anticipation of what was about to be said. 'You should be careful with your heart,' Pandir announced. 'You have not had good luck with women. After the age of 27 I would say there were two girls...'

'Actually rather more.'

'Never mind. You will find a nice girl.' He looked at my bare feet. 'And your married life will be successful.'

'How can you tell?'

'From your feet. When any one of your toes is longer than the big toe it means a happy married life.' Pandir lost interest in my future. He put his right hand forward.

'Now you look at my palm. What do you see?'

His palm was pitted with a complicated maze of deep lines and crinkled ridges. I didn't know what to say. It was all very well reading friends' palms in London. Reading the hand of an Indian professional palmist was another matter entirely.

'You seem pretty healthy,' was all I could manage.

'No matter,' he said. 'Anyway, I am able to see my own future. My hand is a good reddish colour which means my soul is powerful. But look at the mound – the mount of Venus – below my thumb. It is white, meaning my vitality is weak.' He paused for dramatic effect. 'I will only live two or three more years.'

I didn't know what to say. There was silence for ten seconds before Pandir's lower lip started quivering and he broke into howls of laughter, ending in a coughing fit. The philosopher was beside himself with mirth and collapsed in high-pitched giggles. I wasn't sure what to make of all this, but even I started laughing.

'So,' I said between guffaws, 'you've only got another two or three years to live and we're laughing about it?'

'Yes, yes,' cried Pandir.

'Is this what you call a Rajasthani sense of humour?'

'Oh yes. It is a very funny sense of humour that we have in Rajasthan.'

Bansidhar broke up the fun. This schoolboy inanity was not for him, especially when there was the serious business of shadow-reading to be done. While we had been fooling around, he had been scribbling calculations on a piece of paper. He announced that the sun would be directly above Udaipur at 12.35 p.m. today or to be more precise, at 12.35 and twelve seconds.

'I like to be correct,' he said.

Bansidhar and I left the room and climbed the stairs to the top of the house. The heat hit me as we went outside. I did an impromptu jig as the baking stone roof scalded my bare feet. Bansidhar looked up at the sky. 'Good. No clouds,' he murmured. Clouds were the bane of shadow-readers.

He ordered me to stand still with my arms by my side. He consulted his watch and took from his pocket a small piece of wood, a little bigger than a matchstick. We waited for a minute. I could feel the sun burning into my hair. Two small boys playing in the yard below shouted 'hello' at me. I smiled bashfully at them. I have been in some odd situations on my travels, but standing on a roof in Udaipur waiting for my shadow to be measured was the most bizarre yet.

At 12.35 (and presumably twelve seconds) precisely, Bansidhar crouched down and swiftly calculated the small length of shadow that the sun was casting from my right foot to my head. It was about one foot long. The process was over in thirty seconds. Bansidhar stood up with a satisfied look on his face. We had caught the sun at just the right moment.

Back downstairs, Pandir and the philosopher prattled with excitement. Shadow-reading was done very seldom these days and they were eager to discover the outcome. Meanwhile, Bansidhar settled himself in a corner of the room and quietly scribbled away, adding, subtracting and multiplying columns of numbers. He sucked thoughtfully on the end of his biro.

I confess that I had made this shadow-reading a sort of test – I had given Bansidhar no details of my birthdate. He was not in the slightest disturbed by this. He explained that he would base his calculations on nothing more solid than the time we had first met that morning.

'But how on earth can you work out anything from that?' I asked.

'It is a method that our holy men developed many centuries ago. The time that God decided we should meet is very important.'

I don't know what happened, but somewhere Bansidhar's figures must have gone dreadfully wrong; either that, or God had chosen the wrong time for us to meet. A few minutes later he pronounced: 'I would say that you were born at 5.36 p.m., Udaipur time.'

The time difference from Britain is five and a half hours. This made my birthtime 12.06 p.m. Vague though my parents had been, I didn't think they could possibly be ten hours out.

'My mother says I was born at 10 p.m.,' I said quietly. I did not wish to hurt Bansidhar's feelings. He face was expressionless. He shrugged. 'Maybe. Maybe not.'

*****

Even if Bansidhar Shastri's shadow-reading had gone awry, it had been a good illustration of the Indians' devotion to astrology. If a person genuinely didn't know anything about their birth, at least this method would give them some sort of astrological identity which is essential in a star-crazy country like India; and how would they know if the time was inaccurate?

Astronomy is more certain, and this is where India's obsession with the planets began. My next destination was Jaipur, a hundred and fifty miles to the north of Udaipur, and one of India's great centres of astronomy. The city owes its name to the sixteenth-century Maharajah Jai Singh II, a great scholar of his day and the patron saint of modern Indian astronomy.

Jai Singh's famed observatory, the Jantar-Mantar, meaning literally 'instruments for measuring the harmony of the heavens', is still one of Jaipur's main attractions. Of the five observatories that Jai Singh built around India, this is the largest and best preserved. It comprises an extraordinary collection of stone astronomical instruments, up to ninety feet high, that stand in a garden next to the royal palace. I had arranged a tour of the observatory with Jaipur's oldest and most famous astronomer, a man called Bansidhar Bhawan, whom I planned to meet in a couple of days time; but more of him later.

I arrived in Jaipur by bus and took an auto-rickshaw eight miles out of the city to the ancient Rajput capital of Amber, now a sleepy tourist town dominated by Jai Singh's former hilltop fort-palace. This massive construction lies like a stone crocodile on the top of a peak of rocky outcrops strewn with wild bougainvillaea.

I had been invited to stay in the eighteenth-century haveli – a traditional Rajasthani mansion – of some friends, Sunny and Brigitte Singh. It was a stunning house with marble arches, cool stone floors and walls of soft gold. Trickles of sunlight filtered through ornate lattice windows. To the back of the house was a pavilion built around a secret garden. The courtyard was veiled with creepers and perfumed with the smell of jasmine and roses. You could almost hear the Rajput maidens singing love songs to their absent warriors. From the roof there was a spectacular view of the palace.

Sunny was a Rajput prince and a cousin of the Maharajah of Jaipur. He was a noted painter of traditional Rajasthani miniatures and his father owned the world's largest collection of Rajasthani art. Brigitte was French and had met her husband while she was at art school in Jaipur a decade earlier. She ran a textile manufacturing company exporting her designs to Paris and New York.

Besides myself, the Singhs had another house guest, Uma, an American friend of Brigitte's. Uma was a lively woman in her fifties with long black hair tied into a bun. She was a fascinating person who turned out to be one of that rare breed – the original hippies. She was a veteran New-Ager, well schooled in the predictive sciences. She gave my researches an intriguing, alternative angle.

Uma was a hippy who had remained true to her ideals. After turning her back on western society in 1970 she had come to India where she had spent no less than twenty years in a yoga ashram. During a riveting chat on one of the haveli's many balconies, Uma told me how she had rebelled against her upbringing in the suburbs of New York City and Long Island.

'I came to India because my options in life were extremely boring. I had the choice of getting married and being a housewife like my mother which was a life that I would have found intolerable. I looked at my friends and none of them seemed happy. They were all locked in a life of making enough money to live the way they wanted to live, and then not having any enjoyment out of that life because they were so involved in making the money. I could have chosen a career but I didn't have any real talent to become an expert in any field and I felt trapped working the nine-to-five.'

Uma's method of escape was to turn to drugs.

'I took a lot of acid in the sixties – I was working in publishing and the first manuscript I helped to edit was Timothy Leary's *Psychedelic Experience* which tells you where I was at. By the end of the sixties I had been a bohemian, a beatnik and finally a hippy. I had come to the conclusion that the most I could hope for was not to be unhappy. The way not to be unhappy was to have enough money to do whatever I wanted to do and to have lots of affairs, clothes and jewellery. I was resigned to the fact that the best life had to offer was what money could buy.'

Then she met a guru called Swami Muktananda at a yoga symposium in New York.

'For the first time in my life I saw a being who was happy. I felt his love and I felt, ah, there's someone I want to be like, someone I can learn from. I realised I wasn't weird, I wasn't crazy. Baba taught me to see that God dwelled within me, to see God in other people. That is why I went to India, so that I could learn.'

She spent her thirties and forties on Muktananda's ashram outside Bombay. The guru died in 1982 and was succeeded by a woman called Baba Mayi.

'I love Guru Mayi very much. I would not have left the ashram but she said it was time for me to live in the world.'

Uma decided to settle in Hawaii because of the mix of American and Asian cultures. There she ran a business importing Indian carpet bags, while attending a branch of Guru Mayi's ashram a couple of blocks away from her Honolulu apartment.

Uma's years in India had given her a taste for the occult sciences. As well as being expert in astrology, she followed a spirit called Michael whom she contacted via a ouija board. Michael has become a minor New Age cult in America ever since a Californian couple called him up by accident while playing with the ouija board in 1970. Since then thousands of people have contacted him. Uma had been 'using' Michael for ten years. She described him as an etheric librarian who keeps records of everything that has ever happened. When you ask him a question he answers it from a sort of metaphysical data bank.

The Michael theory is that we are born with souls of varying ages ranging from infant and baby, to young, mature and old. Each of these ages comprise seven levels and it takes about two hundred years of life on the physical plane to advance one level. When we die, our slowly maturing soul passes to another person irrespective of age, sex, background or nationality. It is a variation on the philosophy of reincarnation, or karma, that we have been born before and will be born again.[1]

Uma was a mature soul, seventh level.

'According to Michael I have had sixty-eight lifetimes,' she said. 'When I first met Brigitte I knew immediately that I had known her before. I asked Michael about her and he said we had been in loving relationships in many previous lifetimes as friends, sisters, brothers, parent and child and husband and wife. It's the same with Sunny and Brigitte. They've known each other for fifty-two lifetimes.'

How had Michael helped her?

'He validates my perceptions of people,' Uma went on. 'For example, I might meet somebody and have a feeling about them. Then I ask Michael if this is someone I know and he might say, yes, this person was your child in a past life, or maybe this person owes you a debt and that's why you react the way you do. It helps me to understand people better.'

Michael claims that certain countries have a predominance of one kind of soul which determines the nature of that country. This was the

----

[1] Michael's concept of souls is not so different from the teachings of the Theosophical Society, the late nineteenth-century American-Indian movement established to champion the essential spiritual nature of man. Students of theosophy promoted a theory that there is always a limited number of great intellectuals in the world. Century by century, decade by decade, they are transferred from one country to another where they are re-born. Thus the twentieth-century scientists and inventors of the West are reincarnations of the ancient sages of the East. As their souls move around the world, so another country begins to rise.

part that I found most intriguing. Infant souls are mostly found in the remote tribes of places like the Amazon and Papua New Guinea. To them the world is small and womb-like. Infant souls choose that kind of sheltered environment because it is less fearful than twentieth-century civilisation. India is mostly made up of baby souls, wide-eyed and innocent, full of curiosity. They are terrified of letting go of their mothers, which explains why India is bound by tradition and parental teaching and why the caste system remains so strong. Uma remarked, 'Indians who are young or mature souls have a tough time living here. They're usually the ones who have emigrated.'

Beware of young soul countries. They are adventurous, go-getting and aggressive. Thus they include America, Japan, Germany and Israel. Mature souls are more settled. They mostly come from cultured and knowledgeable nations like France, Britain, Italy and Russia. Old soul nations have seen it all and prefer peace to excitement. They are generally pretty dreary – Switzerland, Finland, Iceland, Sweden and the rest of Scandinavia.

After a couple of days resting with the Singhs, I made contact with Bansidhar Bhawan, Jaipur's senior astronomer. He was a man who was said to know the Jantar-Mantar better than anyone. I met him one morning at his ramshackle house in a Jaipur side street where he lived with assorted members of his family. The first rains of the monsoon had come to Rajasthan and the city streets were waterlogged. I had to step through puddles of an unspeakable grey colour to get to the astronomer's house. We talked in an upstairs room furnished only with an ancient electric fan. His 19-year-old grandson, a thin, quiet youth with a struggling moustache, laid down some sun-bleached quilts on the floor for us to sit on.

Bhawanji (ji is an honorific suffix added to names out of politeness or reverence) was a priest-like old man of 79 with a trembling voice. He whistled through his teeth when saying his s's. He was very short, barely five foot, with thick, horn-rimmed glasses that almost covered his mousey face. He was hard of hearing and spent much of the time with a hand cupped behind an ear. His grey-flecked hair was slicked back across his bony skull and he was dressed in the simple, white vestments of the Vedic scholar.

He was a compassionate man with a twinkling sense of humour. He held my hand, gazed at me from the opaque mist of deeply sunken eyes, and took pleasure in telling me how he had been a 'muscleman' in his younger days.

'I may be rather blind and deaf but I am still fit,' he said. 'I eat only simple food, no milk, no sweets, no meat. Only one meal each day in the morning.'

He came from four generations of astronomers and he spoke proudly of his father, Gokul Chand Bhawan, who had supervised the renovations at the Jaipur observatory in 1901. But there was neither money nor prestige in astronomy these days; Bhawanji's son had found work in the marble industry.

'How do you feel about that?' I asked.

'Very bad. But what can I do about it?' At least his grandson was taking an interest in the old sciences. Bhawanji nodded approvingly at his protégé. 'I am teaching him everything I know and he is showing signs of great promise.'

The astronomers of ancient India were highly revered men of learning. As well as being brilliant mathematicians they were also religious men. It was thought that if you could understand the planets, you could also understand mankind and the mysteries of the world. Even if western historians are sniffy about the Indians' claims to have invented astrology, they acknowledge that the Hindus of five thousand years ago were the first people to make a serious study of the heavens. Hindu astronomers were the first to propound the concept of an inherent natural order in the universe. The mathematical precision necessary to establish their theories has become the wonder of modern astronomers. Much of what is known today about the cosmos is based on the legacy of the Hindus' storehouse of knowledge, the Vedas.

The Indian astronomer-mathematicians were not only masters of the laws dealing with the movements of the celestial bodies. They believed that the universe was the result of the development of a creative power, a primordial being. It was too easy to dismiss the orderliness of the skies as merely mechanical. There had to be a greater power at work. Thus the Hindus formulated moral and spiritual laws to correspond to the physical laws. And these were to form the basis of what was to become known as astrology.

Like his forebears, Bhawanji combined both astronomy and astrology. He found nothing strange about this and was keen to point out that he was not a fortune-teller.

'I am just a student of the skies,' he said. 'Once I have discovered the positions of the stars then I can speak about their effect.'

He was in no doubt that the planets had a direct effect on both nature and our behaviour. He had studied the effect of planetary rays on jungles and rivers and had discovered that the profusion of volcanoes in Assam was a direct result of the influence of Saturn and Mars. The stars could tell you much about the wind and its impact on the country. He further claimed to have been clairvoyant in his younger days.

'When my eyes were good I could tell the future of a person just by looking at the way he or she talked or moved around.'

I remarked that western astronomers brought up with Isaac Newton's mechanical view of the universe would have little time for astrology. Few could accept it as a branch of the same science. Why did Indian astronomers think so differently? He smiled tolerantly. The West had a lot to learn. Astronomy and astrology were inextricably linked.

'The true astronomer will know what rays are coming from which planet and what effect they will have on earth,' he said. 'The true astronomer will be so at one with the planets that he will be able to tell you what you have eaten that morning.'

'Does that mean there are no true astronomers in the West?' I asked.

'Let us just say that western astronomers do not have the same mental inclination. There cannot be a difference between astronomy and astrology because they evolved together. The ancients studied astronomy and found that the planets had an effect on us. That tradition remains with us. What is the point of studying astronomy if you cannot benefit the world, if you cannot tell people what impact the planets will have on them?'

His skills were a combination of a gift from God – 'I am a Brahmin and therefore I have a sacred link with God' – and the generosity of the early twentieth-century Maharajah of Jaipur, Madho Singh. He told me how as a seven-year-old he was presented at the Maharajah's court.

'The Maharajah asked me what I was studying and I told him that I was learning English. He shook his head and said couldn't I recite something in Sanskrit out of the Indian scriptures. I remembered a couple of verses connected with God and by good chance they turned out to be favourites of the Maharajah's. He gave me a scholarship of five golden coins a month to study Sanskrit and told me to create a special emphasis on astronomy and astrology because of my father. He considered the wisdom that is India far more important than the influence of our colonial masters. I all but forgot my English.'

Bhawanji grew up to become consultant astronomer and astrologer to the Maharajah's son, Man Singh, dashing former Indian ambassador to Spain and friend of Prince Philip. Better known as Jai, he had an insatiable passion for polo and died in the interval of a match at Cirencester Park polo ground in 1970.

'What was Man Singh like?' I asked. Bhawanji coughed diplomatically.

'He was fine to start with. He respected astrology and spent many hours consulting me about what would happen with the war in Abyssinia. But because of his stays abroad he developed attitudes which were not very Indian.'

'You're trying to be polite, aren't you?' I said.

'All I will say is that he was not like his father. Now there was a true Indian, a one hundred per cent Indian who would seek religious solutions to any problem.'

The present Maharajah, Man Singh's equally polo-mad son, known on the international gossip circuit as Bubbles, was no better.

'He has become westernised,' the old astronomer said bluntly. 'It is no bad thing to be a westerner but it is bad to forget one's own self.'

Bhawanji rose creakily from the floor and stretched his legs. It was time to show me around the observatory. While his grandson held his arm, he shakily slid his feet into a pair of leather slippers. They were about two sizes too big. He took a walking stick that was leaning against the wall and I followed him as he shuffled down the stairs.

We took a cab to the observatory where we were welcomed by a handful of tourist guides waiting for business by the front gate like a pack of scavenging dogs. They all knew Bhawanji, greatest living astronomer in Jaipur. He stopped to chat to his old friends and there was much bowing and kissing of feet. The man on the ticket kiosk refused to let me pay the entrance charge because I was with Bhawanji.

Jai Singh built his first observatory at Delhi in 1724 as a gift to the Mogul Emperor Mohammed Shah. The plan was to stop the feuds that were raging between the astronomers of the emperor's court. None of them could agree on their calculations. They were constantly arguing over the precise positions of the planets and the whole business of astrology was in turmoil. How could predictions be believed if no one was certain of the movements of the planets?

So Jai Singh stepped in to end the quarrels. His Delhi observatory was an instant success, the first time that astronomers had achieved major accuracy. Such was the Maharajah's obsession with astronomy that three years later he began work on his second collection of instruments. He decided to house his new project near his favourite hunting lodge on a deserted plain a few miles down the valley from his ancestral seat at Amber. It was a perfect, tranquil site, well clear of the hills that might obstruct his view of the heavens.

Jai Singh built houses to accommodate his astronomers. A community sprang up around the observatory and soon the Maharajah was spending so much time there that he gave orders for a new palace to be constructed. Within a few years he had moved his court from Amber, and Jaipur was born. It was a city founded as a direct result of a fixation with the planets.

The Jantar-Mantar's instruments are all in working order having been renovated and re-set for accuracy in 1901. Much of the work was done by Bhawanji's father, who was responsible for replacing the marble inlay upon which is carved high-precision measurements for obtaining celestial data.

At first glance, the Jantar-Mantar resembles a huge children's playground. The instruments are up to ninety feet high and one half expects to see a roller-coaster shooting down the giant sundial. Bhawanji's face lit up as we entered the complex. This was his spiritual home, although his failing eyesight meant that he rarely came here these days. He seemed to take on a new lease of life, tottering in his sloppy slippers from one instrument to the next. The old boy was thoroughly enjoying his day out.

'I am happier here than anywhere else in the world,' he sighed. 'It may be daylight but from here it is as if I can see the stars.' His grandson hovered anxiously behind him, terrified that in his excitement he would topple over. Bhawanji rapidly explained everything to me. He brandished his walking stick in the air and pointed at the giant sundial, at ninety feet high the largest sundial in the world.

'It is accurate to two seconds,' he said proudly. 'Better than railway time.'

He tottered on, a tiny figure dwarfed by these bizarre colossi. We reached his favourite instrument, the Yantra Raj, a metal disc hanging like a gong from a wooden gibbet. This was the king of all the instruments, an ancient type of astro-calculator designed to give 'the stereographic projection of heaven on the plain of equator for observing altitudes and thence finding time of all the positions of the heavenly bodies'. Bhawanji caressed the intricate web of lines etched into the metal.

'With this I can prepare an instant horoscope,' he said. 'Far better than a computer.'

I asked him which star sign he was born under. He replied that he was Taurus 'but Saturn is not going well with me at the moment'. Saturn fascinated him more than any other planet. 'It looks like a cycle wheel with spokes,' he said. 'The rays of Saturn are exceptional in that they fall on certain stars and are reflected on to earth where they create impact both good and bad.'

That was the trouble with Saturn – you could never trust it.

'At the moment, Saturn is conniving with Venus to make me suffer physically. That is why I cannot hear properly.' He added that there might be another world war soon because Saturn was having a disastrous effect on Israel and Iran. 'Saturn and Mars are doing terrible things to world peace. No, I've always had great respect for Saturn.'

Halfway round the site we stopped by a wall so Bhawanji could rest. He was wheezing a little. He held my hand and looked up at me through a myopic haze.

'I am old so I do not feel very good,' he said.

'But you obviously love coming here,' I said.

'Very much. In my youth I would spend all night here talking with the stars.'

'What did you say to them?'

'That I loved them.' He laughed like a little boy. 'That because of them I could make a decent living; that I did not have to live in the streets and beg.'

I asked him if he would have liked to have gone to the moon.

'Bah! Man walked on the moon but I never felt the need. You can't grow anything nor keep oxen there so what's the point of going there?'

'Try telling the Americans that.'

'Bah! All the Americans did is get a few rocks. Otherwise it was pointless, just a competition between them and the Russians. I found out quite enough about the moon from down here. The moon came to me.' He laughed again. 'It is like Saturn. Why do I have need to go to Saturn when it has come to me!'

'Do you think that the Indians probably know more about the moon and the heavenly bodies than anyone else?' I asked.

'An astronomer-astrologer in this observatory will know quite enough. It is because his spirit is in it. Spiritually the planets will mean more to him than the Americans or Russians. He will feel more and you must feel in order to understand the heavens.'

We finished our tour and I took Bhawanji home. He had been reflecting on what he had said. Before I left him he admitted that perhaps he had been too harsh in his criticism of the West. There were some positive aspects to western technology. Jai Singh had built his observatories in order to quell the arguments amongst astronomers, but the debates still raged in India nearly three centuries later. 'I have noticed that western astronomers always seem to help each other. The trouble with us Indians is that we are always fighting amongst ourselves. We are still arguing, and always will argue about what the heavens mean.'

I returned to Amber and joined Uma for tea on the balcony. I told her how the old astronomer had said he couldn't see the point of anyone going to the moon when you could study it perfectly well from earth.

'But didn't you know that the Americans already have three secret colonies on the moon?' Uma said. Her tone of voice implied that anyone who was anyone knew this.

'No, I did not,' I said. 'Do tell me more.'

'They're on the dark side of the moon so we can't see them,' she added.

'I see.'

'It's all kept very quiet.'

'I should imagine it is.'

'The Russians and Chinese know about them but they've joined America in a conspiracy of silence. They don't want the public to know there are people on the moon.' Uma looked at me intensely, gauging my reaction. We sat quietly for a moment. A soft breeze blew across the balcony. From the depths of the haveli's basement I could hear a penny whistle being played by one of the kitchen staff.

The US moon colonies theory forms part of the teachings of an alien called Dhrunvalo Malchezezik who lives in New Mexico. He also talks of a race on Venus called the Haphors and a former civilisation on Mars which blew themselves up thanks to too much technology. The survivors migrated to Atlantis, later integrating into American society. Malchezezik claims to come from a constellation called the Pleiades and says he is a 'walk-in' having entered the physical body of a 30-year-old American in April 1972. Apparently his stooge's parents have accepted him without question and are not in the slightest concerned that their 'son' claims to have been brought up in outer space.

Malchezezik's speciality is predicting the future of humanity. He maintains that he comes from the 'order of ascended masters', a spiritual fraternity comprised of assorted ethereal characters, and has a pentagon birthmark on the side of his head to prove it. He receives his information from the mythological Egyptian scribe Thoth, a being that Egyptologists will be intrigued to learn also originated in outer space.

Uma had watched thirty hours of Malchezezik's lectures on video tape. She totally believed in him.

'It was the first time that I had come across someone at the same level as my guru. You can't help but like the guy when you see him. He has great healing powers and he's so ego free that he can't be putting it on. He's extremely lucid and not at all crazy even though his information is quite radical.'

'Radical is a fair word,' I agreed.

Malchezezik's main subject is sacred geometry, the relationship of human beings to the rest of the universe and a sort of road map of how to enter a higher state of consciousness. He claims that between now and the year 2013 we will all be hurled into the fourth dimension.[1] Such is the magnitude of the changes that earth is about to experience that members of inter-galactic civilisations are at this very moment waiting in their spacecraft just outside our field of vision to see what takes place. For what is happening to our planet has never been seen anywhere before in all the inhabited universe.

'What exactly is the fourth dimension?' I asked Uma.

'It's a place where whatever you think instantly happens.'

It sounded pretty chaotic. What did it mean in practical terms?

'Earth will become a world like Venus – barren on the third dimension but inhabited on the fourth,' Uma continued cheerfully. 'It could be caused by a nuclear war or a change in the magnetic poles or an ice age; or the sun is going to give off a tidal wave of energy so intense that the earth will be crisped. It doesn't really matter – whatever happens will be a giant boost in evolution.'

I was lost for words. It was not the sort of evolution I had in mind for myself. I could just about accept Michael and his theory of the souls – but a New Mexico-based alien? I had difficulty keeping a straight face.

'Well, it certainly sounds different,' was all I could manage. Uma noticed my quivering lip. 'You know, Peter,' she said quietly, 'I don't think you and I are on the same spiritual path.'

'No, I don't think we are.'

'So let's just agree to differ.'

'Yes, I think that's best.'

I allowed her the last word. She pointed at the marble table between us.

'It doesn't sound so far-fetched that when looked at under an electron microscope this piece of marble is in fact millions of molecules vibrating at a certain speed. To us it appears to be solid but only energy is holding it together. We've never seen an atom or a neutron and yet all science believes in them. Just because you can't see something, how do you know it doesn't exist?'

----

[1] Western scientists know the fourth dimension as Time. Malchezezik seems to be influenced by the Mayan Indians of Central America. The Mayan calendar began one million years ago and stops in the year 2013 when the Mayans forecast the end of the world as we know it.

The next day I took the bus to Delhi. It was the usual terrifying journey, bumpier than ever thanks to heavy rain that had pitted the road. After tales of aliens and heavenly curators I was firmly back on earth. There is nothing like an Indian highway for returning one to reality.

Fifty miles before Delhi, an accident delayed us for an hour. A bus a few minutes in front of us had struck a lorry on a narrow bridge. The bus had plunged thirty feet down a bank into a field and ended up on its side. The driver and a couple of passengers were dead. A huge crowd had materialised from nowhere. They all stared at the wrecked vehicle. There was no conversation among them, no exchanging of views, just stares, like children. I thought about Uma and her baby souls. It all seemed to fit.

4

A Country Run by the Planets

India has a tradition of rulers taking political decisions by the stars. Indeed, astrology has long been considered essential for strong government. The astral sage Garga, who lived around two thousand years ago, proclaimed, 'As the night without a light, as the sky without the sun, so is a king without an astrologer: like a blind man he erreth on the road.'

Whether a ruler could be guaranteed correct predictions was another matter. Take the case of the sixteenth-century Mogul Shah Jehan. His court astrologers persuaded him to leave his Delhi stronghold because, they claimed, whoever held first rank in Delhi that month would be assassinated. Complying with their wishes, Shah Jehan left the city and embarked on a futile military campaign during which he almost lost his empire. He swore retribution on his seers. The astrologers were terrified. In order to save their skins, they poisoned the Governor of Delhi – the man of most senior rank left in the capital – therefore craftily fulfilling their 'prediction'. The Mogul returned to Delhi a happy man.

Another story concerns Maharajah Ranjit Singh, nineteenth-century ruler of the Punjab, who always consulted astrologers before a battle, most of which he won, thereby increasing his faith in the stars. During his final campaign he was struck down with a fever. His English doctor tried to persuade him to move from his tent in a field to a nearby fort. The royal astrologer, however, decreed that the Maharajah should not be moved until the planets had changed. Ranjit Singh ignored his doctor and spent another few hours in the damp field, his temperature rising rapidly. Later in the fort, he asked how long he could expect to live. The astrologer said he had at least fifteen years. Four days later, the Maharajah was dead.

But the first prize for taking astrologers too seriously goes to a mythical king who ruled in northern India many years ago. The story goes that the king was desperate to fly. He consulted his astrologers and, after considering the position of the planets towards which the king planned to travel, they came up with an ingenious suggestion. First they robbed an eagle's nest of its young, which they reared with great care. Then they built a wooden frame. At each of the four corners they fixed javelins upon each of which was stuck the flesh of goat. An eagle was bound at each corner and the king was sat in the middle with a goblet of wine to soothe his nerves. As soon as the eagles became hungry they endeavoured to get at the goat's flesh impaled on the javelins, and by flapping their wings and flying upwards they raised the throne from the ground, ascending higher and higher through the clouds and conveying the astonished king far beyond his country. But eventually they lost their appetites and the contraption plummeted from the sky, landing in the middle of nowhere. The king eventually died alone of starvation.

India's twentieth-century leaders are no different when it comes to relying on cosmic divination. The prime minister, Morarji Desai, was constantly ridiculed for his beliefs and most members of Jawaharlal Nehru's cabinet were rumoured to employ personal astrologers, who travelled with them across the country. Nehru himself was fairly scathing about astrology, whereupon he was attacked in Parliament by a celestially devout colleague who strongly advised his prime minister to take care whenever the planets were in Capricorn.

Another unnamed Member of Parliament was convinced that Tuesdays were inauspicious for him. He was proved right when the opposition moved a no-confidence vote in him on a Tuesday. The MP quit without a fuss. His resignation was written in his stars, he said.

The ex-prime minister, P.V. Narasimha Rao, was castigated by the Indian press for refusing to visit Bombay following the January 1993 riots over the disputed religious site of Ayodhya. With so many people dead one might have assumed that the prime minister would want to inspect the trouble spot immediately; but Narasimha Rao could not be persuaded. There was a malefic conjunction of the planets at the time and there was no way he would leave the capital.

Like the Moguls before him, Narasimha Rao had his 'court' astrologer: a man called Chandra Swami, a self-styled sage of debatable authenticity. While I was in India I heard only negative things about

Chandra Swami. I got the impression that his relationship with the former Prime Minister had been a dubious one, only a little short of making India's leader the laughing stock of his people.

Chandra Swami is a boisterous character who claims to have been consulted by six thousand and seventy celebrities and heads of state during his visits to nearly two hundred countries. His patrons have included a mixed bunch of spiritual truth-seekers ranging from the Sultan of Brunei and Richard Nixon to Elizabeth Taylor and Prince Rainier of Monaco. Even Margaret Thatcher, a woman one might expect to know better, is said to have been seduced by his claims after he allegedly predicted in the mid-seventies that she would become British prime minister .

Chandra Swami has become rich from his jet-setting brand of sorcery. He charges an hourly consultancy rate of around a thousand pounds – he charmingly describes his fees as 'handling charges' – and he has aroused the interest of India's tax inspectors on the suspicion of possible foreign exchange dodges. His opponents allege that his contact with the former Prime Minister was the only reason that he remained immune from prosecution.

Delhi's more down-to-earth political soothsayers claim that the guru is little more than a highly charismatic public relations man. They say he gets his predictions from a battery of astrologers in his pay, evaluates the common points and then claims the forecasts are his. 'He has put on the garments of a yogi and adopted the roar of a tiger but he doesn't know much,' was one comment. An admittedly far-fetched snippet of gossip alleged that the Swami had been a double agent, reporting to the Americans what Narashima Rao had told him, and at the same time revealing to Rao the personal confidences of his US political clientele. None of this tittle-tattle seems to have done Chandra Swami any harm, on his home territory at least. The joke in Delhi was that Indian politicians were still flocking to see him because they all wanted to be prime minister.

I had hoped to meet Chandra Swami while I was in Delhi. Unfortunately, when I rang his office a secretary told me that the boss was in America. They were not precise about his date of return. Instead, I opted to see another, genuinely admired, soothsayer who is consulted by members of the Indian Government.

Back in Ahmedabad, Mr Patel had told me there was only one astrologer in the capital who was both highly respected and had direct access to the corridors of power. No visit to Delhi would be complete without seeing a Brahmin called K.N. Rao.

Rao, a former senior civil servant, retired in 1990 as a director general in the government accounts department. He is the author of many books and pamphlets on astrology with a special interest in weather forecasting. The Government of India's Meteorological Department has been known to take his advice on monsoon predictions.

I called on Rao at his central Delhi home, a comfortable bungalow in a tree-lined street. The house had been built in the 1930s for civil servants of the British Raj. The mosquito-netted front door led straight into his office, a cluttered room with a high ceiling and the usual muddle that you find in the lairs of Indian star-gazers. Rows of dusty registers containing years of research were crammed onto sagging bookshelves entwined with the cobwebs of long-dead spiders. Halfway up a wall was a platform bearing a silver statue of Ganesh, the elephant-headed Hindu god of prosperity. It was garlanded with strings of dusty, dried flowers. A wooden crucifix was propped up on the mantelpiece.

Rao sat on a pile of cushions behind a low desk overflowing with papers. He nodded politely as I entered and with a formal sweep of his hand indicated that I should sit on a rug-covered bench. He poured me tea from a thermos flask. In his astrologer's garb of white kurta and pyjama trousers he looked more like a yoga guru than a retired civil servant. His hair was neatly combed back, his salt-and-pepper beard carefully trimmed. A pair of spectacles hung on a chain around his neck. He was a shy man who warmed up as we talked.

Rao, a bachelor, had become a full-time astrologer two years earlier after retiring at the age of 60. He claims to have studied five hundred thousand horoscopes since he started practising his art at the age of 12 and learned astrology from his mother. He looked at me through long eyelashes.

'It was not in my stars to marry,' he said. 'My mother used to say that as a mother she felt I should be married, but as an astrologer she knew I should not.'

He was wistful for a moment.

'I had a lot of fabulous offers of dowries, but I said no. I think it is because I used to play a lot of bridge.' He won the Delhi bridge championship three years running in the 1950s. 'My friends at the club were always looking at their watches, saying they'd be in trouble with their wives if they didn't go home. I decided that I couldn't play bridge and be married. I think that is a good enough reason to be a bachelor.'

He was also a noted chess player.

'I won two brilliancy prizes in chess, but chess becomes too much of an obsession. When you lie down, when you walk, all the time the chess pieces are dancing in your brain. Your unconscious gets divided into two halves – the black pieces and the white pieces.'

Like Mr Patel, Rao charged nothing for his readings. He was damning of professional astrologers who 'spouted mumbo-jumbo' and fleeced their clients.

'Astrology should be only for service of the people, a gift from God. Astrologers who get greedy will lose that gift. But professionals who make money out of astrology get annoyed because people can consult me for free. I have a lot of enemies.'

The subject of charging money was Rao's favourite soapbox. Astrologers who gave their services free tended to be more accurate than astrologers who charged. It was as simple as that.

'If you pay me money, I can tell you something which impresses you so that you come back and pay more. If my predictions go wrong, let them go wrong, it doesn't matter to me. I am only a human being, not God. But given a precise birthtime, sixty or seventy per cent of what I say will be right.'

All this said, Rao was recovering from a minor crisis of conscience regarding the financing of his first trip overseas. He had been invited to America later in the year for a lecture tour.

'I asked my hosts how will I manage for money? They said I must charge. I said, okay I will charge the minimum I need to live on because I have not enough money for an expensive place like America and I will not beg from anyone.' He looked at me in resignation. He was still not happy about his decision but this was reality.

There are several astrological societies in India. Some are spurious, grandly titled organisations that have been set up by avaricious astrologers as fronts to further their own business. However, there is one that stands out from the rest. The Indian Council of Astrological Sciences was established in 1981 to promote astrology as a science to be studied. The council's president is India's most celebrated astrologer, Dr B.V. Raman, whom I planned to see at his Bangalore home when I headed south later in my journey.

India's occultists are in awe of Dr Raman, octogenarian founder of the *Astrological Magazine*, who has been at the forefront of his profession for sixty years.

'B.V. Raman is the greatest astrologer not only in India but also in the entire world,' Mr Patel told me with great reverence. 'Quite simply, he is the Wizard.' I couldn't wait to meet him.

Rao is vice-president of the ICAS. He lectures at weekend astrological classes run by the institute's Delhi chapter, the largest astrological training centre in the world. The professions of students joining these courses illustrate how seriously middle-class Indians take astrology. Rao's recent pupils have included seven doctors, two chartered accountants, twenty-six engineers, seventeen bankers, five lawyers (including one public prosecutor), nineteen post-graduates, one industrialist, twelve businessmen, two Indian Air Force wing commanders and a retired army colonel. Furthermore, many of these students were men approaching the age of 60 – no coincidence, according to Rao. Sixty is regarded by the Hindus as a special age, when a man reaches the peak of his intellectual powers.

'Astrology is a perfect occupation in retirement,' he explained. 'It keeps the brain active and your mind glued to the spiritual principles. Apart from that it helps people find an answer as to why certain things have happened in their lives.'

'And I suppose it makes for a good social life,' I said.

'Oh yes, I always have company. I find a common bond when I am discussing astrology with someone I do not even know.'

Our conversation was interrupted by one of Rao's clients, a young man who had dropped by to ask what was in store for the week ahead. The fly-screen banged behind him as he entered the room. He remained standing while Rao consulted a file and gave a brief reading in Hindi. The man left five minutes later, apparently satisfied.

'What was that all about?' I asked.

'His mother is not well,' Rao said. 'I told him not to worry. She will get better.' He allowed a slight smirk. 'Let me tell you, a middle-class Indian is totally unhappy unless he has a few worries.'

Rao poured more tea. He went on, 'Indians are family people. Most of them ask about their little middle-class family problems. Like their daughter's marriage, son's career.'

'Whereas in the West we're only interested in sex and money?' I said. Rao smiled.

'Those are common questions put by foreigners. But in reality there are only six problems fixed in every human life: birth, defects, pain, sickness, old age and death.' Within this cycle, according to the Vedas, are three bodily needs: nidra – a state of quietness of the mind; ahar – a life-sustaining energy force; maithuna – sexual intercourse filled with selfless love so that the body and mind become one.

'At the close physical level of a very inferior man they mean literally food, sleep and sex. In an intellectual man, food becomes career, sleep becomes comforts of life, sex becomes love and family life. When you transfer this to the spiritual level, nidra is awakening man from dead sleep to the spiritual reality of human beings. Ahar is constantly filling people with spiritual thoughts, and maithuna means living without selfishness for the larger society.

'And that is how astrology should be used – to further a person's spiritual life. A nation which is spiritual cannot be wiped out from the earth. It will survive even a nuclear holocaust because of its sheer spiritual force. The reason India has survived so long is because of her spiritual culture.' He cited the examples of Egypt, Iran and Iraq. 'All these countries' original cultures have been wiped out and Islamised. India has the unique history of having been ruled both by Moslems and Christians. Yet today eighty-five per cent of the population is Hindu. Why? Because of our spiritual way of life, which leads to great tolerance. Take Islam. We accept Islam, we accept Christianity. We don't see any contradiction, but we don't see anything new either.'

The other vital condition for a trust in astrology is a belief in karma, or reincarnation. The Hindus believe that a man's happiness or misery is due to his actions in his last life. In other words, as you sow you reap. Hindu astrologers assert that the position of stars at the birth is a God-given index of these previous actions.

Rao was in full flow.

'If you don't believe in rebirth, you can't understand human life. A mother delivers four babies. One is bright, one is dull, one is a cripple and the other is a brilliant sportsman. How do you explain it? I explain it by the planetary positions at birth. And why do people have certain planetary positions at birth? It is the result of what you have done in your past life.'

'It could just be luck,' I suggested. Rao ignored my interruption.

'It is the same with identical twins. Why do they not have identical lives? A belief in the transmigration of souls is the only logical explanation.'[1]

(Not all Indians are as reverent on the subject of karma. In a magnificent outburst of cynicism, the Indian novelist Shrilal Shukla wrote, 'The theory of reincarnation was invented in the civil courts so that neither plaintiff nor defendant might die regretting that his case had been left unfinished. Comforted by this theory, both could die in peace knowing they had the next life in which to hear the judgement.')

---

[1] Multiple births foretell bad news, according to the *Brihat Samhita* which states: 'If two, three, four or more children should be born to a woman at a time . . . the country will suffer miseries as well as the family.'

We moved from the spiritual to the political. I asked Rao about his high-ranking clientele. Understandably he was reluctant to divulge names, but he knew of many government ministers who made political decisions according to their horoscopes.

'Politicians come to me, but many refuse to admit it publicly.' A note of anger crept into his voice. 'They come in the dark of the night and consult me so no one can see them. Yet on the public platform they denounce astrology. They are hypocrites and fools.' He spat the words. 'You see, more than fifty years after Independence, educated men in India still suffer from a colonial inferiority complex.' Rao pointed at his dusty files. 'There are more than ten thousand horoscopes in there, including most of the present government.'

'So you get to know quite a lot about their family lives and sexual indiscretions?' I asked.

A sly look.

'Yes, I do. You could say I am in a trusted position. Like a psychotherapist.'

However, he no longer allowed politicians to visit him at his house. 'Ever since the terrorism at Amritsar in 1984, I have told them that they must send a car for me and I will see them at their homes. Some of my clients are on hit-lists and I don't want terrorists on my doorstep.'

I mentioned a newspaper story I had seen the day before about a woman who allegedly murdered an astrologer, with whom she had been having an affair. Apparently the lady had lost her temper after being jilted. Before killing him, she had removed her soothsayer's testicles with a carving knife. Rao had seen the article. The story was the talk of the Delhi astrological circuit.

'A woman should never consult a male astrologer alone,' he said. 'You see, women have very good powers of intuition, but they also react very emotionally. They can be very gullible. An astrologer can easily exploit them, both sexually and financially.'

Morality apart, there was another problem. 'For example, I'm a bachelor. When a woman comes and talks about certain problems, like her children and servants and her health, I don't have any intelligent appreciation of her difficulties. I'm much better qualified to talk, for example, to a government servant about his office problems.'

I was excited when Rao offered to read my horoscope. Mr Patel had enthused me with his predictions and now I was in the presence of one of the most highly regarded astrologers in India. Before leaving England, friends had teased me along the lines of, 'You don't believe in all that rubbish?' I had replied that I wasn't sure and was keeping an open mind. An hour later, after Rao had finished with me, I was beginning to think there was something to it.

Rao asked for my birthdate and time. I repeated what I had told Mr Patel: 'About 10 p.m.' Rao seemed happy with this. He picked up the telephone, dialled a number and spoke to a man who drew up computer horoscopes. Rao gave the man my details and replaced the receiver. 'There are some pandits, [Hindu men of learning] who do not want to accept modern science and refuse to use computers. But to me a computer is a gift of God. It is much quicker than working out all the planetary positions by hand.'

A maid served us watermelon. We chatted for an hour before a messenger arrived with my chart. Rao settled back on his cushions and studied it. He took a pen, leaned forward and scribbled in one of his registers. I asked how honest he was if he foresaw something dreadful. Did he give sugar-coated predictions? He gave an imperceptible side-to-side bob of the head.

'I'm cautious, I don't like to tell bad things. One reason is that your horoscope might be wrong. Or your horoscope may be right, but you may be a good man and therefore the planets will not give you so much trouble. With good deeds you can ward off the evil effects of planets.'

And was, heaven forbid, the astrologer ever wrong? Rao countered with a neat argument.

'Maybe. It is very difficult to get hold of the horoscope of an astrologer. But if you do, you may find that he is passing through a bad time astrologically himself and will make mistakes.' He mentioned a colleague of his from Calcutta whose speciality was predicting longevity. 'All his predictions were going wrong so he asked me to see his horoscope. It was very bad. He died a few weeks later.'

Cultural problems also arose when reading westerners' horoscopes. 'A Norwegian lady came to me and I could see that something scandalous had happened to her in 1965. She thought for a moment, didn't seem at all worried, and said that all that had happened in 1965 was the birth of her daughter . . . out of wedlock. My Hindu background got a jolt. It wasn't at all scandalous to her, but if this had happened to an Indian girl she would have been thrown out of the house. She would have probably beaten me for simply mentioning it – even if it was true.'

There had been similar incident with an American woman.

'I saw in her horoscope that for the sake of her career she would go to bed with her boss and had done so with several employers. She was stunned when I told her and admitted it was true. If I had put that to an Indian lady she would have slapped her slippers around my face.'

Birds whistled in the trees outside. Rao thumbed through one of his astrological manuals. He began to talk. Much of what he said about me was correct, including the fact that I was not married (and had encountered one or two problems in the area of relationships).

'There should also be some mark on your stomach.'

Astonishing.

'Yes. Mr Patel in Ahmedabad told me the same thing.'

'And you were once fired from a job? It happened quite nastily.' He gave the precise year.

'Spot on.'

'And are you a little irreligious?'

'I pray, and I go to church on Christmas day. But that's about it.'

'I see.'

Rao then told me about my sister. This was the part where my faith in astrology took a leap. Through reading *my* horoscope Rao was able to tell me that my sister was an actress. Correct. Furthermore, she was married to a man who worked much of the time with non-Christians, probably Moslems. Correct. My brother-in-law was spendng several months of the year on business in the Arabian Gulf. Then Rao moved onto my mother with equally astonishing results.

'According to your horoscope, she needed a lot of help in April 1992.' Correct again. This was when my mother stood for Parliament. (And as a Conservative candidate in a Labour-held marginal, she needed all the help she could get!)

We reached my future. It was good, with an exciting, prosperous life to look forward to. Before he finished, Rao announced that my birthtime of 'about 10 p.m.' could not be accurate. Judging by my profession and various aspects of my character, he declared that it was more likely that I had arrived in the world at 9.56 p.m.

'Does four minutes really make that much difference?' I asked.

Rao scratched his beard thoughtfully.

'It is only through perfection that we can be accurate. And astrology is the perfect science.'

*****

I met K.N. Rao a few more times during my stay in Delhi. We talked at length about the occult sciences in India and he suggested people who might help my researches. Among them was a 16-year-old boy called Brajendra Singh and his 13-year-old brother Dharan, who lived with their family in a small village called Taroli south of Delhi in rural Uttar

Pradesh, one of India's most populous and backward states. Rao told me little about the Singh brothers except that as small children they were famous for their exceptional clairvoyant gifts.

'Brajendra was particularly outstanding,' Rao said. 'I would be interested to hear how he is getting on.' He added wistfully, 'I used to know the family well, but that was a long time ago.' Rao sounded quite mysterious about all this, but I agreed to visit the boys and report back. I wondered what I was letting myself in for.

My companion and interpreter for the trip was a Delhi film-producer friend called Sudhir Nair. Sudhir was in his late twenties with a bushy shock of hair and a permanent smile. He had limited experience of fortune-tellers, although a couple of years ago he had visited an astrologer.

'I gave him fifteen hundred rupees plus another five hundred towards a frock for his daughter.[1] Then he told me exactly what I'd told him about myself a few minutes earlier. He must have thought I had a very poor memory.'

On another occasion, while researching a film, Sudhir had discovered a group of dirt-poor Rajasthani musicians living in a hut near Jaisalmer.

'They said they knew everything about the future. They said they were experts in astral projection and claimed they had each been round the world four times. They were difficult to take seriously.'

We hired a taxi early one morning and set out on the main Mathura road. Neither Sudhir nor the driver had heard of Taroli and it wasn't marked on my map. We stopped several times to ask for directions. The drive was not made easier by the first rains of the monsoon. Soon after we left Delhi we were plunged into a torrent. The combination of flood water and greasy tarmac transformed the road surface into a skidpan. Even more crashed trucks than usual languished on the verges. The air was heavy with exhaust fumes and smoke from roadside chai stalls.

One hundred and fifty kilometres south of the capital, we turned off on to a muddy country lane fringed with pampas grass. Either side were saturated paddy fields where a few miserable cows wandered in search of vegetation. Barefoot villagers, heads covered with scraps of polythene to keep the rain off, stared at the car, a rare sight in these parts. A battered local bus, advancing like a thunderbolt, threatened to squeeze us off the road. Our driver took evasive action. The pampas grass swished alarmingly along the taxi's nearside windows.

----

[1] Nearly forty pounds – a small fortune considering that an exceptionally well-paid Bombay clerk would be lucky to earn fifteen a week.

In the sunshine, this district of Uttar Pradesh probably looked quite quaint and rustic; in the wet season it resembled the hellish aftermath of a particularly vicious barrage on the Somme: great ruts in the road and the smell of dirt and poverty. This is not the colourful, jolly India that tourists jabber about. Yet little more than fifty kilometres away is Agra and the Taj Mahal, where armies of carpet salesmen feverishly rake in the dollars.

A mile from Taroli we asked a farm worker with hair hennaed the colour of tangerine if he knew where the Singh brothers lived.

'Ah, you want they who can foretell,' he said. In return for the promise of a small tip, he climbed into the taxi and showed us the way. I marvelled again at how in India you will always find someone to act as a native guide in return for a rupee or two.

Taroli consisted of a depressing collection of mud huts with patched straw roofs as scabby as the backs of mangy dogs. It was still raining heavily as we trundled over the water-filled pot-holes in the main street. A few people huddled under the canvas awnings of fruit stalls. Skinny hens strutted under the overhangs of the huts and scratched at whatever dust hadn't turned to mud; water buffalo, tied to posts outside the huts and staring dozily at nothing in particular, seemed to be about the only creatures enjoying this weather.

We drove to the far side of the village and stopped outside a house with green walls and red pillars. Here was the Singh family residence, one of the few brick buildings in the village and a picture of opulence compared with the huts.

The rain thundered on the roof of the car. Sudhir remarked, 'If these brothers really are clairvoyant they should know that we are coming to see them.' We leapt out and ran into the porch of the house. Several faces peered at us from the gloom inside. As it turned out, the Singh family had no idea we were coming. On the contrary, they seemed amazed that an Englishman was visiting them on possibly the wettest day of the year.

Brajendra and Dharan came out to meet us. They were barefoot and dressed in grubby dhotis and faded T-shirts. With them was their older brother, who introduced himself as Vijet. He told us we were lucky that our car had got through the mud. I explained that I was a writer from England and a friend of Mr Rao. The brothers showed us into a dimly lit living-room, basically furnished with iron beds and simple chairs. Inside the house there was a farmyard atmosphere with the sickly smell of dung and buffalo urine. A cockerel pecked at the lumpy earthen floor; open doors led into a muddy courtyard where bony goats chewed on maize stalks. The boys' mother was in the kitchen preparing food; their father was in Delhi for a couple of days. Chairs were pulled up and we all sat down. Brajendra let fly with a burst of Hindi. He was an anxious, fidgety boy with a pinched mouth and wide, staring eyes. On his wrist was a Casio digital watch. Sudhir took over the role of interpreter.

'Where is Mr Rao?' Brajendra asked.

'He's at his home in Delhi,' I said.

'And why have you come here?'

'To ask you questions.'

'Ah.'

Brajendra told me he had been clairvoyant since the age of 15 months. He also boasted faith-healing powers, claiming he could cure fatal diseases within ten minutes of meeting his patient. An Indian heart specialist had written a book about his miraculous powers and thousands of people used to visit him as a child. But very few people came these days, he admitted. He acted as if he was unconcerned by this, although I'm not sure that I believed him. He said his ambition was to devote his life to Shiva and to build temples around India.

'Whatever you are doing, you should offer it to God,' he said. 'What is yours today was somebody else's yesterday and somebody else's the day before that. So just hand it all over to God.'

Was there any rivalry between him and Dharan? The boys chattered together before Brajendra spoke.

'We have similar thoughts, but we have a problem. I say I am strongest and he says that he is. We fight about it.'

This was Dharan's cue to talk about God. For a boy of 13 he had a mature approach to spirituality.

'One who doesn't make any mistakes is God, one who doesn't realise his mistakes is Satan and one who makes mistakes and changes is a human being.' He spoke in a squeaky, unbroken voice. 'The poor are afraid of the rich, the weak are afraid of the strong, all these people are afraid of a person with a high character. One who is afraid of God is not afraid of anyone.' He paused to let this sink in. He added, 'God is everywhere. A flower still remains a flower even if it is confined to ashes.'

By local standards the family seemed exceptionally well-off. I asked if their neighbours were jealous.

'Some people don't like us,' Brajendra said. 'We have to be careful because this is a dangerous locality. If a man says he will kill someone tomorrow, he usually does it. But jealousy is a natural thing – even the gods had rivals.' He spread his arms as if to demonstrate his forgiving nature. 'I am like the sun, which has so much strength that even if I throw a handful of dust in front of it, I will still feel its heat.'

There is a method that has long been used by parents in country areas for producing clairvoyant children. However, it is very dangerous. Put a tub of water outside overnight. In the early morning, the birds come and drink from the tub. Give a few teaspoonfuls of the remaining water to your newly born baby. This is risky because ninety per cent of babies die from infections contracted from the birds, but if your child does survive, it will develop supernormal powers. The brothers' parents, however, had not indulged in this superstition and had nothing to do with their sons' powers. Instead, the boys claimed that their clairvoyance was a gift from God. Brajendra was also convinced that he had been murdered in his previous life – not unusual among psychic child prodigies. Studies have revealed that many believe they suffered violent deaths in their previous lives.

Brajendra and Dharan got up from their chairs. They indicated that Sudhir and I should follow them. Vijet trailed after us like a lonely Rottweiler. He was about 20 with a scrubby, under-developed moustache. He appeared to be acting as his brothers' 'minder'.

We went to the next room, which doubled as the boys' temple. A flickering oil lamp threw shadows on to a small altar shrouded in faded red silk. A cluster of incense sticks created vapour trails of smoke that wound around statues of Shiva and the monkey god Hanuman. We sat in a circle on bits of sacking on the dirt floor. The earth smelled damp and musty. We stared at each other for a few moments. Then Brajendra began with a mind game – his way of breaking the ice.

'What is your favourite flower?'

'Oh God, I don't know. A rhododendron?'

Sudhir translated. The boys looked puzzled. We had not got off to a good start.

'What sort of flower is that?' Brajendra asked.

'It's a big wild bush with pretty pink flowers. They look lovely in May in English country gardens.'

'Ah. And what is your favourite type of water?'

'Spring water.'

'And your favourite force or strength?'

I thought of the murky weather outside. I longed for sunshine.

'The sun,' I said.

Brajendra looked pleased. He said that by revealing my favourite flower I had subconsciously told him my ideal type of partner.

'You like wild and pretty girls.'

'True enough.'

The water was a metaphor for my eyes and an indication of what was going on inside me. By saying that I preferred cool spring water it meant I was happy with myself. The 'force' was how I viewed society. Brajendra seemed satisfied with my answer. He declared that I was generally a sunny sort of person. Then, out of the blue, he added, 'But you must take care never to eat lemon or potato on a Tuesday.'

I could hear Hindi music on a radio coming through the walls from the next room. Banks of sweeping violins accompanied a girl singer with a high-pitched voice, which rose and fell as the rain battered on the ground outside.

'Lemon or potato?' It seemed a funny combination.

'Lemon or potato,' Brajendra repeated. 'They are bad for you on Tuesdays.' He gave no further explanation. His word was final. Simple as that.

Brajendra began to exercise his clairvoyant skills on me. He continued talking normally and did not have to psyche himself specially for the occasion in the way that many mediums do. He was entertaining to listen to, but he offered no startling revelations.

'You keep thinking a lot about the future.'

'True,' I said.

'And you are not married.'

'No.'

'How many brothers do you have?'

'None.'

There were more comments about my work and love life. Then Dharan took over. He was more relaxed than his older brother with a smiling, angelic face. But when he started on the serious business of prediction his features became distorted and intense.

'Have you had any illness recently?' he asked.

'Nothing serious, but I've had excruciating toothache in the past few days.' I explained that a filling in one of my back teeth had fallen out. It was still painful.

Dharan looked thoughtful. He told me to close my eyes and put a finger on the offending tooth. He muttered a mantra, tapped my cheek lightly and slapped it hard.

'Now remove your finger,' he ordered. He then told me to drum my feet hard on the floor. I drummed hard. 'How is it now?' he asked. I opened my eyes. Perhaps it was my imagination, but the pain seemed better. Dharan scooped up a small pile of incense ash from the altar and poured it into a plastic bag. 'Rub it on your tooth if it aches again.' He explained that the ash would make me a doctor. 'If anyone has any pain you should repeat the name of Hanuman five times and put the ash on the part that hurts. While the incense is with you no harm will come to you. Ever.'

Brajendra butted in. I got the impression that he did not like little brother hogging the limelight for too long.

'Within the next two years you could have more serious illnesses,' Brajendra said. 'You have a bright future ahead, but we will have to do some special puja so you have no problems.'

'What is "special puja"?' I asked suspiciously.

And now came the rub. I could have kicked myself afterwards, but I fell straight into a cunningly laid trap. Brajendra adopted a 'butter wouldn't melt' expression.

'How many kilometres from here is your home?'

I thought he was just being inquisitive, so I answered as accurately as possible.

'Let me think . . . eight housand kilometres. No, probably closer to seven thousand. Why do you want to know?'

'To find out how much special puja will cost.'

I looked at Sudhir. He raised an eyebrow.

'And how much is that?'

'It will cost twenty-five paise a kilometre.'

Prayers charged by the kilometre? This was a new one.

'I think,' I whispered to Sudhir in English, 'that I smell a very large rat. If I'd known what was going on, I'd have said three thousand and I bet they'd have been none the wiser.' The Singhs' ingenuity was too much for Sudhir. He broke into a broad grin. The brothers looked deadly serious.

Brajendra continued, 'And it will be another five hundred rupees for special puja articles which we will send to your country.'[1]

I decided to swallow my pride, if only for reasons of journalistic enquiry. I reluctantly brought out my wallet and handed over some notes. I parted with two thousand two hundred and fifty rupees, around forty-five pounds at the current exchange rate and a huge sum in India. Brajendra curtly nodded his thanks and handed the cash to Vijet. There was silence while he carefully counted it and stuffed the wad into his trouser pocket.

----

[1] As I write this, six months have passed and still no sign of my 'special puja' kit!

Dharan began talking about God again. God was strength, he said. The body was no more important than a piece of cloth, but the soul lived for ever. I felt I had witnessed a tough emotional struggle. The presence of a foreigner and his money had been too much for the brothers' greed. Now they had the money, perhaps guilt was forcing them to return to some sort of piety. It was all very human and quite sad. For a moment I felt sorry for Brajendra. He seemed frustrated, torn between greed and spirituality.

We returned to the living-room. The boys' mother appeared from the kitchen with a tray of tea and sweets. She was a thin woman, in a cheap, cotton sari, with gnarled hands from working in the fields. Brajendra was proud of his mother. Apparently her talents included rifle shooting. 'She is a crack shot,' he explained. 'Give her any weapon and she hits the target.' Mrs Singh said nothing, but beamed with delight at her son's compliments.

Dharan was fiddling with my camera. He had reverted to the role of normal, curious 13-year-old boy. He asked me if I had any 'coins of my country'. I scowled and reluctantly found a pound that was lurking in my camera bag.

I was irritated at having parted with so much money, particularly since neither of the boys had stunned me with their so-called powers of prediction. Sudhir was more impressed. Perhaps on the basis that I had spent so many rupees, Brajendra and Dharan had given Sudhir a free reading. They had told him that his sister was due to have an operation next month, which was correct. So, despite their dubious business practices, they did have some clairvoyant powers after all. Even so, I was pretty frosty.

'Can't you tell *me* anything I don't know already?' I asked sulkily.

Brajendra replied, 'Next time I will tell you everything.' I bet you will, I thought. Especially when I hand over more money. I reminded Brajendra that he had claimed earlier that he never cheated anyone. How did he plan to spend my cash? What did the 'special puja' entail? Would he hire a troupe of dancing girls? Or men playing drums? My question brought shifty looks. Vijet looked particularly uncomfortable. Brajendra, who was turning out to be by far the brightest brother, neatly parried my enquiry. 'I can only talk about the puja while I am performing the puja.'

Sudhir and I left soon after that. The downpour continued as we headed back to Delhi and my anxiety level rose as the taxi skidded along the flooded road. I was still in considerable pain. Mrs Singh's sticky sweets were playing havoc with my tooth, despite Dharan's mantras and my sachet of holy ash – in a moment of desperation, on the expectation that a dollop of faith might relieve the ache, I had rubbed some of the stuff in my mouth. It felt gritty, tasted like chalk and was absolutely no use.

The journey wasn't helped by the fact that the taxi's windscreen wipers packed up after twenty kilometres. Our driver seemed remarkably unconcerned that he was peering through a windscreen that resembled frosted glass. Sudhir put the fear of God into me by suggesting that the broken wipers might be the brothers' doing.

'Maybe they have put a curse on us,' he said.

'Why? Because of my cynical remarks at the end about dancing girls?'

'You never can tell. Some people say these clairvoyants and their pujas can have evil effects as well. People have gone insane, lost all their money.'

*****

I visited K.N. Rao that evening. He was eager to hear my news.

'How did it go?'

'I think I got conned.' I felt weary and short-tempered from the travelling. I told him about the day's events and how I was still confused about whether the brothers were genuinely clairvoyant or not. 'There was a lot that didn't add up.'

'I see.'

Rao looked sad. He settled back on his cushions and told me the story of Brajendra as he remembered the boy. Rao first met the Singh family in the early 1980s. He had been spending the weekend on a pilgrimage at Brindawan, a small town in Uttar Pradesh where Lord Krishna is said to have spent much of his childhood. He was with a friend, who had heard of a small boy with supernormal gifts twenty kilometres away in a village called Taroli.

'My friend was curious and wanted to go and see him. I was not interested in going. I had seen so many of these children in the country and I couldn't be bothered to see another.' His friend insisted and Rao reluctantly agreed to accompany him. They arrived on a Monday morning. The Singh family were living in wretched conditions. Their home was a hut with a simple thatched roof, two small rooms and a puja shrine in the corner.

'A large crowd had gathered outside,' Rao continued. 'I was standing at the back and suddenly this tiny child pointed at me and said, "He will come and worship with me."'

Brajendra was aged five. He walked up to Rao, took the astrologer by the hand and led him into the hut where they said prayers together before the shrine. Brajendra asked Rao if he wanted to ask any questions.

'I said I had nothing to ask. I said I had heard about him and I had just come to see him out of curiosity.'

During the conversation, Rao referred to the boy by the affectionate, shortened 'Brajend'; in return, the child referred to his new guru as 'Babuji'. Rao continued, 'Brajend reacted beautifully. He climbed on to my lap and said we were together in a previous birth at Barrackpore, a town north of Calcutta on the Hughli River. He told me he would only accept my orders and would go wherever I wanted him to.'

And so Rao became the child's guru. A few days later, Brajendra joined the astrologer at his house in Delhi. The boy's father, a village farmer, came with him; his mother remained in Taroli to look after her other children. Brajendra's fame spread rapidly through Delhi. Each day a big crowd gathered at Rao's house to see this miracle boy.

'He was brilliant, outstanding. Everyone was amazed by his predictions.'

Brajendra's prophecies were short-range, which, according to Rao, was typical for a child with minor supernormal powers. Nevertheless, he was astonishingly accurate. Rao recalled, 'I was due to take a new job as accountant general in Madhya Pradesh. Brajend was walking with me along the road and he suddenly pointed at a house and said, "You will not leave Delhi but you will move into this house." A few days later, my move was cancelled, I got a new job at Delhi municipal corporation and that very house was allotted to me.'

Rao witnessed extraordinary faith-healing sessions.

'I once saw him treat a boy with polio. Brajend simply told him to get up and walk and he did. Similarly, if you had seen him at that age, he would have taken one look at you and told you everything about yourself.'

'He told me nothing amazing,' I said.

'No. It saddens me, but I am not surprised.'

Brajendra became nationally famous. Newspaper articles were written about him and he was examined by parapsychologists from Britain and America. It all got out of hand. Rich people in air-conditioned Mercedes would turn up for consultations. Disturbing stories began to filter back to Rao. He learned that while he was at his office during the daytime, Brajendra's father was charging large sums of money behind his back. Rao confronted the man.

'I was very annoyed. I told the father that a person with supernormal powers will lose them quickly if he charges money. In these cases you must not put a strain on the mind of the child. The boy must say spontaneously whatever strikes him, he cannot make predictions to order. Supernormal powers are meant only for service to people.'

The rumours continued.

'One day I scolded Brajend and said, "What do you mean by this? You know the spiritual law, which says you cannot afford to exchange your powers for money." I told him that poverty is absolutely necessary for saintliness. Poverty means: "Whatever God gives me I live on it." It was okay for him to take a few little presents off people, but only if they gave voluntarily.

'But Brajend was a helpless child and he said, "What can I do? My father is greedy." I said, "This is becoming impossible and Delhi is becoming a bad place for you. People will gossip that Mr Rao is also taking his commission. I can't afford that. People come to me for free astrology. Now they will say that Mr Rao has gone into business."'

Rao's patience snapped. He told father and son they were no longer welcome in his house. He warned them that if the exploitation continued, Brajendra was likely to get sick. The pair returned to Taroli where they continued to do good business. By now, Dharan was nearly three. He was also displaying remarkable clairvoyant powers and, if anything, he was even more impressive than his brother.

Big changes took place in Taroli. From being a collection of hovels, the village became a small pilgrimage centre with the Singh brothers as the resident 'saints'. When their rich clientele complained about the poor road into the village, one of their patrons, a chief government engineer, arranged for it to be specially resurfaced to take the expensive cars.

'I wonder what the road is like now,' Rao remarked. 'It's in Uttar Pradesh, where road maintenance is almost unknown. Is it bad?'

'Awful,' I said. 'Like a mud track.' As Brajendra's popularity had waned, so the pot-holes had grown.

A year passed. Then Rao found himself back in Uttar Pradesh on another pilgrimage. On the way back to Delhi, he dropped in at Taroli. His timing could not have been better.

'It was like God had sent me there. Brajend was very ill and he was surrounded by big businessmen and their expensive doctors.

'The moment he saw me, he got up from his bed, jumped into my lap and said, "I will go with Babuji."'

The boy stayed for a month at Rao's house in Delhi and soon recovered. Rao forbade him to make any predictions and encouraged him to play like a normal child. Before Brajendra left, Rao tried again to convince him to stop charging money. He even offered to pay for a private school in Delhi.

'I told him that he had become a predictor for rich men only and that the poor could never see him.' But far worse, Rao warned that if the boy continued this way of life, he would lose his psychic power. Rao's pleas made no difference. Brajendra returned to Taroli and the exploitation continued. The family earned even more money by going on tour around India as a travelling roadshow. The astrologer had had enough. He finally severed all connections with the Singhs in 1984 and had not seen them since. Rao's droopy eyes seemed sadder than ever. These were times he did not want to remember. With considerable feeling, he added, 'You know, when I first met the family they were such good people. Brajendra's mother was a wonderful cook. She produced very tasty village food. On my last visit to them she had the food cooked by her servant. It was not tasty. I said I would not eat in their house again.'

The story of the Singh brothers had turned out to be a tragic account of hype and exploitation.

'So your visit was not a great success,' Rao concluded.

I nodded. I mentioned Sudhir's remark about the broken windscreen wipers. 'I just hope they didn't put a curse on me.'

'I doubt it. My guess is that since childhood Brajend has lost seventy per cent of his powers.' It wasn't exactly what I wanted to hear, but it went some way toward putting my mind at rest.

*****

I stayed a few more days in Delhi, continuing on the political theme. I learned that little arouses the fascination of India's network of prophets more than the subject of the most famous Indian political dynasty of them all – the Gandhis.

The assassination of Indira Gandhi in 1984 and of her son Rajiv in 1991 is said to have been foreseen by astrologers all over India. In 1984, several articles appeared in newspapers saying that Mrs Gandhi should take extra care of herself in November of that year. Among them was a piece written by K.N. Rao in the October issue of the *Astrological Magazine*. Rao warned of the 'Ides of November', and predicted that the government was about to suffer 'significant and tragic' changes. Mrs Gandhi was murdered by her Sikh bodyguards on 31 October 1984.

When Rajiv Gandhi succeeded his mother as prime minister he decided to take action against what he saw as a gross breach of privacy by the country's seers. These insolent astrologers could not be tolerated. How dare they speculate on his mother's life? They must be gagged. The result was that one of the most archaic pieces of twentieth-century legislation to be passed anywhere in the world ended up on the Indian statute books – the Terrorists and Disruptive Activities (Prevention) Act passed by Rajiv Gandhi's government in 1987 illustrates the extraordinary influence that astrologers exercise over the Indian people. The act states that action will be taken against anyone who 'predicts, prophesies or pronounces or otherwise expresses in such manner as to incite, advise, suggest or prompt the killing or the destruction of any person bound by oath under the constitution'. Minimum penalty: seven years imprisonment. The thinking behind this law was that if a potential assassin, particularly one spurred on by religious fervour, read that the stars foretold his victim's death, he would be more likely to carry out his task.[1]

The Indian act, which lumps star-gazers with terrorists, has become an Aunt Sally for astrologers. Ironically, it was Rajiv Gandhi himself who was to become the first victim (if that is the right word) of the new law. Rao claims that he and his colleagues were convinced that Rajiv Gandhi would be in mortal danger around the middle of 1991.

'Rajiv's planetary positions made it very obvious that he had to be very careful, and it would be fatal for him to travel south during that month.' In August 1990, Rao wrote in *The Times of India* that the country could look forward to 'a time of risks and dangers, daredevilry, cataclysmic changes, which can be both fatal and spectacular. There will be attempts on the lives of big leaders.' The following April, a Calcutta astrologer reported, 'A sensational political assassination is likely before the elections, an attempt at it a certainty.' Rajiv took no notice. On 21 May 1991, he was blown to bits by a human bomb at a political rally near Madras.

Following Rajiv's death, the media mocked Rao and his friends for not having been more specific. Why didn't they have the guts to name

---

[1] The last English law to discriminate against astrologers was Section 4 of the 1824 Vagrancy Act, which applied to 'every Person pretending or professing to tell Fortunes, or using any subtle Craft, Means, or Device, by Palmistry or otherwise, to deceive and impose on any of His Majesty's Subjects'. The last prosecution under this act was in 1917; it was repealed as late as 1989.

names? Or were they were afraid they might be wrong? Rao said, 'The trouble is that if I'd written that Rajiv Gandhi should not travel south in May, I'd have had the security forces on our doorsteps. Because of this law, I have to be damned careful.'

There is one soothsayer in Delhi who knows all about security forces on his doorstep. Step forward Dr Ramesh Paramahamsa, an outspoken guru whose irrepressible ego once led him to publish a pamphlet entitled *The Entire World Is Mine*.

If K.N. Rao was reluctant to discuss his political clientele then Dr Paramahamsa couldn't wait to blow the whistle on his most famous patron: Indira Gandhi herself.

I met Dr Paramahamsa at his West Delhi headquarters, an establishment called the Institute of Psychic and Spiritual Research. When I arrived, he was lighting incense sticks and muttering prayers by a little shrine in a rose garden in front of a large white building. He abandoned his meditation and greeted me warmly. We walked inside to his office, which was an airy room with a tall ceiling hung with rippling fans.

Dr Paramahamsa was the antithesis of the modest Rao. He was good-looking, wildly flamboyant and peppered his sentences with asides like 'I have a brilliant brain' and 'I am very, very arrogant, but . . .' Here was a thinking person's guru; a yuppie of the paranormal world. He was a man of immense charisma and indeterminate age, perhaps late fifties or early sixties. He wore fashionably baggy pantaloons and had meticulously styled black hair that curled rakishly over the high Nehru collar of his white shirt. With his lightly coloured skin, he could have passed for an Italian playboy.

Paramahamsa described himself as a clairvoyant and tantric – a man blessed with the supernatural powers of tantra, the study of primordial energy. The Institute was financed chiefly by yoga classes, but this was a tiny part of Paramahamsa's plans for world recognition. His ambition was to give Delhi a fifty-two-storey skyscraper embodying primordial energy. It was to be designed by a two-thousand-year-old Tibetan hermit whom the doctor claimed had developed a unique breathing system that could solve the world's problems.

The doctor's association with Mrs Gandhi began back in 1977, the year when she was thrown out of office and into what looked like political oblivion by Morarji Desai's Janata Government. Indira had heard of the doctor's powers and, as a last resort, asked him if there was anything he could do to help her.

'When Indira Gandhi first came to see me, she was very depressed and thought she would never be in politics again,' Paramahamsa said. 'I told her not to worry.'

On the night of 1 October 1977, Mrs Gandhi and her son Sanjay arrived at the Institute for a special Hindu fire ceremony, known as a yajna. The festivities, conducted by Paramahamsa, lasted all night. Large amounts of wood and clarified butter were burned, and mantras chanted.

'Indira's stars were very bad,' Paramahamsa confided. 'But by sitting before the fire, she invoked the supreme power and that made everything okay.' He brushed away a strand of hair that had fallen over his face. 'Perhaps, my friend, it is difficult for a foreigner to understand this, but the yajna can change anything. I have tested it hundreds of times and it is always a sureshot.'

The doctor sat back in his chair, looking pleased with himself, and adjusted his horn-rimmed glasses. He allowed his voice to rise a notch.

'And do you know what happened? Indira never looked back and within three years she was in power again.'

'So do you claim responsibility for Mrs Gandhi's success?' I asked.

'I certainly do. What's more, she never denied it.' I was not surprised. Whatever her views, a politician of Mrs Gandhi's stature was unlikely to enter a public debate with a self-styled wizard, who claimed to be acquainted with a man aged two thousand. I resisted an urge to say this, although the doctor was so wrapped up in himself that I doubted anything I said would have upset him.

The yajna was not the end of the story. A few months before Mrs Gandhi was re-elected, Paramahamsa performed another ceremony, this time a fortune-telling session in which he threw five rudraksha seeds like dice. The seeds from the rudraksha tree, which grows in the Himalayas, have been revered by holy men for centuries. The name rudraksha comes from two Sanskrit words, rudra meaning Shiva, and aksha meaning eyes. Thus rudraksha is the 'eye of Shiva'.

The seeds are believed to possess spiritual properties and are usually worn in a string of thirty-two or twenty-seven around the neck. They usually come in four colours – white, golden, reddish and dark brown. White and golden are the rarest. Lines run over the surface of a seed, dividing it into a number of crescent-shaped sections. Seeds with five sections are the most common, but there may be any number from one to fourteen. A seed with one section is exceptionally rare and is said to be sacred to Lord Shiva.

According to Paramahamsa, throwing the rudraksha is very special, the ultimate method of divination.

'It is a serious procedure that I learned from my guru, a great spiritual man in Rishikesh. I look at the way the seeds are positioned when they fall. Then I get the vibrations. I do this very seldom, perhaps once every five years, and only in very serious cases. I do it with people who will try to dodge me and I knew that Indira Gandhi had that tendency.'

The rudraksha-throwing session took place at Mrs Gandhi's Delhi residence, 12 Reddington Crescent.

'The seeds revealed that she would return to power. But I told her, "Don't think that Rajiv and Sanjay are your only family. The entire people of India are your sons and daughters. Proceed with this in mind and you will find happiness."' Paramahamsa was visibly moved as he recalled this epic day. I was sprayed with a shower of spittle as he yelled, 'You know what happened? She came back to power!'

Paramahamsa visited his client a few more times at her official residence.

'She would try to get me to talk while we were standing outside on the verandah but I would only talk to her if she was sitting down and listening. She would reluctantly sit on a sofa, ramrod straight, bolt upright and I would pull up a chair.

'She seemed to hear whatever my advice was, but she was only being polite. I would talk about removing the people of India from poverty, but I don't think she took any notice. If any advice was not quite to her liking, she would dismiss it completely. Especially spiritual things. She was very arrogant, very screwed-up, she always knew best, always selfish about her own well-being.'

Paramahamsa claims that it was Indira's arrogance that led to her murder.

'The precise circumstances of her death are irrelevant,' he thundered. 'Above all else, the thing you must remember about the rudraksha is that if someone tells you something is in the seeds you must follow their advice. If you don't . . . well, see what happens!'

While Mrs Gandhi had tolerated Paramahamsa's noisy prevarications with good-humoured patience, her son Rajiv was not so understanding. In 1984, Paramahamsa became a marked man when he established his own political party called Janata Congress. Being aware that his outspokenness might land him in trouble, he launched the party in the name of his five-year-old son, Sanjay Siddarth. He nominated Siddarth as 'prime minister' of 'Bharatvarsha', a specially invented country of 'spiritual harmony' that comprised India, Iran, Afghanistan, Pakistan, Nepal, Bangladesh, Sri Lanka, Cambodia,

Bhutan and Burma. The message was simple – abolish nuclear weapons and love thy neighbour.

It seems almost unbelievable, but Rajiv and his government took the doctor and his plans for a new country seriously. So seriously, in fact, that Paramahamsa ended up on the Intelligence Bureau's list of undesirables. This setback did not deter Paramahamsa, who continued to needle away. He further aroused Rajiv's anger by declaring in a newspaper article that the biggest threat to India (and presumably Bharatvarsha) was Italy – a sideswipe at Rajiv's Italian-born wife Sonia. The last straw was when Paramahamsa published a leaflet criticising Rajiv's twenty-point plan for India. He patriotically pointed out that rather than controlling the country's population, it should be allowed to double, thereby flooding the world with all things Indian.

Paramahamsa and his various dotty bandwagons sound like excellent material for a Monty Python sketch. In most other countries he would have been treated as a mild pain in the neck. But Rajiv did not see the joke. The doctor ended up on charges of sedition and treachery.

Paramahamsa recalled, 'I was sitting here one morning with an American who had come to have his stars read. Suddenly this American looks through the window behind me and says, "My goodness, there seem to be a lot of police in your garden." There were police all over the place. The American said maybe he'd come back another time and left very quickly. Then I was taken down to the police station and thrown in a cell.'

He decided that the best course of action was to invoke his clairvoyant powers.

'I got in touch with Indira's spirit and I said to her, "Look, I was never very nice about you, but at least you never put me in jail. Now your son has imprisoned me for merely writing a leaflet attacking his policies. What's going on?"'

He was released on bail two days later – on 19 November which also happened to be the birthday of Indira Gandhi. The case was thrown out when it came to court two years later.

'So do you believe that Indira was still smiling on you?' I asked.

'No doubt about it. The coincidence was too great.'

I voiced my surprise that the government had bothered to take action against him in the first place. During our conversation, Paramahamsa had become excitable and tub-thumping. Now he exploded with indignation as if relishing his image as a power-driven maverick.

'The duffers who rule this country,' he bellowed, a strand of hair dancing wildly on his forehead, 'don't have a brain between them.' His mood suddenly changed. He took on a look of humility (genuine or false, I'm not sure) and lowered his voice to a confidential whisper. 'What I want you to know, Mr Holt, is that for the first time I have been doing my clairvoyancy on myself.'

'That sounds interesting,' I said.

'And you will see that what I am about to say will happen.'

'And what's that?'

He took a breath.

'The time is coming, in four years to be precise, when I will be prime minister of India.'

'Er, right.'

'It is true.'

'Fine.'

It was time to leave. I hired a cab outside the Institute. The driver spoke a little English and, by way of conversation, I showed him a copy of Paramahamsa's autobiography that the doctor had given me. Had the driver ever heard of the meddlesome doctor?

'Oh yes, sir. Very great man.'

This was not the answer I had expected.

'And do you think he would make a good prime minister?'

'Oh yes, sir. Yes indeed, sir.'

'Well, he thinks he's going to be prime minister within four years.'

'Oh certainly, sahib. No problem.'

'And your friends think the same?'

'Oh yes.'

I am aware that there are people in this world who say things in order to please you. But this man's response to my questions was utterly spontaneous. A clairvoyant in charge of India? I wondered how the United Nations would take to Bharatvarsha.

Before leaving Delhi, I visited K.N. Rao again. I mentioned the demon doctor and his extravagant claims. Rao raised an eyebrow but to give him his due, he made absolutely no comment. He was not prepared to criticise a fellow star-gazer.

'I do not believe I have heard of this man,' he said evasively. I dropped the subject. Rao asked me what my plans were. I replied that I was flying north to Ladakh to visit a Tibetan oracle. Rao hoped I would not be conned.

'When you meet a genuine sage in the country that is luck. But finding the right person is a problem for us Indians, let alone a foreigner like yourself. You will find many quacks who give snapshot predictions. Be careful!'

His concern touched me. I promised to report back with my discoveries. Rao issued a final warning.

'Watch out for people who are interested only in dazzling you and making money. I have seen many and I can't stand them. My test of a sound, good occultist is one and one only – he does not show any greed.'

5

Attacked by a Tibetan Oracle

The flight over the Himalayas to Leh, capital of Ladakh, was enlivened by a conversation with a businessman in the seat next to me. Ravi was a 40-year-old plastics salesman from Delhi. I told him about my meeting with K.N. Rao and how accurate he had been about my past. Ravi had little time for astrologers. His brother-in-law, he explained, was an amateur astrologer.

'He's an old-time retired army colonel. You know the type: a big bugger with a big bugger's moustache. Utterly obsessed by the stars.'

A couple of years earlier, Ravi was offered a new job. He'd never had much faith in astrology, but he thought he'd ask his brother-in-law what his prospects were. The colonel took it all extremely seriously and drew up Ravi's horoscope.

'He told me that this job was perfect for me. He said, "Absolutely wonderful, you take it immediately, don't waste a second."'

Ravi took the job. Three months later he was fired.

'It was awful. I hated the work, my boss hated me, and it was the first time in my life I'd ever been sacked. I went back to my brother-in-law and said, "This is bloody nonsense. What the hell's going on?"'

The colonel was beside himself with remorse. The reputation of his beloved science lay in tatters. A post-mortem was called for, urgently. He frantically contacted his astrologer friends in Delhi. They gathered at his house and spent all day poring over Ravi's chart trying to establish what had gone wrong. As dark was falling, one of the astrologers cried 'Eureka!' The colonel had failed to note a tiny star, perhaps the tiniest in the universe, but one with evil tendencies, that had been passing through Ravi's horoscope the day he started work. It was this wretched star that had caused all the fuss. The delighted colonel reported back with the news. Ravi was not pleased.

'I thought it was complete, bloody nonsense. I don't think they had a clue what they were doing.'

We reached Leh and the plane made a steep descent that scattered the thick clouds over the mountains into vaporous wisps. The flight path into Leh is so hazardous that only a handful of Indian Airlines pilots are qualified to land there. The valley seemed to climb around us, the hillsides so close that we could almost touch them.

At the airport I teamed up with an Australian backpacker called Kevin. He was a quiet, craggy man, with two marriages behind him. At the age of 51 he had quit his clothing business in Melbourne to pursue a long-held dream to go around the world. He had arrived in India from Thailand and was *en route* to Africa. Like me, Kevin had come up to Ladakh to escape the heat. Leh lies at three thousand five hundred metres and visitors must adapt slowly to the high altitude – the exertion of walking less than a kilometre can leave a new arrival gasping for breath.

We found a guest-house on the outskirts of town. It was a magnificent building decorated with traditional Ladakhi wood carving and the rooms had panoramic views of the mountains. Willow and eucalyptus trees shaded the terraced garden where bluebells thrived in the cool sunshine. The owners were an elderly Ladakhi couple, who were Christians – rare in this centre of Buddhism. On the wall of the guests' sitting-room there was a copy of Psalm 23 and a notice proclaiming: 'Christ is the head of this house, the unseen guest at every meal, the silent listener to every conversation.'

Ladakh was a welcome relief after the stickiness of the plains. I explored Leh with a new feeling of freshness and vigour. The town was plastered with posters demanding that Ladakh become a separate state of India. At present it comes under the jurisdiction of the state of Jammu and Kashmir. The Ladakhis feel aggrieved. They say that they are culturally very different from Jammu and Kashmir, and have more in common with Tibet than the rest of India. There were also allegations of corruption. It was rumoured that central government funds given to the state were more likely to be spent on Kashmir because the majority of the J & K officials are Kashmiris.

The threat of unrest was being kept in check by the Indian Army. A few soldiers armed with .303 rifles patrolled the streets. A couple of Israeli girls I met were pretty sniffy about the weaponry. They had each served two years in the army and were as tough as hell. They declared that .303s would not be much use in a scrap.

Meanwhile, the many Tibetan refugees in Leh were quietly hoping for a return to their homeland, which has been under Chinese occupation since 1959. The well-worn topic of conversation in the back-street cafés was of the death of Tibetan Buddhism and culture with monasteries destroyed and the monks butchered as 'counter-revolutionaries' by the Chinese. China has flooded Tibet with seven million of its own people. The years pass and the refugees have assumed the Ladakhi identity. But the Tibetans pray that one day the old men ruling China will go and the 'land of snows' will revert to its ancestral ways.

In Leh bazaar I found a book about Tibetan superstitions. I read that the Tibetans believe that if dogs howl at dawn, something unpleasant is about to happen. The night before the Chinese invasion of Tibet, dogs were heard howling like human beings, and in the streets of Lhasa, the sacred Tibetan capital, the dogs dug holes in the ground until their paws were bloodied. This was interpreted as digging graves.

Like Hindus, Tibetans consider cats are jinxed. They say that whereas a dog feels sad that its master might die soon, a cat will curl up near the pillow waiting for its owner to die so it can eat his brain.

There are many superstitions relating to childbirth. Tibetans believe that if, by chance, a horse steps over a pregnant woman, or even if its shadow falls on her, she will be 'polluted' and will remain pregnant for 12 months, the length of time a mare gestates. Tibetans also believe that a child in the womb may disappear after a thunderstorm. Thunder is the cry of a dragon, they say, and a dragon will take away unborn children. There is another saying that if the child is a boy and the father is present at the delivery, the child will not arrive easily because the mother feels shy before his father. Tibetans also believe that it is very unlucky to buy or to make clothing for an unborn child. Stepping over anyone's clothes is considered a terrible sin and is believed to degrade one's personal deity. If you walk over your toddler's clothes, the child will trip over frequently. On a happier note, if a child bends over and looks backwards between its legs, it means its mother will be pregnant soon – it is said the child is looking to see who is coming after him. When an infant's grip is tight, the Tibetans say the baby has a wish-fulfilling gem in its hand and does not want it taken away.

Like most cultures, Tibet has a recipe for wart removal – on the fifteenth day of any month, the person with warts goes up on to the roof of his house and pretends to sweep away the warts with a broom.

Someone down below should call out, 'What are you doing?' The person with warts replies, 'I am sweeping away the warts'. Less practical, but said to be just as efficient, is to rub the warts on the place where a hare has slept, but only while the place is still warm. However, be warned – never count your pimples because they will only increase.

Of course, there is marriage advice. A girl with a gap between her two front teeth will not make a good wife and she will probably die young; avoid a woman who doesn't wear earrings – she will be born a donkey in her next life. Toes are of great importance – when standing barefoot, if a woman's little toes do not touch the ground she will become a prostitute. If the third toe does not touch the ground, she will be quarrelsome and a raised second toe means she will be unfaithful.

The Tibetans believe it is unlucky for a man to be over-endowed. He will be a rich and good husband if his penis is no more than six finger widths long. But if while squatting, the penis reaches to the bottom of the heels, his life will be full of sorrow.

The Hindus have similar beliefs. According to the *Brihat Samhita*, a big penis can only mean trouble – the man will be poor and will have no sons. If his member is straight, small and sinewy he will be rich. A penis inclining towards the left indicates poverty. If a man has perfect, matching testicles of the same size he will be a king and if they're not matching, he'll be fond of sex. If the glans penis be depressed in the middle, the person will father daughters and be poor; if it is raised in the middle, he will have many cows; if it's not very large, he will be rich.

Semen is also important. If it smells like honey, the man will be rich; like salt, he will be poor; like fish, he will have many children. If it is thin he will have daughters and live in great comfort. Finally, forget the superstud routine if you want a long life. A person whose sexual intercourse lasts for a minute or so will live long, but prolonged bouts of rumpy-pumpy will lead to an early death.

On the subject of women, the *Brihat Samhita* says that a woman will be happy if 'her thighs be like the trunk of the elephant, without hair and firm, the genital organ be broad and triangular, the part just above it be large and high and like the shell of the turtle, if the clitoris be hid from view'. But she will suffer grief if 'the calves of the leg be found to grow larger as they approach the knees, or if the shanks be covered with muscles, without flesh or with too much flesh or covered with hair, if the genital organ be sunk, small, with the hair growing from right to left, and if the belly be like a pot'.

Snow cuts off Ladakh for eight months of the year and the savage sub-zero weather is held in great respect by the locals, who have struggled for years to survive on subsistence agriculture and rainfall of little more than two inches a year. Before antibiotics, there was a high death rate each winter, and faith-healers were much in demand.

I asked local people if they knew of a Buddhist oracle I could visit. There are several in Ladakh, most of them living in areas that are out of bounds to foreigners because of their proximity to the Chinese border. Kevin was keen to come along and I learned that it would be no problem for us to visit a 60-year-old grandmother, who lived ten kilometres outside Leh. As well as having a reputation as being one of the most impressive oracles in the state, she was also known as a great faith-healer.

I heard about the lady at Saboo from a local trekking guide called Tashi. He was a 22-year-old science student, born and brought up in Leh, who earned money during the tourist season to pay for his studies at Bangalore University in South India. He was a quiet young man with a keen sense of propriety.

'It is very nice to see British people in Ladakh, sir,' he told me politely.

'Please call me Peter,' I insisted.

'No, sir. I will call you sir, sir. Otherwise it is not respectful.'

I hired Tashi as interpreter for the visit to the oracle. He knew her well and was convinced of her potency. He claimed that she had cured him of a stomach ailment.

'I had been to many doctors, but no good. The oracle removed the poison and I got better.'

Most of the oracles in Ladakh are women. There are strict rules to prevent fakes. Anyone claiming to have supernormal powers must first be examined by a group of senior oracles. In the first test, a bowl of seven black stones and seven white stones is placed before the blindfolded novice. He or she must pick out the white stones. If the novice selects just one black stone, it means the person is not a true oracle and there is an evil spirit lurking within them. Then four boys and girls hand over some personal items, like watches and pens, which are put in a pile. The novice has to pick out the objects and hand each one to the right child. Finally, the novice's occult powers of healing are tested. An animal like a cow is made to swallow a pin. The novice must force the pin out through the flesh using psychic energy and so that no harm comes to the animal. Pass these exams and you are a true oracle.

The woman we were about to see was called Sonam Zano. Tashi explained she would go into a deep trance before speaking through a goddess called Tsering Chenmo, one of the three hundred and sixty

Tibetan deities and a protector of the Dalai Lama, spiritual leader of Tibetan Buddhism.

Sonam's native language was Ladakhi, but while possessed by the goddess she gave her predictions in Tibetan. Both her mother and father had been oracles and Sonam had first gone into a trance aged four. The experience did not happen again until she was nine when the oracle briefly returned. The deity left her again, but came back when she was 19. Since then she had been practising as a full-time oracle, going into a trance about once a week.

The Indian Army presence was obvious on the outskirts of Leh. Large sectors of rubbish-strewn wasteland were fenced off with barbed wire; signs warned that this was a mine training area. We drove east along the Indus River valley, a lush belt of green pastures with grazing cows and the occasional yak. Women with water urns and monks in orange robes strolled on the path alongside the river. The Indus was little more than a meandering trickle of melted snow; droopy willow trees hugged the banks. It was a warm day, the crisp blue sky dotted with puffy clouds.

We turned off on to a rough track that pointed towards a range of brown, jagged hills. The snowcaps of the Himalayan peaks lay in the distance. The driver stopped at an army checkpoint manned by a member of the Indo-Tibetan border police. The guard was immaculately uniformed with a marvellous plume on his hat and spotlessly white puttees. Tashi explained that the police checked vehicles containing foreigners. They did not want tourists wandering off into the mountains.

We left the greenery behind and headed on over arid terrain with neither trees nor bushes. The track was marked with stone piles to show the way when the snow drifts came. A sharp wind whipped up spirals of sandy dust. After a mile the track petered out into nothing. We left the car and picked our way over the rocky ground to a small house that stood alone in the barrenness. It was single-storey, built of mud and brick. The flat roof was topped off with the ubiquitous television aerial to which was attached a string of prayer flags, flimsy pieces of tattered cloth inscribed with invocations that the Tibetans believe will be blown on the wind to the gods. Outside the front door were a dozen or so metal plates containing black, sticky stuff. Tashi informed us that this was the poison that the oracle had sucked out of her patients. Kevin grimaced. I think he was beginning to have second thoughts about the visit. We left our shoes in the doorway and Tashi led us into the main room of the house, which was crowded with people.

The oracle was kneeling on a platform at the far end of the room. She looked much older than her 60 years. Her face was weatherbeaten and her nose was aristocratic and hooked like a scimitar. Kevin, Tashi and I weaved our way through the crowd and found a space on the floor next to the platform.

We had arrived just as Sonam was going into a trance. It was as if she had been hit by a lightning force. Her body jerked as the goddess entered her. She shook with tremors and her breath became short and sharp like an asthmatic. She made busy movements like a hen in a state of extreme agitation. Then she picked up a bell and rang it ferociously while manically mumbling a long prayer. To the side of her was a small table laid out like an altar. A row of copper vessels contained offerings to the goddess: barley, rice, water and tea. Her dress, a bizarre mixture that might have come from a child's dressing-up box, consisted of a black tunic down to her ankles, silk shawl and nursemaid's black apron, a gold headdress shaped like a castle, and, most macabre of all, a blood red scarf tied like a cowboy mask around her mouth. Her plaited hair dangled innocently below her waist like a schoolgirl's.

Clouds of smoke rising from an incense burner added to the intense atmosphere. A single, bare lightbulb hanging from the ceiling glowed dimly. The room was packed with people sitting on the wooden floor and, with only small windows, was hot and airless. The people were mainly locals who had come to have their ailments cured. Worried-looking women cradled crying babies close to their chests. An American woman had arrived before us. As well as having a loyal local following, Sonam was gaining notoriety as an off-beat tourist attraction.

Tashi explained that people came from as far as one hundred kilometres away; and not only Buddhists, but also Moslems, Hindus and Christians. One of Sonam's regular visitors was an Indian Army brigadier, who often drove down from his posting near the Pakistani border to ask her advice. She was famous for handing out amulets, in the form of knotted pieces of string, to members of the Indo-Tibetan security forces. Tashi insisted that wearing one of these would protect you against anything – even Pakistani or Chinese bullets.

The oracle beckoned a mother and baby forward. The child had a nasty stomach upset. The oracle chanted a prayer and took the baby in her arms. The floor creaked as she leaned forward. After gently pulling up the baby's woolly jumper, she blew and sucked noisily on its stomach. She took a small bowl from beside her and spat out a mouthful of what looked like black bile. There was no mark on the baby's stomach – it was as if the oracle had sucked the substance straight through the skin. The bile coagulated in the bowl.

'She is removing the poison, sir,' Tashi whispered. This repulsive display could either have been a magic trick (a small sack of chicken blood hidden in the mouth perhaps?) or a homespun version of an obscure medical practice known as 'cupping'. This treatment involves the practitioner drawing contaminated blood to the surface of the patient's skin by the partial vacuum within a heated glass.

The oracle handed back the baby. The mother muttered her thanks and hugged the infant tightly to her, cooing reassuring messages. She returned to her space on the floor. A girl came forward. She was in her late teens and wore heavy make-up, baby-doll eyelashes and plastic earrings. She looked worried and complained of an eye problem. The oracle blew on the girl's face and murmured incantations. She repeated the sucking process. When it was over, the girl handed over a gift of a white muslin scarf, a traditional Tibetan symbol of goodwill. The oracle took it and draped it over her head-dress.

'Would it be okay if I took a photograph?' I asked.

Tashi nodded.

'Yes, sir. But afterwards you should keep it in a frame like a holy picture.' Like the other Ladakhis in the room, he was greatly in awe of this lady's power.

The oracle resumed her chanting and bell-ringing. Now she turned her attention to her grand-daughter, a pretty girl of about ten, who had been lurking at the back of the room. Granny called her over. The girl looked horribly awkward.

Tashi explained that she was doing so well at school that her classmates were jealous of her. A couple of days earlier, Granny had noticed that the girl was unhappy. One of the girl's rivals had put a 'bad feeling' on her and it was Granny's job to remove it. The oracle lightly tapped her grand-daughter on the cheek and blessed her with a prayer. Despite the 'cure', the girl didn't seem much brighter. She self-consciously brushed a strand of hair from her face and returned to the back of the room. This was an intriguing family relationship. I wondered how healthy it was for a child to be brought up in such a bizarre environment.

After dealing with half a dozen more patients, the oracle glanced in our direction. She pointed a finger at Kevin and me, and indicated that we should ask our questions. Kevin had been wide-eyed and squeamish during the blood-sucking.

'Your turn, Peter,' he said.

'No, I'm sure you've got something much more important to ask.'

Each of us feigned politeness, but in truth we were both terrified of approaching this lady head-on. I went first. Tashi prepared for his job of interpreting. It was a complicated business, which involved using the oracle's son, a tall, excitable man of about 25, as a go-between. His mother replied in Tibetan, the son translated the words into Ladakhi and Tashi spoke to me in English.

'What do you want to ask her?' Tashi said.

'What do people normally ask?'

'Like have you lost something? Or do you want advice on how to get on with your family?'

This sounded rather dull.

'How about asking if I'm going to be very rich?'

Tashi looked as if he hadn't heard properly. 'What?'

'Am I going to be very rich?' I repeated.

'No, sir!' Tashi was appalled. 'She will get very angry if you ask that. She will say you are very selfish.' There was no way he was going to ask my question.

I felt severely admonished for my western materialism. I remembered the Hindu saying: 'Man makes money, so man is more important than money.'

'How about, "When will I get married?"'

Tashi still looked unhappy. Anything related to sex was out as well. I desperately tried to think of a selfless question. After some soul-searching, I suggested: 'Is my work going to be successful?' Tashi wearily agreed that this was acceptable.

He passed on the question to the son. The son repeated it to his mother, who did a little dance on her knees. She picked a little drum in one hand, the bell in the other, and began banging and clanging.

'Now she is predicting,' Tashi said. 'She is calling up the spirit.'

The oracle launched into a high-pitched chant creating a mad cacophony like a brigade of fire engines. This went on for ten minutes. Then all hell broke loose. The oracle took a handful of rice and hurled it violently in my direction. It hit me in the face. Tashi cowered away. Kevin was speechless. The woman was distraught. After breathing fast and deeply like a swimmer who has come up for air after several minutes under water, she broke into a hacking cough, which sounded like a cat being sick. Then she violently pounded her chest with her fists and began shouting at me. A bolt of fear moved through me.

Her son rapidly translated her words to Tashi. Tashi turned to me.

'The goddess is very angry,' he said. 'She says this is an unnecessary question you are asking her. And if you are not asking a true question, she says you have some doubt in her.'

'You look worried, Tashi,' I said.

'I am scared, sir. I don't like her being angry with you. Perhaps she will be angry with me for bringing you. It's a kind of sin for us if she gets angry.' He was also worried that the woman might hit me. Oracles had been known to punch people. The oracle wagged a finger at me. Mindful of Tashi's words, I backed away. She jabbered on in a little girl voice. Her son struggled to keep up. There were a lot of words exchanged, but Tashi was keeping the translation to a minimum. He seemed reluctant to translate exactly what the woman was saying.

Tashi repeated,

'She says you should not ask unnecessary questions. She says if you don't pray in this life you will be born in hell in the next.' From the look on his face I could only imagine that the woman was being much ruder than that. Tashi was being diplomatic. He was caught in a no-man's land where his conscience was playing havoc. His inborn superstition would not let him defy the oracle and yet he did not want to upset his foreign guest.

'Well, what should I ask her?' I said tersely.

'Sir, the problem is that you asked your question in a doubtful manner. She is angry because you do not have faith in her. She does not like unbelievers in the room.'

The oracle was burbling and chattering away in the background. Beads of sweat had gathered on her brow; she grasped and tugged at her clothes like a lunatic in Bedlam. Pain showed in her screwed-up eyes. Her anguish was the stuff of a Breughel painting. Everyone in room was staring at me with blank faces that gave nothing away. One of the babies began crying. The oracle flicked more rice in my direction. I felt embarrassed; and unloved.

'She is angry, sir, because she is a powerful deity and yet you doubt her.'

'Of course I have doubts,' I said irritably. 'For a start, I was brought up in the Church of England and it's the first time I've met a Tibetan oracle.'

Tashi sighed.

'I told you she would get angry if you asked unnecessary questions.'

'I suppose she gets angry with all the foreigners she meets.'

'No, sir. You are different.'

To prove this point, the woman was much calmer while talking to Kevin. Her voice descended an octave. Perhaps this easygoing Australian had the faith? He asked a few questions about his family. She talked gently to him for a couple of minutes. He seemed encouraged by

Above: The temple of Somnath, Gujarat. According to Hindu mythology, Somnath is the oldest place in creation, the place where man first walked on earth. Hindus believe that the temple should be their first pilgrimage destination

Below: Wall painting at the Palace of Udaipur depicting sixteenth-century Maharana Udai Singh consulting his court astrologers. The first seer is blindfolded so that he may not know to whom he is giving his predictions

Above: The Maharanas of Mewar, rulers of Udaipur, believed that they were directly descended from the sun. It was obligatory for the family to pray to the sun before eating and imitation gold suns are dotted around the Palace of Udaipur so that worship could continue during the cloudy weather of the monsoon

Below: Udaipur astrologer Bansidhar Shastri, one of the last experts in India of the ancient art of 'shadow reading'

Above: Bansidhar Bhawan, Jaipur's senior astronomer, standing by the Yantra Raj, his favourite instrument at Jaipur's sixteenth-century observatory. *Jantar-Mantar* means literally in Sanskrit 'instruments for measuring'. 'With this I can prepare an instant horoscope,' he said. 'Far better than a computer'

Below: K. N. Rao, said to be one of the most accurate astrologers in India whose predictions are taken seriously by the Indian Government

Left: Sixty-year-old Ladakhi grandmother Sonam Zano in her guise as a Tibetan oracle. Sonam is in a trance, speaking through the Tibetan goddess Tsering Chenmo. I took this photo shortly before she attacked me

Below: Varanasi. Classical vedic astrologer Pandit Rajmohan Upadhyay, ex-dean of the faculty of Oriental Learning and Theology at Benares Hindu University.
His speciality is reading the moles on a person's body

Right: Ujjain. Effigy of Kaal Bhairav, commander of the celestial armed forces. Kaal Bhairav is a much-feared Hindu deity with strong connections to the supernatural

Below: Priest at a temple in Ujjain feeding alcohol to a statue of Kaal Bhairav, most feared of the Hindu deities. I saw the statue appear to drink the liquor. Later I looked closely at the effigy. There was not a trace of liquid to be seen. Nor was there a hole in Kaal Bhairav's mouth. The statue is made of solid wood

Above: Amalapuram, Andhra Pradesh. Nadi reader Ramajogeswara Rao with some of the palm leaves he uses to predict a person's destiny. This was the man who used his special powers to stop my tape recorder from working.

Below: Madras beach. The author listening to his horoscope being read by what looked like an old cereal box with knobs

Above: Top Madras sex astrologer Mr K. Parthasaarathy, whose speciality is revealing whether or not your partner is having an affair

Below: Octogenarian yoga guru Gitananda Giri at his ashram outside Pondicherry. Canadian-born Swami Giri is an expert at foot reading. He claims the west's problems lie with its use of shoes. 'Shoes kill you. They stop all the natural energy from leaving your body. Sandals are okay, but bare feet are best of all'

Left: Preparations for the asta mangela at the village of Alathirakkal in Kerala. Mr Krishnyer, the troubled priest, is on the left. An asta mangela is a cosmic investigation into why certain evil events have happened either in your family or at your temple

Below: B. V. Raman, India's most famous astrologer, at his Bangalore offices. Raman is known as 'The Wizard'. He warns that the world faces a period of tremendous change

her answers. The American woman said she would like to ask a question. When would the Chinese leave Tibet? Now it was the son's turn to get angry.

'Never! Impossible,' he shouted scornfully. He held his head high like a camel's. The oracle began chattering.

'Not a chance!' the son repeated. He was very certain about this.

'Quiet!' the American woman snapped. She was quite tough. 'I want to hear what the oracle says. You just translate exactly.'

The son was not used to being spoken to like this. He listened to his mother and then replied sulkily, 'It will take time for Tibet to be free, but she says it will happen.'

The oracle took fifteen minutes to come down from her trance. It was like a scene from *The Exorcist*. She banged her drum louder than ever – perhaps to clean the room of my unhealthy influence? The deep breaths began again. She panted heavily, cleared her throat and made little 'cack, cack, cack' noises like a bird. Then she whistled like a doodlebug, clicked her tongue, knelt forward so her head touched the floor, and began a series of dry retches. She clenched her fists and struck herself on the back as if in heartbroken agony. There was more gulping and retching, a horrible mixture of animal sounds and motions that must have put a massive strain on her body.

The spirit suddenly left her. It was all over. The room was silent. Then people quietly began to leave, melting away from the smokey gloom. The woman removed her headdress and mask. The tension left her face and she broke into a weak smile. She looked exhausted.

We stayed for a while. The mood changed to one of domesticated family life. We were joined by the son's wife, who passed round milky tea and biscuits on a cracked plate. Another of the oracle's grandchildren, a boy of two, climbed on to his grandmother's lap. The strangulated cries of Granny's trance did not appear to have disturbed him – he had spent the time playing happily with a pink, fluffy teddy bear, shrieking with delight whenever Granny banged her drum.

Sonam remembered nothing of what had happened. As soon as the goddess left her, she was a perfectly normal person again with no special powers. She knew very little about Tibetan Buddhism, had never been to school and didn't even know how to count to ten.

'Doesn't she remember getting angry with me?' I asked Tashi.

'No, sir. But she thinks maybe you had some doubt and that is why the goddess got angry.' Sonam said something. Tashi grinned. 'She says you are lucky she didn't beat you. You are lucky that she is old. The younger oracles often hit people.' I looked at Sonam and mimicked the way she had wagged her finger at me.

'But you were very angry with me,' I said. 'I felt like a naughty schoolboy.' Tashi translated. Sonam chuckled and gave me a lovely smile.

'And you threw rice at me,' I added.

'She thinks you are funny,' Tashi said. 'She says why don't you try another oracle? Then you can see if you get scolded again.' I left Granny giggling with delight.

*****

After a week in Ladakh I returned to Delhi. and paid a brief visit to K.N. Rao. He was keen to hear about my experiences with the oracle. When I got to '. . . and then she nearly hit me', he allowed a hint of a smile.

'And did she charge you money?' he enquired. I said that there had been no demands of any kind. Local people usually donated one rupee and Tashi had said that whatever I gave should not matter to me. I had given fifty rupees, the equivalent of a pound. Rao approved.

'That is how these people should be,' he said. 'Using their occult powers for the common good.'

A short man of about 30 was seated on a nest of cushions in the corner of Rao's study. Rao introduced him as Pandit Ganada Watwva, a thumb-reader from Nagpur, three hundred and fifty miles south of Delhi in the state of Maharastra.

Pandit Watwva was staying for a few days in Delhi as Rao's house guest. He was said to have impressive powers of divination from looking only at a person's thumb – known in the Vedas as 'angustha sastra' – and Rao was inviting his friends round to test Watwva's skills. Also in the room was a middle-aged woman in a voluminous yellow and green sari. I failed to catch her name. Rao introduced her as a lady doctor. She was his former pupil and one of the best female astrologers in Delhi.

Pandit Watwva was dressed entirely in white with a Gandhi hat stuck lopsidedly on his head. He said little but smiled a lot. Rao suggested that he read my thumb. Watwva beckoned me over and I sat next to him on the cushions. He produced a magnifying glass from a yellow cotton bag, gently took my hand and peered at my thumb.

'This is a form of astrology that has been all but lost in tradition,' Rao intoned from across the room. 'Thumb-reading is one of the great secrets of Indian prediction. All the planets and how they affect you can be found in the thumb.'

Watwva scribbled some calculations in a notebook and asked a question in Hindi. The lady doctor translated for me.

'He wants to know which nostril you are breathing through,' she said. 'Left or right?'

The use of nostril breath in divination derives from a powerful type of yoga called swarodya. Experts in swaroydya claim that they can predict the health of a person according to the amount of breath coming out of each nostril. From merely examining the pressure of the breath from the nose, yoga gurus have been known to forecast the time of their own death down to the last second.

I shut my mouth and blew through my nose on to my hand. By moving my hand around I could just about work out which nostril was blowing hardest.

'It's difficult to tell but I think it's my right,' I said. 'But what on earth has it got to do with my thumb?'

'It is all part of who and how you are,' the lady doctor said.

She translated my words into Hindi and Watwva nodded delightedly. Breathing through the right nostril was lucky if you were a man. For a woman it should be the left.

'It's all to do with your cerebral spinal system,' the lady doctor said. 'The nerves come from the nose down the spinal cord and right down to the base of the spine.' For good measure, she added, 'It is all part of the ancient Vedic tradition and has been scientifically detailed.'

The problem with my thumb is that it is horribly crooked. If I try to hold it upright, it bends backwards at a nearly ninety-degree angle. Watwva gently wiggled my digit.

'Hold it up straight,' the lady doctor barked.

'But that's how it is naturally,' I protested. 'It bends right over. See?' She laughed in a motherly way.

'So that is how it is. It shows a very malleable, flexible nature perhaps?' She turned to Watwva and translated 'malleable' and 'flexible' into Hindi. He nodded. She was absolutely right. He went on to describe my life from the age of seventeen to the present day. He talked for about twenty minutes. I cannot say what he said made much sense and he filled me with gloom at the prospect of medical problems by the age of forty-five. Frankly, he was not very revealing, although I did not want to say so in front of Mr Rao.

I spent a week in Delhi before making another excursion into the Himalayas. I intended to visit the Dalai Lama's personal oracle at Dharamshala in Himachel Pradesh. Kevin had flown back from Ladakh a few days earlier and also wanted to see Dharamshala. I was glad to have a travelling companion and we arranged to meet at Delhi railway station. I should have taken greater notice of my horoscope in that day's copy of the *Indian Express*. 'Travelling may be difficult,' it had said.

A few days earlier, I had visited a colleague of K.N. Rao's called Mr N.P. Thareja, a retired bank manager in his sixties who lived in a suburb on the edge of Delhi. Mr Thareja was a thin-faced man who sat behind a desk creaking under a heap of books. As well as being a traditional astrologer, he was a goldmine of information regarding auspicious days for travelling as laid down by the ancient Indian sages. As a traveller, he declared that it was important I should have this data. He produced a sheaf of yellowing notes and proceeded to tell me on what days and in which direction a person should travel:

Good days to travel . . .

East – Sunday, Tuesday, Thursday, Friday

West – Monday, Saturday

North – Thursday, Friday, Monday

South – Wednesday

Bad days to travel . . .

East – Monday, Saturday

North – Tuesday, Wednesday

South – Thursday

West – Sunday, Friday

By the time I reached Delhi Station I wished that I had listened more attentively to Mr Thareja. It was a Tuesday, a bad day to go north. The north-bound Jemal Express to Pathankot, from where we would take a bus to Dharamshala, was late; worse, no one knew when it would arrive. We sat it out on the platform. It was a stinking hot night and my patience was tested to the limit.

I was in an intolerant mood. Earlier that day I had escaped being cheated by one of the many Sikh fortune-tellers plying his trade on

Janpath, Delhi's main tourist street. Mr Rao had warned me about swindlers like this, that they used nothing more mystical than common conjuring tricks. Even so, the Sikh was so persuasive that I found it difficult to drag myself away when he accosted me. He was a huge man with a warrior's beard and a mighty blood-red turban. He produced a pair of stools from a doorway in a side street and we sat down.

About the only vaguely interesting thing he told me was, 'Don't cut your fingernails on a Tuesday,' a piece of information that I shall cherish. He quoted a ludicrously high fee – five hundred rupees (ten pounds) – in return for telling me my mother's name. I was aware of this trick. The idea was that I would write a name on a piece of paper. Unknown to me, there would either be a piece of carbon paper underneath the notepad, or the trickster would glance at what I had written by using sleight of hand.

'Okay,' I said. 'But I'm not writing anything down.'

This foxed him completely. Bang went five hundred rupees. But he wouldn't give up. He grabbed my hand and studied my palm. He traced a finger along my life line and said I would live to 85.

'What does the island on my life line mean?' I asked.

'It means nothing, Sahib.'

'Nonsense,' I countered. 'According to professional palmists I've met, it means I'll be seriously ill at around 75 and lucky to live longer than that.' The man looked aghast. I added, 'I don't think you know what you're talking about.'

I was enjoying myself enormously. The Sikh tried to recover lost ground.

'That will be a hundred rupees,' he said. I gave him five rupees. The Sikh snarled as I walked away.

Now I was at Delhi Station suffocating in the fetid air. The platforms were swarming with people. Kevin saw off a couple of suspicious-looking teenaged boys who were eyeing our luggage. Thieves had stolen his camera on a train at Lucknow and he was not taking any chances.

Most of the trains were running late. Despite promises by railway officials, the Jemal Express had still not arrived by 4 a.m. We spent most of the night trying to ignore a beggar. He was crippled with rickets and dragged himself up and down the platform on hands protected by plastic flip-flops. Exhausted by his nocturnal prowl, he eventually fell asleep on a pile of mail bags.

A blind man stumbled along the platform, tripping over the rows of sleeping bodies. A few people hastily moved when he crashed into them. An elderly middle-class woman recoiled with repulsion when he shuffled too close to her. From the look on her face he might have been a demon. He staggered past her and headed straight for the edge of the platform. No one tried to stop him. Kevin and I grabbed him and steered him to a safe place in the centre of the platform.

Our rucksacks were positioned next to a family of four. Father and two children slept while mother stayed awake, gently fanning her brood. She noticed that Kevin and I were wilting in the heat and she fanned a little harder so that we might catch the cooling breezes. This simple act of kindness contrasted with the way the blind man had been treated.

At 5 a.m. the station began to wake up. Able-bodied beggars carried their limbless colleagues down the steps on to the platforms to begin their day's work. The hawkers arrived. Everyone, from newspaper sellers to chai stall owners, seemed to be shouting. I was pestered by a padlock salesman weighed down by the chains around his neck. Small boys clustered around a man selling plastic machine-guns. As if there wasn't enough noise already, we now had to suffer an excruciating ratter-tatter as the children sprayed passers-by with imaginary bullets. As the rising sun began to cook us under the corrugated iron roof of the station, I longed for a cold shower to sooth my sleep-deprived nerves.

There is a lesson to be learned in India about tolerance and patience, but I was not in the mood to receive it. I felt exceptionally bad-tempered. At 6 a.m. I approached a guard who was wearing a sleep-rumpled shirt with a dirty collar. I asked what had happened to the Jemal Express. He scratched his groin. He neither knew nor cared.

I tried the enquiries counter. I barged past a huddle of people asking about delayed trains and walked into the office. There was a muddled blackboard bearing the names of various trains. Most of them had been crossed out.

'What's happened to the Jemal Express?' I demanded.

A small man came forward. He was the enquiries office manager.

'We are very sorry, sir, but the Jemal Express got lost somewhere between Pune and Delhi. It is always late on a Tuesday.'

'But now it's Wednesday. And if it's always twelve hours late why don't you just cancel the thing and reschedule it for a later time?'

'A good idea, sir. I will suggest it.'

The manager promised that the train would arrive at 8 a.m. I asked for the platform number. He said it would be announced over the loudspeakers. I said that I couldn't understand the announcements because they were in Hindi.

'No, sir. Actually they are in English.' The manager was truly apologetic. 'I know it sounds like Hindi, but I am afraid it has to do with the quality of the loudspeakers.' He added cheerfully, 'But do not worry, sir. We will do something about it.'

I returned to Kevin who was guarding our bags. Ten minutes before our train was due, the announcements began. The announcer spoke very, very slowly, in the best Oxford accent he could muster: 'The Jemal Express, Number 4677, will arrive on platform three.' He repeated it . . . and repeated it again. He must have made the announcement thirty times in the hope that Kevin and I, the only foreigners amongst thousands of Indians at Delhi Station, would hear it. As we drew out of the station, we could still hear the announcer's cultured tones. Kevin and I lay back on our second-class bunks and laughed with sheer joy at this act of thoughtfulness. The frustrations of the previous twelve hours vanished. I put it down as one of the best moments of my life.

*****

Dharamshala is one of the eighty hill stations established by the British in the last century. The town is split into two parts with most of the tourist action concentrated at the village of McLeod Ganj, which lies at eighteen hundred metres in one of the most spectacular settings in India. The views from the hillsides are of thick forests and of the spur of granite mountains that form the Dhauladhar range. The scenery is almost Scottish – the Viceroy Lord Elgin was especially taken by the majestic hills because they reminded him of his beloved Highlands. He is buried at St John's-in-the-Wilderness, a quintessentially British church built to last out of sturdy, grey stone. It stands in a glade of fir trees a little way from the town.

After the Chinese occupied Tibet, much of the land around here was designated as a permanent base for the Dalai Lama and the Tibetan Government-in-Exile. McLeod Ganj has become a tourist centre scattered with cheap hotels, trinket shops and cafés run by Tibetan refugees who far outnumber the local Indian population. When I arrived, the Dalai Lama (or the 'DL', as his colleagues call him) was in South America on a speaking tour, but over a cup of tea in a café I happened to meet a young man who worked in his office. I gathered that the Tibetans had little time for the Indian authorities, particularly the Indian Office of Internal Affairs, whose responsibility it was to approve His Holiness's daily audience list.

'They're always making sure that the Dalai Lama is not just seeing westerners and Tibetans and we're always having to change the list to make sure he's got enough Indians in there as well. The Indian Government have a bit of a chip on the shoulder about it.'

There was a strong foreign influence in McLeod Ganj. The place was crammed with Westerners attending meditation courses, although I wondered if their serene 'n' happy looks had more to do with the quality of the local marijuana than the perspicacity of tantric philosophy. The nights at my guest-house, a wooden chalet perched precariously on the side of the valley, were disturbed by a group of guitar-playing American students puffing and partying until dawn. The local Buddhist monks benignly tolerated this behaviour. I had the feeling that as long as the tourists spent money, they could do what they liked.

Midway between McLeod Ganj and Dharamshala is Nechung Monastery, home to one of the most extraordinary psychic curiosities in India. The Nechung State Oracle of Tibet is consulted up to fifteen times a year by the Dalai Lama and the Tibetan Government-in-Exile. The god manifested through the oracle is Dorje Drakden, one of the protector divinities of the Dalai Lama. In pre-Chinese days, Tibetan Buddhism's leader would even take his spiritual oracle on foreign trips; but since the Chinese occupation, the oracle remains at Nechung, a modern monastery complex perched on a hillside a mile below McLeod Ganj.

The Dalai Lama admits that the idea of deciding government policy on the opinion of a clairvoyant may sound far-fetched to Westerners. He writes in his autobiography, *Freedom In Exile*:

> Even some Tibetans, mostly those who consider themselves 'progressive', have misgivings about my continued use of this ancient method of intelligence gathering. But I do so for the simple reason that as I look back over the many occasions when I have asked questions of the oracle, on each one of them time has proved that his answer was correct.

The ceremony of the oracle is a raucous occasion with much chanting and playing of horns, cymbals and drums. After the oracle has entered his trance, his fellow monks dress him in a bulky embroidered costume. A huge helmet is placed on his head and a sword in his hand. His face and body swells like a bullfrog's. He twitches violently. His respiration diminishes to a breathless hiss and he dances wildly. If the Dalai Lama is present, the oracle prostrates himself before the great man.

'When I was small, it was touching,' His Holiness recalls. 'Nechung liked me a lot and always took great care of me. For example, if he noticed that I had dressed carelessly or improperly, he would come over and rearrange my shirt, adjust my robe and so on.'

After receiving local people to be blessed, the oracle is taken into a back room and questioned by members of the government on matters of state – no one is allowed to ask questions about their own welfare. When the oracle emerges from his trance he is carried out of the hall in a catatonic state.

The Dalai Lama virtually dismisses the monk through whom Dorje Drakden speaks. He is no more than a medium, or kuten, a Tibetan word meaning literally 'the physical basis'.

No oracle ceremony was planned while I was in McLeod Ganj, but I was keener to meet the medium as a normal human being. After all, this monk has arguably the toughest job in the Tibetan Government. Since he took on this duty, his real name has been all but forgotten and today he is known simply as Nechung Kuten. I met him one morning at the monastery.

It was a hot, sticky day. There was a hint of monsoon in the air. Rain was forecast and thunder rumbled in the hills. My clothes were damp with sweat after the forty-five minute walk down the hill from my guesthouse to the monastery.

I was welcomed by the administrator, a young monk called Karma, who spoke English with the trace of an American accent. His voice was soft with that dreamlike quality you find on a Californian meditation tape.

After showing me into the monastery office, Karma left me alone while he went to find Nechung Kuten. The office was clinical and tidy after the cardboard-box mess of temple offices I had visited in Hindu India. It was a long, bright room, newly whitewashed and with a highly polished red linoleum floor. A regiment of multi-coloured biros was neatly lined up on Karma's desk. A polished boardroom table was surrounded by folding garden chairs draped with Tibetan rugs. The decoration was limited to a portrait of the Dalai Lama – in his habitual tinted *Easy Rider* spectacles – hanging alongside pictures of Mahatma Gandhi and the Pope. Through the windows I could see gardeners at work on a herbaceous border. Birds twittered in a magnolia tree.

I was sleepy from the thundery weather and unsure about meeting the oracle. Karma had told me that Nechung Kuten did not usually give interviews. The monastery hierarchy was worried about what might be written. In order to improve my performance, I tried an ancient trick that the palmist Pandir had told me about back in Udaipur: grab a length of hair halfway down the crown of your head and tug it gently for a minute. Doing this was said to trigger a pressure point on the scalp that helped concentration. I tried it. Perhaps it was my imagination, but it seemed to wake me up.

Karma reappeared. Behind him was a monk with a wan, delicate face. He stooped as he walked hesitantly into the room. Despite his gentle smile, there was something unhappy about him. He struck me as a melancholy man.

The pair gathered their saffron robes about them and sat at the other side of the table. Karma introduced Nechung Kuten, who had become a monk at the age of 13 after escaping from Tibet with his family. As well as being an oracle, he had a normal 'day job' in the monastery. Thanks to his artistic talents, he was 'ritual master', in charge of making the cakes and butter sculptures used during religious ceremonies. Since the monastery was undergoing a programme of renovation, Nechung Kuten was currently employed in the distinctly unmystical role of chief painter and decorator.

Nechung Kuten and I established that we were the same age. It was a small matter, but it seemed to create a feeling of warmth between us. Despite the culture gap, we were pleased to have at least one thing in common, and we congratulated ourselves for both looking far younger than our years!

There were great celebrations in the monastery when Nechung Kuten had fallen into his debut trance. The medium before him had died in 1983 and the Dalai Lama and his government had been without an oracle for four years, a situation that worried them greatly. Everyone wondered when the next oracle would appear, if at all. That all changed at 7.30 a.m. on 31 March 1987.

The Dalai Lama had been giving a series of lectures in McLeod Ganj and the town was crowded with monks who had travelled from all over India to hear His Holiness. That morning, the monks at Nechung were conducting the traditional ceremony of the oracle in the packed prayer hall. In the absence of a medium, they carried out the rituals in front of a statue. Nechung Kuten was in his usual role as ritual master, ensuring that all was well with the butter sculptures. As the chanting began, the head monk noticed that his colleague was behaving oddly. His eyes were popping out as if on rice stalks and his head was drifting from side to side. Nechung Kuten was going into a trance.

'It was like an electrical shock.' Nechung Kuten told me. 'It happened right out of the blue. I had never known anything like it.'

He had felt excited and restless the day before, but he did not anticipate the new feelings. He was terrified, particularly as he had no idea that he possessed psychic powers. As a child, the only clue that he was different from his playmates had been that he had a 'strong desire to recite mantras'. Otherwise, he had always considered himself a perfectly normal human being. Nechung described the extraordinary mental voyage, which had repeated itself many times since that morning.

'As soon as I begin praying, my vision becomes blurred and sounds get further away from me. The light becomes dim and then it's like falling asleep.' It was similar to disappearing down a long tunnel. 'My feelings fade away and the outer world disappears. They say that I am sometimes in a trance for one hour, but when I wake up it feels like only five minutes. I can't remember what I have said.'

'So you can't give me any great predictions about the future of the world?' He smiled tolerantly at my cheekiness. No, he could not.

'Is going into a trance a nice feeling?' I asked. Nechung Kuten frowned.

'No, it is frightening, like losing control. My whole body gets a vibration. Afterwards, I feel very exhausted.' He looked sadder than ever and sighed. 'It is not very nice. I am totally drained.' I had heard that trances of this depth could put a great strain the body.

'Without being too grim about,' I said, 'it is supposed to have an effect on life expectancy. Do you worry about damaging yourself?'

A hullabaloo of cymbals and kettledrums started up somewhere else in the monastery. A dog barked. I had asked an awkward question. Nechung Kuten struggled to find a reply. He conferred with Karma. They talked rapidly in Tibetan. After a pause, Nechung Kuten spoke.

'I think I may have problems with my heart,' he said slowly, as if unwilling to admit it. The muscles around his mouth tightened in fear. 'As I go into a trance my heart pounds quickly.' He struck his chest to emphasise this. 'Really pounding.'

'Are you worried about that?'

Karma interrupted hurriedly, 'It doesn't really help to worry.' He seemed unhappy with the direction in which our talk was going.

'I have never thought about worrying about this,' Nechung Kuten joined in. 'Looking at it in a Buddhist way I feel satisfied whether negative feelings come to me or not. The main point is that through this work I am able to benefit many people. When I look at it that way, then I am more happy than worried.'

I suggested that if he developed serious heart problems, the Dalai Lama might have pity on him and tell him to take a break from his arduous job, maybe stop doing it altogether. After all, His Holiness had the reputation of being a reasonable sort of man. Surely he did not want one of his brothers to suffer. The monks looked at me as if I was joking.

'Once I have been possessed, it is a lifetime duty,' Nechung Kuten said bluntly. 'Being oracle is not something that I have personally achieved in my lifetime. The post requires a lot of karmic relations from previous lives and I have been specially chosen. It is completely different from any other work assignment. People can be assigned administrative jobs in the monastery and after a while they can retire. My role is very different.'

'And His Holiness wouldn't make you a special case on medical grounds?'

'No.'

'It's a tough job.'

'Yes, it is tough. But the best thing a human being can do is to help other people. I feel happy that I am helping other people.'

I wanted to find out more about this shy man, but my questioning was making him uneasy. He announced that it was time for him to return to his decorating. He got up, smiled his melancholy smile again and gently shook my hand. Karma showed me out and I began the humid climb back up the hill to McLeod Ganj.

While the Nechung State Oracle is forbidden to answer personal questions, there are several monks in Dharamshala who will happily tell you your future. The most revered expert in prediction in McLeod Ganj is a septuagenarian, reincarnated monk called Khamtrul Rimpoche. Rimpoche is a Tibetan Buddhist title given to an abbot or spiritual personality. Khamtrul had a reputation for mind-blowing accuracy. He used the traditional Tibetan method of dice divination known as MO, which calls on the power of the Buddhist saint of wisdom Manjushri. It is a system sanctioned by the Dalai Lama through the Tibetan deities.

Divination ran in Khamtrul's 'family' of reincarnation. He was born under a totally different name and became a monk aged four. Four years later he was recognised as the reincarnation of the third Khamtrul Rimpoche, a man, who along with Khamtruls One and Two, had been a distinguished seer at Khamtrul Monastery in Tibet. In his new, elevated position, Khamtrul the Fourth was expected to learn the secrets of Tibetan prophecy, a subject at which he quickly became expert.

As a child, he read every book on Tibetan divination to discover what was meant by each particular fall of the dice. He learned through meditation how to concentrate the mind and invoke the power and advice of Buddhist deities like Tara, a protective goddess who is said to help people cross safely from birth to death. It had taken many years to develop his intuitive powers.

The day before I left, I visited the monk at his ground-floor apartment in a concrete block across the road from the Dalai Lama's official residence. I talked to him in his living-room, a dark chamber lit with candles. Since he spoke no English, our conversation was interpreted by his daughter Chimey, a strikingly beautiful student in her early twenties.

Khamtrul was a relaxed man with a chubby face and that big, Buddhist smile. He began with a lesson in humility. Chimey explained, 'My father says he will not have anything to offer to your researches.' I replied that he was being far too modest and that local people had attested to his great skills. Chimey translated this. The old man beamed in appreciation.

It turned out that his job was more like that of a counsellor. He was not in the business of straightforward fortune-telling, and would only answer specific questions about everyday problems. Many of his clients were other monks.

'He can help you make decisions,' Chimey said. 'For example, if you are sick and you do not know which doctor to choose, he will tell you who to see.'

I wondered if Buddhists were as inquisitive about 'sex and money' as everyone else.

'Yes, some people do ask about getting married or which business they should be in.'

Did Khamtrul worry about giving a wrong answer? He was a little perplexed by this question. Wrong answers did not come into it.

'He does not worry about such matters because it is not his own knowledge,' Chimey said. 'The answers come from the gods. Even if he has given very good and correct answers he will never take the credit upon himself.'

Khamtrul agreed to answer a question for me – how long should I spend in India? When was the right time for me to go home? Bad idea. I wished that I had kept my mouth shut.

The monk picked up a little silver box and opened it. A set of dice lay inside. One of them was inscribed with Manjushri's holy mantra: OM AH RA PA TSA NA DHIH. Khamtrul took all the dice in his liver-spotted hands and clenched his fists. Shutting his eyes, he screwed up his face in concentration. There was a long silence broken only by the clicking of dice as he shook them gently. Several times he opened his eyes to sneak a glance at me. Then he shut them tightly again as if playing Grandmother's Footsteps. He blew on the dice and threw them hard into a silver bowl. They made a loud clang as they struck the metal. He looked at them and repeated the throwing process four more times. Still with his eyes closed, the old man made his pronouncement. He mumbled quietly in Tibetan.

'Actually there's not much difference whether you stay for a long time in India or whether you stay for a week,' Chimey said. 'But if you stay in India for some time, at some stage you might have some obstacles in the form of losing your things, maybe your passport, maybe anything. So go home to England after a week.' I was aghast.

'But I'm supposed to be here for another two months.'

'Then stay if you like. But this is what the goddess says.' Khamtrul's prophecy troubled me for days. I swore that this was the last time on my travels that I would ask a leading question. As it happened, the goddess turned out to be wrong. My belongings were still intact when I eventually returned to London six months later.

Before leaving Khamtrul's house, I asked him if his neighbour the Dalai Lama had ever come for a personal consultation. The monk thought this was the funniest thing he had heard in years. He let rip with a stream of giggly Tibetan.

'His Holiness does not have to ask questions,' Chimey translated rather stiffly. 'He knows everything already.'

6

The Silent Baba

A journey around cosmic India would not be complete without a visit to Ujjain. For if we believe the Hindus' claim that they were the first people to study planetary power, then Ujjain is where astrology took root. Ujjain was for centuries the starting point for Hindu astrologers. It stands in N latitude 23° 11' 10', the first meridian of longitude for Indian astronomers, who believed that the Tropic of Cancer passed through the city. As further evidence of Ujjain's astrological past, it was also the birthplace of the sage Varaha Mihira, author of the *Brihat Samhita*.

Ujjain is one of the seven sacred cities of Hinduism, and one of the least known when compared with famous names like Varanasi and Ayodhya. Once an important link in the trade route to Mesopotamia and Egypt, Ujjain lies in the middle of the state of Madhya Pradesh, known as the Heart of India because of its central position in the country.

Today Ujjain – population three hundred thousand – is little more than a provincial town with a sacred past. Its astrological connections have all but disappeared. For hundreds of years, astrologers relied on the *Ujjain Ephemeris*, the book of tables giving the position of the heavenly bodies at certain times. It is still published today, but sales are few. Serious astrologers prefer to use N.C. Lahari's government-approved *Ephemeris* published each year in English by Calcutta's Astrological Research Bureau.

After returning from the Himalayas I stopped briefly in Delhi and transferred to the sixteen-hour night train to Ujjain. The town, which rests on the grassy banks of the River Shipra, was a refreshing change from the polluted capital. Life moved at a slow pace; a suburban drift of university students, bicycles and bullock carts. I found a room in the

Atlas Hotel, a dog-eared boarding house by the bus stand. The friendliness of the staff compensated for the swarm of mosquitoes in my room.

There may be no great astrologers in Ujjain today, but the site retains a mighty vibrational spirituality. The earth beneath the city is said to possess magnetic forces so powerful that planes tremble when they pass overhead. In another nugget of Ujjain folklore, there is said to be a secret tunnel leading from a cave temple near the river four thousand kilometres north to the pilgrimage site of Haridwar.

Ujjain's largest temple emphasises the potency of the area and the town's prominence as a centre of tantric worship. Mahakaleshwar Temple enshrines one of India's *jyoti lingas* – twelve stone phalluses around the country which are believed to generate their own energy. The *jyoti linga* is the symbol of Shiva's power. At 3 a.m. each morning the temple priests pay homage to the *linga* by covering it in a mixture of curd, butter and milk into which they then rub the ashes of a newly cremated body. They believe that Shiva himself enables them to do this, for it is said that everyday without fail at least one man or woman dies in Ujjain. There are always ashes to put on the *linga*.

Ujjain's mysterious quality could have something to do with the legend of Uma's elbow. The story goes that Shiva's wife Parvati was reborn as a goddess called Uma. Uma was desperate to marry Shiva again, and he wooed her in the disguise of a wandering holy man. The pair wed, much to the disgust of Uma's father, who did not consider Shiva smart enough for his daughter. Uma was so ashamed that she burnt herself in a sacrificial fire (the prototype for the ceremony known as suti at which Hindu widows burn themselves after their husbands' deaths). Shiva was so upset that he gathered her bones and danced around with them in a frenzy, finally scattering the remains to all corners of the earth. Uma's elbow fell near Ujjain on the banks of the River Shipra thereby giving the area a special, if somewhat sinister, vibrancy.

The city is also a centre of worship for one of the most obscure religious cults in India; a cult that fills its adherents with joy and fear alike. For here is one of the few temples in India dedicated to the deity known as Kaal Bhairav.

Kaal Bhairav is the manifestation of Lord Shiva in his guise as commander-in-chief of the celestial army. His name derives from the Sanskrit word *bhaya* meaning fear, or in some circumstances, death. There is a high rock near Girnar in Gujarat known as Bhairava Jhao, or 'leap of death', where Hindus tempted by the promise of a happy next life traditionally went to commit suicide. The practice was outlawed in the 1850s.

The warlike Kaal Bhairav is portrayed in statues with an orange, Halloween-pumpkin face. He is solid, round, obese, with heavy, black eyebrows. He has a mocking, ghoulish grin and none of the grace found in images of other Hindu gods. A ferocious dog is sometimes seen by his side. So great are his occult powers that, using no more than his little fingernail, he was able to decapitate Brahma, creator of the universe. Disciples of Kaal Bhairav are said to be able to invoke their master's supernatural energies. They can gain extraordinary powers ranging from simple prediction to diverting a person's destiny.

There are several ways of worshipping this awesome deity. The first is to sit and pray totally naked in the open air from between the hours of midnight and 2 a.m. This is the time when Kaal Bhairav prowls the earth. He a god who sleeps by day and is awake by night and he is associated with the ghosts of people whose spirits will not rest in peace, such as those who have suffered unnatural deaths through accidents or murder. While these spirits roam, Kaal Bhairav leads them on. Before you pray, you should draw a special tantric design – or yantra – on the floor and sit inside a triangle in the centre. After several weeks of chanting mantras a person will obtain supernormal powers.

The second way to worship Kaal Bhairav is more gentle and is designed to encourage the god's loving nature. The devotee makes the same design but instead of sitting in the triangle he burns a fire there. The ceremony is carried out fully clothed and during the daytime. It is mainly done for people with health, business or family problems.

The third type of puja is the most sinister and takes place in a graveyard. A devotee sits amongst the graves at night until he has managed through his powers of prayer to 'capture' a spirit. If you possess great spiritual strength you can accomplish this in two days. The devotee brings the spirit home and lets it do the work. For example, if you have a friend living a thousand kilometres away who is having marital difficulties, you can dispatch the spirit to sort out the problem. However, this method can be fraught with problems. There are stories of devotees coming home with 'bad' spirits, which then cause havoc in their lives leading eventually to their deaths.

The fourth ceremony is exceptionally rare and is believed to have been performed only a few times this century by the late millionaire cult leader, Bhagwan Shree Rajneesh. It is not widely known that during Rajneesh's reign as India's top international guru in the 1970s and '80s he was manipulating the power of Kaal Bhairav.

In this puja, a hundred couples go into a room and remove all their clothes. One of the couples have sex on a stage while the others anoint the writhing pair with alcohol. The men say prayers to the goddess Devi and the women worship Kaal Bhairav. Then all the couples make love. The tantric who has organised the show does nothing but watch. He is believed to obtain supernormal powers through the sexual vibrations in the room.

Devotees of Kaal Bhairav insist that the Bhagwan's much publicised love-ins at his Pune ashram, dubbed Club Meditation, were not the actions of a dirty old man. They were a variation on this ancient ceremony that has been performed for thousands of years and were a perfectly acceptable, if somewhat extreme, way of manifesting the power of Kaal Bhairav. What Hindus did object to was Rajneesh's greed and his statement that he wanted only rich people to be his followers.

For Kaal Bhairav has no time for greedy people. Abuse his trust and you will lose your power, but do something good for a person and your powers will grow. It is said that the god will forgive only twice. The third time he is offended, that person will meet with a violent death. One can only speculate that Rajneesh, with his vast personal wealth including a Lear jet and ninety-seven Rolls-Royces, offended Kaal Bhairav a lot more than twice, which perhaps explains his four hundred thousand dollar fine for violating US immigration laws leading to his deportation from America; and why his principal aide walked out on him declaring, 'To hell with the Bhagwan.' He died from heart failure in 1990 aged 58.

Ujjain's best-known devotee of Kaal Bhairav was a middle-aged gentleman called Mr Dabral. He was the antithesis of Rajneesh. By day he was a humble accounts clerk at Ujjain University. Out of working hours he was a medium of the highest rank, summoning the power of Kaal Bhairav in order to predict the future and to counsel people with problems.

I met Mr Dabral early one morning at his consulting chambers in a small, terraced bungalow near the city centre. Even at 7 a.m. there was a long queue of people waiting to see him. It was like visiting a doctor's surgery. His 'patients' included men and women, children and babies.

We sat on a long wooden bench that was shiny from years of use. Every so often a person emerged from behind a curtain behind which lay Mr Dabral's inner sanctum. Another client went in to see him and we shuffled and slid up the bench. Eventually it came to my turn. I pushed past the curtain and disappeared into the gloom. The room was dark, lit by a single oil lamp that threw murky shadows around the walls. The sage was seated on the floor in front of a small shrine dedicated to Kaal Bhairav.

Dabral was a small man in his fifties. A necklace of sacred rudraksha beads tumbled around his neck into his lap. He was dressed in a tangle of white robes and his hair was a badly cut jumble of tufts that twisted upwards like a schoolboy's. As I entered the room, his crooked, rabbity teeth parted and he gave me a huge welcoming smile.

Our talk was not a wild success. An acquaintance of mine, a prominent politician in Madhya Pradesh and a keen student of the occult sciences, had warned me that great secrecy surrounded the cult of Kaal Bhairav; devotees were reluctant to talk to outsiders. I had heard that Mr Dabral performed a nightly puja at one of the riverside ghats, or landing places, near Mahakaleshwar Temple where bodies are cremated on open fires. When I tried raise the subject he appeared not to understand me. Instead I was treated as just another punter wanting to know about his future.

I sat on the floor next to him. He had a dainty manner, constantly touching my arm with tiny hands. The presence of a foreigner seemed to amuse him. After giggling softly to himself, he asked, 'What do you want, baba?' He talked in a whisper with the hint of a lisp. I had difficulty understanding him. I explained why I was in India and that I was meeting all types of experts in prediction.

'And I bring greetings from Mr Rao in Delhi,' I added. Rao had met the psychic a few years earlier; the astrologer insisted that he was one of the greatest mediums in the country. Mr Dabral returned the compliment.

'Ah, Mr Rao. He is good, baba.' Mr Dabral panted like a dog. He took sharp little bursts of breath between sentences. 'That's fine baba . . . first thing, baba . . . blessing to you, baba . . . everything is okay, baba.' He took my hands in his. They were soft and strong. Heat radiated from his palms. I could feel a force burning into me. 'Ah, baba,' he soothed. 'Everything is okay, baba.'

In five minutes he told me more about myself than the Singh brothers had managed in two hours.

'First, baba, today you are looking for some peace of mind.' This was not a particularly stunning piece of information, but he was right all the same. I was wound-up from the travelling and longed to sit and do nothing on a beach. He knew immediately that I was unmarried, but insisted that my single status would change in a year or two. 'And you will get some good children and a male child also and your family life will be spiritual and you will get some love, faith and everything.' They were kind words of reassurance. I could see why he was so popular; he offered divine comfort in a world of uncertainty. He paused for a moment before placing his right hand against my cheek.

'Ah, baba,' he sighed. 'There is some pain here.' He had found my lingering toothache. I had seen this kind of psychic diagnosis once before, performed by a Russian faith-healer who was visiting London from Georgia. But I was still impressed. Mr Dabral caressed my cheek. 'No worries, baba. Your health will be okay soon.' (The pain eventually disappeared a week later after a dentist prescribed me antibiotics for a root infection.)

Mr Dabral fell silent. My session with him was over. He presented me with the head of a rose taken from his shrine and a plastic card bearing the image of Kaal Bhairav holding the holy trident of Lord Shiva. I asked who else I should see in Ujjain.

'Mauni-Baba, you will get some gain from him. And say prayers at the temple of Kaal Bhairav. Then you will get everything.' I thanked him for his time.

'Blessings to you, baba,' he said. 'Do come again.'

Even if Mr Dabral had not told me anything of great consequence, his words had a remarkably calming effect. My meeting with him had swept away the stresses of India for an hour or so. I was in a euphoric mood as I set off in an auto-rickshaw for my next appointment.

Several people I had met on my travels, including K.N. Rao, insisted that a visit to Ujjain would not be complete without meeting a man called Mauni-Baba. His name meant Silent Man in Hindi, and he had not spoken a word for forty years. He lived on the banks of the River Shipra on the outskirts of Ujjain. He was one of the most respected holy men in India and an expert in divination. Years of meditation in the Himalayas were said to have given him extraordinary supernormal powers.

Rao had told me why the Himalayas were such a popular retreat for gurus like Mauni-Baba: 'There are too many distractions in a big city. Even in the countryside there are too many people. If I want to be all alone for six months, I must cut myself off and sit on a mountainside. Only there is it possible to maintain a physical, emotional, spiritual and intellectual discipline. Rishis have sat in the Himalayas for thousands of years so the vibrations are brilliant. A place where a man has done a lot of worship before you becomes sanctified, so that your worship progresses faster.' In Rao's words, Mauni-Baba was 'a very great saint'.

'Don't expect a common clairvoyant. He will give predictions only five or six times a year to people close to him. He can tell you something which is going to happen maybe fifty years ahead, but he rarely does.'

Such predictions were usually of profound importance. Rao added chillingly that he had recorded an instance of a rishi telling a man that within six months his wife and children would die. The prophecy had come true.

From the way Rao and others talked about Mauni-Baba's great humility and spirituality I had a romantic vision of a much-venerated hermit living a lonely life in a simple hut by the water's edge. In my mind, I could see his followers bringing this impoverished mystic gifts of food and flower garlands in return for words of wisdom. Wrong.

Mauni-Baba did not live alone; far from it. His home was an modern ashram set in an agricultural estate that enjoyed half a mile of river frontage. At a rough estimate, I guess he employed a dozen people. He occupied a substantial bungalow (TV satellite dish on the roof) and visitors could stay at the ashram guest-house which amounted to a small hotel. In the car-park was a fleet of buses used for conveying devotees from afar. I was intrigued to see that the ashram's guest lavatory (with avocado green suite) featured the first bidet I had seen in India.

Admittedly, the complex was nowhere near as grand as, say, Sai Baba's retreat at Puttaparthi, Karnatika, which glories in a small airport; but still, it was very comfortable. I mused that if there was a guidebook rating to Indian ashrams, Mauni-Baba's would merit three stars.

Everyone was rather vague about who had paid for it, although local gossip hinted that municipal funds had found their way there thanks to the co-operation of local politicians. The official line was that the great man enjoyed the patronage of many rich devotees.

I arrived at 8 a.m. and found one of the ashram helpers, who was preparing breakfast in the dining-hall. He was a cheery man of about 20 with Chinese features. His name was Kemal and he struggled to understand me.

'Does anyone here speak English?' I asked.

'Yes. Mauni-Baba,' Kemal said brightly. The very mention of his guru's name lit up his face.

'But I understand that he hasn't spoken at all for forty years.'

'Yes.'

'Well, how on earth is he going to speak to me?'

Kemal mimicked the act of writing.

'Ah, I see. So he writes things down.'

'Yes.'

'Can I see him?'

'No. With other people.' The great man's appointment book was full until 11 a.m. He was presently engaged with an architect who had come seeking blessings for plans for a new office block.

I asked if there was another English speaker, who could tell me about the ashram. Kemal went into the kitchen and reappeared with a woman in her mid-forties and swathed in a white sari. Hot from her culinary exertions, she wearily dumped a plate of chapattis on the floor and wiped her brow.

'Lady name Pushpar,' Kemal explained.

'Hello, Pushpar. My name is Peter and I gather that you speak English.'

Pushpar shook her head.

'So you don't understand English?'

Pushpar nodded furiously.

'Kemal, what's going on here?' Kemal laughed.

'Silent lady. No speak.'

Pushpar sucked her lips. She dug into the folds of her sari and produced a pen and notepad. She wrote, 'I have not spoken since 1972,' adding, 'I used to be a librarian at Ujjain medical college.'

The elation I had felt after leaving Mr Dabral was evaporating rapidly. Here I was in an area of India where hardly anyone spoke English and the only two who could had both taken vows of silence. Pushpar smiled broadly. I could have sworn she almost laughed.

'Is it a problem not speaking?' I asked. Pushpar scribbled away.

'No problem. But it was difficult in the beginning.'

'But Baba showed you the true path?'

'Mmm.' Pushpar grunted a noisy and enthusiastic affirmative. Her mouth remained firmly shut.

I moved to a shady corner of the ashram courtyard and settled on a stone bench overlooking the river. It was a tranquil spot with cooing pigeons and the perfume of lilies. The water looked cool and peaceful. A man slowly polled his raft through purple-pink clumps of water hyacinths drifting downstream; goats and cows grazed under the ashoka trees on the opposite bank. Eleven o'clock came and went. I was informed that Mauni-Baba was still busy and could not see me until after lunch. Kemal brought me the ashram's answer to elevenses, a bowl of bananas sprinkled with raw chillis. I spat out the first mouthful. There are some aspects of Indian cuisine that I will never understand.

I occupied the time helping Kemal with his English. He was a gentle man and I learned that he came from a peasant family in Tripura, one of the north-eastern tribal states on the Burmese border. He was a devout Hindu and had come to live at the ashram aged 12 because his parents could no longer afford to keep him. He showed me an elderly English language textbook that was his prized possession. The wording was wonderfully quaint I flicked through the book and pointed at the phrase, 'As long as I live I will not forget your kindness.' Kemal read the Hindi translation and grinned. I added, '. . . as long as you never give me bananas and chillis again.' He chuckled like a child.

There was one other foreigner visiting the ashram. He was a Czechoslovakian violinist called Ivo, who was spending a few days here on holiday from an Indian classical music course in Bombay. Ivo joined me on the bench. Despite the strong sunshine, his face was chalky and drawn. He had that sickly, eastern bloc pallor with a painful, pink glow on his forearms. The day before, he had entertained Mauni-Baba with a private concert on his violin.

'What's Mauni-Baba like?' I asked.

'He is a nice old man. But different. He eats no solid foods and lives only on milk and fruit juice. And he doesn't allow any physical contact so don't try to shake hands with him. You can ask him any questions you like, but he is in such a state of mind that he won't be affected by them.'

I could hear the ring of an electric bell. Kemal left his duties in the dining-hall and sprinted across the courtyard to Mauni-Baba's bungalow. Ivo explained that because the master could not speak, he used the bell to summon his staff whenever he needed anything. Ivo leaned towards me confidentially and added, 'He's got a Panasonic cordless telephone next to where he sits, but I presume other people speak into it. There's also a fax machine. I suppose a fax is ideal if you can't talk.'

Ivo went off to practise his instrument and I read for a while. We met later for lunch in the dining hall where we sat on the floor and ate rice and vegetables off palm leaves with our hands. By 2 p.m. there was still no sign of my audience with Baba. He was now enjoying his siesta, I was told. He would be free at 5 p.m. I was becoming impatient at being kept waiting. Everything in the ashram was 'Baba this, Baba that' with people running at his every whim. I was irritated by this attendance on ceremony, by this amazing devotion to a human being with little more than impressive psychic powers. Perhaps I would change my views when I finally met him, but for the moment I was feeling less than understanding.

There was a 'no smoking' rule in the ashram, so I sneaked out for a quick cigarette. I walked past the little Shiva temple that lay outside the ashram grounds and sat on the bathing ghat, or steps, leading down to the river. One of the ashram boys, a spindly youth called Sunil, followed me. He cadged a cigarette and we hid on the far side of the temple so that none of his colleagues could see him smoking.

'Baba wouldn't like it,' he explained.

'Well, Baba's not going to know, is he?'

Sunil was not so sure. He claimed his guru's sense of smell was so acute that the man could smell tobacco smoke at fifty yards. He devoured the cigarette in a few, frantic puffs before scuttling back to his duties.

The afternoon was hot and sunny. Birds sang and a haze of butterflies danced above my head. A squirrel with a stripey back appeared from the bushes to investigate me. The creature moved closer, flicking its tail nervously. Then it retreated, stopping to scratch its ears with a hind leg. Down on the river, electric blue kingfishers skimmed the water. A family of peacocks took off for the opposite bank. It was an enormous effort for them. They flew low and clumsily, as if they were about to fall out of the sky.

My afternoon peace was interrupted by a barefoot sadhu, who came to pray by the water's edge. He was a villainous sight, dressed in black ankle-length robes, a heavy chain of rudraksha beads and a massive, matted beard. The mark of Shiva was daubed in three lines of silvery ash across his forehead. He chanted in a resonant moan. His litany to the river completed, he tossed some flowers into the water and sprang briskly back up the steps towards me. He explained in broken English that he came from the Hindu pilgrimage town of Haridwar and had not sat down for twelve years. He lifted his robes to reveal legs of knotted muscle. He then demonstrated how he slept by walking over to the temple and leaning on his forearms against a pillar. I was at a loss for anything to say. I settled for, 'It can't be very comfortable.' The sadhu bared his rotting teeth and smiled.

'Standing sleep for Shiva,' he said. 'Like horse.'

I was about to give him some money in return for a photograph when I was rescued by Kemal, who was with another man I had not met before. From their disapproving looks, I gathered that the sadhu was an old acquaintance who was not well thought of in the neighbourhood. Kemal took me aside.

'No give money, no speak to sadhu. Not good man. Like beggar.'

'So you mean that he was lying when he said he hadn't sat down for twelve years?'

'Oh no. He not sit down long time, but still he bad man.' I was amused that although Kemal accepted the sadhu's claim, this extreme act of devotion did not prove him to be a 'good' person. I reckoned that anyone – bad man or not – who had not sat down for twelve years was worth a tip. Kemal sent the nuisance packing with a burst of Hindi invective. The sadhu took no notice of the insults. He gave his nose a wipe with the back of his hand and happily sloped off, apparently used to this kind of treatment.

Kemal introduced me to his friend, a man in his mid-thirties called D.V. Bindra. D.V. had little time for sadhus: 'If I am totally illiterate and I am thrown out of home because I am lazy, I will come to a temple, I will do some cooking or some other service, and I will smoke ganja all day. Then I will call myself a sadhu.'

I liked D.V. immediately. He had a no-nonsense approach to metaphysics and described himself half-mockingly as a 'freelance contemplator'. He was employed as a clerk in a Ujjain medical company and came to the ashram after work each day at sunset to meditate and listen to (or rather, read) Baba's wise words. Born in the Punjab, he was originally brought up as a Sikh.

'But I couldn't cope with all the long hair, so I cut it off,' he joked. 'Then I got the job in Ujjain, met Baba and became a devotee of Shiva.'

He was also an amateur artist, whose work hung in the temple. His paintings included one of Mauni-Baba, halo around his head and beads in his hands, gazing downwards like Christ.

'Before I met Baba, I was roaming the world with no destination. Today he is my spiritual adviser, he has inspired me to do creative things. Baba is a heavenly saint.' I was touched by his love for the voiceless old man. 'Silence is such a nice medium,' he added. 'It speaks so many things we cannot say with our tongues. We have been provided with only one tongue, but we have two of everything else. There is a message there somewhere. When we keep silent our ears and eyes and nose become very sharp.'

We walked down to the river as the sun began its descent. We sat on the bank and stared in silence at the water. Rising fish created ripples on the surface. Every so often there was a splash as a brown dipper dive-bombed its prey. D.V. trailed a hand in the water and flicked drops on to his face.

'In India we worship rivers like the mother,' he said. 'The river is like the lap of the mother. Here we flourish. If there is no water, there is nothing.'

D.V. meditated for a few minutes, while I thought about what I would ask Mauni-Baba. When my friend had surfaced from his rumination, I asked him about Baba's powers of prediction.

'Is that why you have come to see him?'

'I suppose so, yes.'

'The person with real power will flatly refuse to tell you about the future.'

'So how do we know that he has powers of foresight in the first place?' D.V. smiled as if he expected a foreigner to ask questions like this. 'A diamond doesn't have to show its quality because it is so evident. The same goes for great saints. Baba's silence tells you everything.' He came down to earth a little and added with great civility, 'The point is, Mr Peter, Baba is not like a lot of other so-called gurus who try to impress you with magic tricks. The nice thing about him is that he doesn't levitate.'

It was nearly dark by the time we left the river. We climbed the steps and passed under a thousand roosting starlings shrieking in the trees above the temple. Strings of coloured fairy lights lit up the ashram as if to welcome us. I eventually met Baba at the evening puja in the temple. Before the great man arrived, D.V. reiterated the 'no touching' rule. Devotees were allowed no closer to their master than his wooden sandals, which they were allowed to kiss when removed from his feet.

'I've never asked why he doesn't like people touching him,' D.V. remarked. 'I imagine it is because if he allowed it, he would be surrounded by sycophants touching him in order to get his energy.'

D.V. and I were joined by a rich Calcutta industrialist and his wife, who were staying in the guesthouse. The wife was ill and they had travelled to Ujjain specially to seek Baba's blessings for her health.

Kemal, Pushpar and the other ashram workers entered the temple in a procession. The guru followed, clutching a writing slate. He crossed the stone floor with slow strides. He turned, acknowledged his followers with a nod, and sat down on a carved wooden throne. Everyone bowed to him except for the man from Calcutta who threw himself prostrate on the floor and kissed the sandals.

Baba was the perfect image of the Indian yogi. His beard was black and long and his eyes sparkled as bright as highly polished mahogany. He wore only a white loin cloth. A string of rudraksha seeds tumbled over his bare concave chest and protruding belly. His body was fit, but his face was old with sun-shrivelled skin and sunken cheeks. No one was certain of his age, but I judged him to be around 75.

I could see the drawbacks of not speaking for forty years. Baba constantly rolled his tongue and licked his lips. He pulled all manner of funny faces, presumably to exercise the muscles around his mouth and prevent the sinews from seizing up.

The puja was a deafening thirty-minute ceremony of drum-banging, bell-ringing and chanting. The guru clapped his hands and tapped his foot in time to the cacophony. One of the ashramites had brought along his toddler daughter. Baba beamed at the little girl. He waved his arms and indicated that she should join in. She shrieked with joy and clapped back at him. The prayers over, it was time for my audience. D.V. led me forward.

'You must bow, Peter,' he whispered.

I knelt and touched the floor with my forehead. I didn't much like doing it, but I thought I had better humour the old man, in the same way that I might address an elderly gentleman as 'sir'. I raised my head. Baba was smiling at me mysteriously. I had the feeling that he knew exactly what I was thinking.

Mauni-Baba took his slate and wrote on it with a stub of chalk. D.V. and the man from Calcutta peered at the spindly scrawl. They had difficulty in understanding what he had written. I was amused that despite his years of silence, Baba had made no effort to improve his handwriting. Baba held up the slate. D.V. read the words, which I imagined to be a holy man's version of small-talk.

'He is telling you about Ujjain,' D.V. said. 'There are strong magnetic forces in the earth here. That is why aeroplanes vibrate when they pass overhead.'

'I had heard that.'

'And in May and June the planes vibrate even more.'

'Why is that?'

'Suction from the superatmosphere.'

I explained that I was visiting experts in divination around India. I added that I brought greetings from K.N. Rao. The guru tilted his head in approval.

'Baba remembers meeting K.N. Rao in Delhi. Baba says that K.N. Rao is the best astrologer in the world. He can give you the future.'

'I know,' I said. 'But can *you* give me the future?' More scribbling.

'There is no one in Ujjain who can tell you better than K.N. Rao.'

I was getting nowhere. My knee-caps ached from the hardness of the stone floor. Mauni-Baba saw that I was in pain and indicated that I should sit. I rearranged myself to a more comfortable cross-legged position and rubbed away the soreness. Everyone's eyes were on me. I stuttered, 'But I've been told that you, Baba, can tell me exactly what will happen in the future.' Silence. Then the man from Calcutta spoke.

'No, no.' He raised his eyebrows and tut-tutted disapprovingly. 'Baba is a spiritual baba. He is not a fortune-teller.'

'I'm aware of that. But people have told me that I should go to Mauni-Baba and he will tell me everything about my past and my future.' The man from Calcutta laughed pityingly.

'Oh dear, these stories about people predicting the future are always going around. It's so boring. It happens all over India.'

Mauni-Baba understood our conversation. He wrote on the slate. D.V. reported, 'He says that he can see into the future.' Baba wrote some more. 'He said that in March there would be less rainfall and that happened.'

Everyone in the temple laughed. It took a moment for the joke to sink in – there is *always* less rainfall in March. The guru was grinning like hell. There was nothing like taking the mickey out of an Englishman. He continued to write.

'He is being serious now,' D.V. said. 'Earlier this year he foresaw there would be many plane crashes in the world and there were. And he says that soon there will be an epidemic of skin diseases in India. Most people will suffer.'

'Does he say anything else will happen?'

'No.'

And that was the extent of Mauni-Baba's predictions, that the country was headed for a plague of itching. Baba stood up. I too rose. My interview was over. Baba rolled his tongue and licked his lips. He made some hand signals. D.V. said, 'He is asking if you like his ashram.'

'I have enjoyed myself very much.' Baba gave me a doubtful look and sternly flicked a finger at me.

'No, you haven't,' D.V said. 'This afternoon you were angry that Baba kept you waiting.'

'But how can he know that if he didn't even see me?' The temple echoed with laughter. D.V. gazed in admiration at his guru.

'Baba knows everything.' Deep dimples appeared in the old man's cheeks and he twinkled his naughty smile again. He left the temple followed by his adoring disciples.

The next day I continued on the trail of the mysterious Kaal Bhairav. D.V. took the morning off from work to show me the temple dedicated to the warrior god. My friend picked me up at the Atlas Hotel and we set off on his scooter into the countryside on the edge of the town. The sun had risen but the air was cool as we sped through small lanes flanked by high hedges. Rural India was waking up. Women pumped water from wells and boys assembled teams of oxen ready for work in the fields.

The temple lay at the end of a rutted track. A rag-taggle of sleepy young souvenir salesmen mooched around by the usual collection of trinket stalls at the main gate. Hindi religious music blared from loudspeakers strung up in the trees. We walked up a long flight of grey stone steps pitted with weeds. D.V. pointed out that the temple lay on the site of a three thousand-year-old fort. Bearing in mind Kaal Bhairav's military status and immense power, I speculated that this was probably more than a sinister coincidence.

The story of Kaal Bhairav is a typical Hindu tale of bad boy made good. The moral of the story is that everyone should be given the chance to earn respect however great their shortcomings. Brahma was overcome with pride when he created the earth. So proud was he that Shiva decided to bring him down a peg or two and gave birth to Kaal Bhairav through his third eye. Kaal Bhairav gained a reputation for violence. He got into a fight with Brahma and killed him. The gods found him guilty of murder and sentenced him to many years roaming the wilderness. After some time he arrived at this temple where he did penance. Eventually he found peace and the gods pardoned him.

'They say that if Kaal Bhairav has noticed someone, he will be attracted to this temple because of the deeds of his past birth,' D.V. explained.

'Do you think that's the case with me?' I asked.

'Almost certainly, but perhaps you will never know the reason. Maybe you worshipped Kaal Bhairav in your past birth and that is why he is attracting you.'

Kaal Bhairav's bizarre nature is best illustrated by the puja offerings made to him. For whereas most Hindu idols are presented with flowers and fruit, the commander-in-chief's unpredictable temperament is kept at bay with a supply of alcohol. I noticed the rank, bitter-sweet smell of stale liquor the moment I entered the temple's inner sanctum. Three middle-aged men sat on the floor. They were local peasant farmers who had come to pay their respects to the god. One of them clutched a quarter-bottle of hooch. A priest sat opposite them next to a bright orange effigy of Kaal Bhairav. The statue was round and bloated with piggy eyes that seemed about to burst. Decaying flower garlands tumbled over its baby face.

The priest took the bottle and attempted to open it with an iron Shiva trident that was leaning against the statue. The cap refused to budge. The priest dug around behind the statue and produced a proper bottle-opener. This did the trick and the cap popped off. The priest muttered a prayer and poured the cloudy white liquid into a saucer. He carefully lifted the overflowing saucer to the statue's mouth and tilted the liquid into the opening.

'Kaal Bhairav is offered liquor as food because he is a tough man,' D.V. whispered. The stench of raw alcohol was overpowering. I silently agreed that you'd have to be tough to drink this stuff. Local legend claims that this wooden effigy actually drinks the alcohol. I peered closely at the statue. The priest saw my look of scepticism. He smiled at the unbelieving foreigner and beckoned me closer. He allowed me to put my finger into the statue's mouth. It was damp, but I could see no hole in the carved wood. The priest said something in Hindi. D.V. translated.

'The god takes the liquor,' he said simply.

'Is this another example of Kaal Bhairav's supernatural powers?' I asked.

The priest nodded. The god was so mighty that his statue had a life of its own. He was so powerful that he could give a devotee whatsoever he desired.

The priest poured the remains of the bottle into clay cups and gave it to the three men. They drank down the liquor in single gulps. He offered some to D.V. and me. We both refused. I asked the priest if he drank alcohol. No, he never touched a drop. It was ironic that a Brahmin priest remained abstinent, while his god was allowed to drink.

After the farmers left the temple, D.V. and I hung around outside while the priest tidied up. After a few minutes, the Brahmin said goodbye to us and walked across the temple grounds to his quarters. D.V. was determined to discover the secret of Kaal Bhairav.

'I'm sure there must be a tube and the alcohol goes into a bladder underneath the statue,' he said. 'These local people are too ignorant to ask questions. I'm going to have a look.'

'Well, you can count me out,' I said. I did not fancy being caught out by the priest; nor did I want to invite the wrath of the terrifying Kaal Bhairav. D.V. checked to make sure the priest had gone and darted back into the temple. He returned two minutes later.

'Nothing,' he said. 'There is nothing there.' There was no secret tube, no hidden receptacle. No sign of the alcohol.

'Maybe it evaporated,' I suggested.

'What? A whole bottle in ten minutes? Not possible.' We laughed nervously. I glanced back at the statue. Kaal Bhairav's piggy eyes seemed more enigmatic than ever. His disconcerting gaze remained with me for the next two days on the train as I headed north-east across India to Hinduism's holiest city, Varanasi.

7

From Moles To Gemstones

Bhaskar and I sat on a wall at Manikarnika Ghat at midnight and discussed our favourite London nightclubs while we watched the corpses sizzle. A burning ghat on the banks of the River Ganges seemed a curious place to be remembering the fleshpots of Mayfair and Soho.

Bhaskar was a journalist and documentary maker I had met through friends in Delhi. He was in Varanasi finding musicians to play in a festival later in the year at the infamous troublespot of Ayodhya. The show was to be a non-denominational protest against Hindu-Moslem violence.

I had joined Bhaskar in Varanasi that morning. We could not recall meeting before but we reckoned that we must have bumped into each other in the early eighties when we had both been ardent nightclubbers. Dives like Tramp, Tokyo Joe, Legends, Maunkberry's . . . we'd done 'em all while I had been writing a newspaper column on pop music and he was producing movies with the likes of David Bowie. We agreed that our favourite haunt had been the Embassy Club in Bond Street.

'The Embassy closed down, didn't it?' Bhaskar said.

'Yes, some time in the mid-eighties,' I said. 'But it was never the same after Stephen Hayter stopped running it.' Hayter had been one of the great, flamboyant characters of London clubland, a man who nicknamed his barmen Faith, Hope and Charity.

One of the domes, the men tending the funeral pyres, swore as an arm dropped off a fire. He took a pole and casually flicked the limb back on to the embers. A procession of mourners carried a body up the steps from the river where it had just been anointed in the waters of Mother Ganga. The corpse was laid on a rude wooden stretcher, enshrouded in flower garlands and multi-coloured tinsel. A couple of domes heaved it on to a newly lit fire and a shower of sparks spluttered into the night air. The heat from the blaze was stifling. Sweat poured down our faces. We stared at the flames, mesmerised by the hideous contortions of the charred body.

'And what happened to Stephen Hayter?' Bhaskar asked. I shook myself as if returning from a dream.

'He died in New Zealand. Terribly sad. Knowing his sense of humour I think he'd have liked the idea of us discussing him on a burning ghat at Varanasi.'

'Oh I'm sure he can hear us now.' Bhaskar lazily waved an arm towards the sky. 'He'll be up there somewhere.'

Despite an English education and an impeccable BBC accent, Bhaskar's true home was India. He had spent most of his late twenties and thirties in Britain but was now back to stay. Varanasi had a strong hold on him and he was considering moving here from Delhi with his wife and two-year-old son. He held strong views on how the West had much to learn from India, particularly in the area of bowel movement. He had once written an article as a riposte to American complaints about pollution in the East. He argued that if India excreted at the same rate as America, the core of the earth would crumble: 'I estimate the Americans must shit five times as much as us because they consume so much more food. Then they flush their loos with large amounts of fresh water and use paper to clean themselves which means cutting down more rain forests and clogs up the sewers – all wastage that the earth has to bear. But the average Indian goes into a field, has a comparatively small shit because he hasn't eaten so much, and uses just a little pot of water to clean himself. Far more environmentally sound.'

I was staying with Bhaskar and some friends of his in a crumbling old property at Assi Ghat at the southern end of the city. The building consisted of a series of cells around a courtyard and had been originally occupied by an order of sadhus. It was now occupied by several middle-aged bachelors who shared the cooking and washing facilities. Bhaskar knew them all well, having dropped out there in the post-flower power years of the early seventies.

The windows of my room looked directly on to the Ganges although the view was marred by a fly-blown rubbish tip that had appeared during the past year. No one could explain why local people had suddenly started using this stretch of the river as a dump. It was just one of those things that happened in India. The enraged inhabitants of Assi Ghat were petitioning the council to have the eyesore removed.

The Varanasiphiles, like Bhaskar, were worried that the city was losing its identity as the holiest place on earth. Hindus come to Varanasi either to learn or to die. They learn Sanskrit, music and traditional Hindu culture at one of the many colleges. They die here because to die in Varanasi means you escape the cycle of karma and are not born again. You are for ever. According to Hinduism, Varanasi is not really on this earth. It lies at the tip of the light emitting from the middle prong of Shiva's trident. This shaft of light has no beginning and no end. If you die in Varanasi, your soul enters that stream of light and you will go upwards, beyond the realm of the gods. Death is a joyous event, a moment of liberation. Manikarnika Ghat, where we were sitting, is said to mark the exact spot where Shiva's light penetrated the earth. Many believe that it is the most auspicious place to be burned in India.[1] But now, horrors, more Hindus are coming to Varanasi as tourists than pilgrims.

'A bath in the holy Ganges used to be an essential religious ritual for any Hindu,' Bhaskar said. 'But the middle-class Indian of the 1990s will not let his family bathe in the river because it's too dirty. He thinks there's too much shit and half-burnt bodies and he's terrified of cholera.'

I had always heard that Ganges water was supposed to be surprisingly pure considering what was dumped into the river. Don't you believe it, said Bhaskar. He still bathed here but many people wouldn't. This was the age of bottled mineral water and the best water filters that money could buy. As far as the middle-classes were concerned, the notoriously hardened Indian stomach was a thing of the past. As well as the latest Sony hi-fi (now assembled in India), increasing prosperity had brought a greater susceptibility to bacteria.

Bhaskar noticed more changes each time he returned to Varanasi.

'There are fewer Sanskrit schools and you see more people wearing trousers and less dhotis. People are busier and have video and satellite television. They have less time for religious sing-songs and get-togethers. The way people worship is changing. Rituals are getting shorter. Whereas a certain ritual might have taken three hours, people are finding ways of getting it over in forty-five minutes.'

But little had changed at the burning ghats. The fires at Manikarnika still burned twenty-four hours a day like they had for centuries; and the domes still had their black sense of humour. The domes are untouchables.

....

[1] Varanasi is also known by Hindus as Kashi, meaning 'City of Light'. Most locals still refer to the city by its old Moslem name, Benares.

They are the lowest of the low, without caste. You will see them, turbans wrapped around their dark, glistening faces, waiting in the alleys above the ghats at Varanasi. A funeral procession approaches down one of the narrow lanes. The first dome to see the chief mourner (in other words the man with the money to pay for the cremation) shouts out something like, 'The man with the blue shirt . . . he's mine,' and gets the job. It is up to him to bargain how much it will cost to burn the body. Add the cost of firewood to the dome's fee and a reasonably decent blaze will cost around six hundred rupees (fourteen pounds). But if that is too expensive you can always go to the new, hi-tech electric crematorium a few ghats up the river – a hundred and fifty rupees and said to be more ecologically acceptable (if less auspicious) since none of your beloved's bits end up in the river.

There was much shouting and laughing amongst the domes as another cadaver was dumped on a fire. They gleefully prodded it with their bamboo poles. I was surprised that there was no smell of burning flesh, just clouds of smoke and the faint scent of sandalwood. I remarked to Bhaskar that considering the domes' grisly jobs, they seemed a remarkably cheerful bunch.

'They have a pretty coarse sense of humour,' Bhaskar said. 'It must do something to you, burning dead bodies everyday. Death becomes so normal. It's like someone who cleans toilets and is unworried by shit.'

Bhaskar translated a conversation that was going on between two domes a few feet away. He put on a cockney accent to give me a good feel of what they were saying: 'Oi, there's a bit of leg still there . . .' 'Well, give the fing a bloody good poke with your stick then.' 'Old bugger won't burn . . . '

Soon only the skull remained. One of the domes smashed it with his stick. The blackened bone collapsed with a pop. The dome balanced the skull on the end of the stick and flung it over the heads of the mourners into the river. The mourners took a last glimpse at their relative and left the ghat.

'The smashing of the skull is the final ritual, the final liberation,' Bhaskar said. 'It's something to do with your soul being in your head.'

'Is this where you'd like to end up,' I asked.

'I know I'll end up being burned but I don't know if it will be in Varanasi. Perhaps in my next life. There's a legend that if you come to this city once you will die here in your next lifetime.'

'So I've got something to look forward to.'

'Certainly. At least at the end of your next life you are assured eternal salvation.'

It was 1 a.m. and still more fires were being built, more bodies burned. We left the ghat and walked up the steps past an all-night kiosk where a boy was sleepily advertising his wares: 'Cold drinks . . . mineral water . . . ' We hired a rowing boat to take us back upriver to Assi Ghat. The Ganges was smooth and quiet after the turmoil around the fires. The sacred waters lapped against the side of the boat. The night was clear and humid. Bhaskar and I lay back on the splintery planks and gazed at the stars. Bhaskar sighed contentedly.

'To put a rather sixties expression on it, this river has such a lot of good vibes,' he said. 'A bath in the Ganges gives you your best thought of the day.'

I asked him what he thought about astrology. He said that the planets held little interest for him, although he wore a pearl around his neck to attract the power of the moon.

'It's to keep my wife happy, she quite often visits astrologers, but I don't really believe in all that stuff.' On the birth of their son he had commissioned an astrologer to produce a traditional birth chart in the form of a scroll about twenty feet long crammed with diagrams and the positions of the planets throughout the boy's life.

'Is your son going to have a good life?' I asked.

'Absolutely no idea. It's just a lot of lines and wiggles that mean nothing to me. My father had a chart done when I was born and that meant nothing to me either.'

Hindus insist that Varanasi is a seat of extraordinary supernormal inspiration, the like of which exists nowhere else in the world. It is said that you will be astonished by the results of whatever work you carry out in Varanasi. It is even more astrologically important than Ujjain. Indian astrologers insist that Shiva's divine band of light makes the rays of the planets stronger here than anywhere else in the country. As a result, Varanasi is home to many astrologers, mostly from the classical, Vedic tradition of astrology.

Despite his ambivalence towards the planets, Bhaskar asked his friends who would be the best astrologer for me to visit in Varanasi. He came back with a name. There was one man who could be considered truly brilliant – Pandit Rajmohan Upadhyay, ex-dean of the faculty of Oriental Learning and Theology at Benares Hindu University, and head of BHU's astrology department for twenty years.

Upadhyay belonged to the pure, classical tradition of Hindu astrology. As well as studying the planets he was also expert in the Vedic science of face-reading, analysing a person's physiognomy. For him all the answers were in the Vedas and he would not be influenced by the West. He was the closest you get to an astrologer of ancient India.

Later, back in Delhi, K.N. Rao told me that traditionalists like Upadhyay were an endangered species.

'My type of astrology is not complete but what he does is correct according to the Vedas. He will combine a deep sense of intuition with your horoscope. For instance, you come to my house with totally dishevelled hair, ill-kempt dress and behave in an ugly manner. If I look into your horoscope and I see a very talented, intellectual man, I will stick to the horoscope ignoring your pretensions. You might pretend to be illiterate but I will not be mistaken. The classical astrologer will be misled because he will over-emphasise your manner. Methods like face-reading might be documented in the Vedas but they can lead to terrible confusion.'

There can be other problems if faces are taken too seriously. The Hindus say that the sight of the first face in the morning influences that day's luck. Indians tell a story about a king who, first thing one morning, saw the face of a barber. The king stumbled and fell in his garden, and ordered the barber to be hanged. The barber said, 'Please sir, do justice. For what offence am I being hanged?' The king replied, 'Because your face is so unlucky that I stumbled.' The barber pleaded, 'Oh king, by seeing my face you only stumbled, but by seeing your face I am being hanged. Whose face is more unlucky?' The story goes that the king was delighted and forgave him.

The classicists of Varanasi loathed to admit that times had changed. They were suitable for the pastoral age of two or three hundred years ago but they offered little help to the Delhi citizen of the 1990s. Rao went on, 'They will take a very puritanical view of a horoscope. For instance, throughout history the male has dominated and the female has been suppressed or derided. Today a woman can have fifteen lovers and still be very talented and a great social worker, writer or whatever. But the traditionalists will condemn her as a whore.'

The same was true with politicians. Rao claimed, 'There will always be an element of corruption and lying in the horoscope of a politician from anywhere in the world. No question about it. But if I call him a criminal I am doing him an injustice. The traditionalist has a high level of idealism and automatically dismisses him as a gangster.'

The next day I took an auto-rickshaw to Pandit Upadhyay's home, a large, concrete cube in the suburb of Sunderpur. About thirty men of varying ages were waiting in the front yard to consult the master. His 20-year-old son, Rajendra, showed me into his father's office. It was painted lilac and on the walls were displayed the usual Shiva and

Ganesh pictures. I noticed a couple of medals awarded to Upadhyay at past Sanskrit conferences in Varanasi.

The pandit lay sprawled on a bed, his back propped against a bolster. He was a large man of about 70 with a florid face and thick red lips. He was dressed in Druidic white robes and he hid behind impenetrable sunglasses which looked suspiciously like Rayban copies. On his forehead was a swipe of grey, holy ash. He said nothing as I entered the room but gave me a languid smile. He directed me to a chair with a rather camp sweep of his arm. He was immensely laid-back.

Upadhyay had lived in Varanasi since the age of nine when he had left his home village sixty miles away in Uttar Pradesh. He had come to the city with his brother and together they had studied Sanskrit. He had learned astrology and face-reading from his grandfather.

Since the astrologer spoke no English, his son translated our conversation. It was not an easy chat. Upadhyay was dry and plodding. He gave the odd dramatic swish of a hand, flashing a large, gold signet ring, but he was otherwise unexciting. It made me think that the Vedas must have been rather dull. Later sages must have fiercely edited the original writings, ending up with only the most interesting bits.

Upadhyay admitted that BHU's astrology classes were not going well.

'We cannot say that the astrology course is very popular at the moment,' Rajendra said flatly.

'Why is that?' I asked.

'Too many of our people are running after the West. They are not interested in the old sciences of India.' It was an old story, although it was ironic that westerners who came to study in Varanasi often worked harder than Indian students. 'My father likes western students,' he added. 'They are very scholarly.'

K.N. Rao accused the Varanasi classicists of being stuck in the past. Their teaching methods were too heavy for most people, who could not be bothered to memorise lengthy chunks of Sanskrit. It took BHU a full year to teach what Rao and his colleagues managed in eight weekends. Upadhyay asserted that memorisation and laborious study was the only way to teach astrology. It might be unpopular in today's modern world but the declining number of students was only a passing phase.

'My father says if there is some knowledge it will never vanish altogether. In the same way that the shape of the moon is always changing, you could call this a slowing down period. But it will rise again and people will come to realise the importance of the Vedic sciences.'

Upadhyay blamed this downward trend on Kali Yoga, the period of time in world history which the Hindus say we are presently in. I had been waiting for this. You will hear that magical phrase Kali Yoga many times in India. You will hear that it is an epoch of moral degeneration, of the breakdown of the fabric of society. The nation's woes, the warping of the country's youth, the evils of the West, are all blamed on Kali Yoga. From the way people talk you would think we've been in Kali Yoga for a hundred years or so (since the moral decline following the Victorian age perhaps?) and that things are going to get progressively worse over the next decade.

Actually, Kali Yoga has been going on for more than fifty centuries – 5,094 years as of 1996, to be precise. Furthermore, we're only in the first phase, by no means particularly bad, with another 38,109 years to go, by which time our standards will have dropped so low that they'll make Sodom and Gomorrah look as depraved as a Tunbridge Wells whist drive. Brahma, the supreme being, will draw in his last breath and all matter will vanish. For the time being, we can relax and be relieved to know that Kali Yoga is a lot easier to live in than the preceding four yogas as laid down by the ancient Hindus.

First came Satay Yoga, which began 1,726,000 years ago. This was a time of pristine religion when people did nothing but pray twenty-four hours a day. Such was the level of devotion that they did not even need to eat. Treta Yoga, starting 1,296,000 years ago came next – seventy-five per cent prayer and the rest of the time learning the skills that a human being needs to survive. Then Dwapar Yoga, 864,000 to 432,000 years ago, and a more reasonable twelve hours a day on one's knees.

In Kali Yoga, the winter of the Universe which began on the day that Lord Krishna left his corporeal form to become a god, only twenty-five per cent of the world follow any sort of religious ritual. The ancient sage Veda Vyas said that in many ways Kali Yoga is the best age to live in. There is more time to get on with life and the development of the sciences; only remember God and your worship is complete.

Pandit Upadhyay was not at all happy with Kali Yoga and I got the impression he would be happier spending his days at prayer. But he was doing his best to keep the ancient occult sciences alive, particularly the art of face-reading. He could also tell something about a person by analysing the moles on their body. It was an obscure method of divination that I found most fascinating. Far from being a trivial fortune-telling technique, mole-reading, known in Sanskrit as *til sastra*, is a serious Vedic science. Our moles tell us about our previous life. One can avert misfortune by being warned of the effects of a certain mole.

Moles on the right side of a man's body are generally believed to bring good luck; moles on the left side mean bad luck, and vice-versa for women. Brown and red moles are auspicious; black moles are inauspicious. Thin, long, hairy moles foretell wealth and fame; thick, short, hairy moles indicate poverty and unhappiness. The position of the mole is also relevant:

On the forehead

Men: on the right side it means wealth after the age of 30. On the left it denotes worries and loss of money. In the centre, the man has a harsh temper.
Women: on the right side, wealth; left, a pious, elegant lady. In the centre, wealth and good children.

On the nose

Men: on the tip of the nose, very lucky, he achieves success very quickly in everything he attempts; on the right, a great traveller, more fond of the outdoors than being tied to a desk; on the left, untrustworthy, oversexed.
Women: on the tip, a determined lady, will get what she wants at any cost, loved by her husband; on the right, her husband will be unfaithful; on the left, happy domestic life.

Ears

A mole in either ear indicates a rich man or woman.

Cheeks

Men: on the right, wealthy, famous and loved by all; on the left, a respected, virtuous life.
Women: on the right, she will have more sons than daughters. If it's on the lower right side she will be promiscuous; on the left, a happy married life but a selfish lady. A mole on the lower left side denotes a passionate nature and unusual sexual gratifications.
If moles are found on both the cheeks of either men or women, success will only come after hard work and struggle. A mole on the cheek where tears fall indicates domestic unhappiness, widowhood or death of wife.

Shoulders

Men and women: on the right, a wise and prudent nature; on the left, quarrelsome. A mole found anywhere between the shoulders and the loins indicates a sudden downfall in health and wealth.

Chest

Men and women: a devoted lover with a sharp mind. Generally misunderstood by their partners and highly distressed if deceived in love affairs.

Breasts

Women: on the right, she will have more sons, she leads an ordinary life, is fickle, fond of opposite sex and dies before her husband; on the left, she is good-natured, becomes a mother early; between the breasts, she has a comfortable life, a love of fine arts and poetry. A mole on the breast touching either nipple signifies a woman who is immoral, avaricious, over ambitious, probably a high-class prostitute.

Back

Men and women: a mole on the back indicates wealth, a God-fearing nature and happy domestic life.

Stomach

Men: in the middle, fond of good food and lead a happy, prosperous life; below the navel, loss due to theft, gluttony and a nasty temper.
Women: a mole on the stomach just below the breasts means she will die before her husband; a mole anywhere else indicates a moderately wealthy lady.
Note: a green-coloured mole anywhere on the stomach of either sex means unnatural sexual indulgence such as bestiality.

Armpits

Men: right armpit, a man of moderate means with occasional interludes of poverty; left, a man craving for women who dies without realising his dreams.

Women: right, a sensual lady, could be a hooker; left, frigid, avoids sex, spends her time at prayer.

Arms

Men: on the right, happy life, wealth; left, makes a fortune, successful.
Women: right, success in everything, enjoys sex; left, success in social life, command over her husband.

Elbows

Men: right elbow, riches, luxury, sensual pleasures; left, a womaniser and sex fiend.
Women: right, haughty, quarrelsome but good administrator; left, passionate, fond of opposite sex.

Forearms

Men: right, difficulties in childhood, rich after early middle age; left, becomes rich through hard work, a good planner.
Women: right, difficulties, bad relationship with in-laws; left, happiness, success in all her efforts.

Wrists

Men: right, honour, wealth through the arts; left, good artist, earns well but spends on women and drink.
Women: right, selfish, scheming and determined, probably a good actress; left, wealthy, domesticated, may be an artist.
A mole on the right wrist near the thumb indicates all-round success for either sex.

Back of the hand

Men: right, wise, success in all enterprises, an easy life; left, success with delay, economical in spending, fond of fashion, women and wine.
Women: right, very auspicious, assuring happiness and artistic achievement; left, wealthy either through birth or marriage, domestic happiness, artistic.

Knees

Men: right, wealthy, successful, happy marriage with beautiful, accomplished lady; left, bad temper, meanness, hasty nature, likes low women.
Women: right, financial difficulties, unhappiness due to ill-treatment by husband; left, marriage to a man of high position, controls husband and family.

Legs

Men: right, strength, courage, success, energetic; left, lazy, henpecked, coward.
Women: right, argumentative, fond of gossiping; left, noble and affectionate wife, will sacrifice everything for the good of the family.

Ankles

Men: right, pious, religious, leads a peaceful life; left, moderate means, easily pleased, respectable.
Women: right, poverty, hard work, immorality; left, virtuous, leads a happy comfortable life.

Right side of feet

Men: right, shrewd, intelligent, tactful, successful; left, disrespectful to elders, leaves his wife and family, suffers from mental and physical illness.
Women: right, lack of interest in family, craves men, suffers from venereal diseases; left, prosperous, happy, devoted to God.

Left side of feet

Men: right, shrewd, intelligent, successful, religious; left, respectable, secretive, of moderate means.
Women: right, homely, respectful to husband, religious, may contract venereal diseases; left, devoted wife, wealthy with all comforts of life.
If moles found on both feet of either sex it indicates unexpected misfortune and sudden illness. A mole on any part of the sole means frequent journeys, ambitions and wealth. A mole in the centre of the sole of a man shows a romantic nature. For a woman, it means she is

secretly seeking the company of other men.

Pandit Upadhyay did not like reading the moles of Westerners.

'You white people have too many and that will dilute any reading,' Rajendra translated flatly. 'Indian people only have a few moles.'

I showed the astrologer the mole on the palm of my right hand. He raised his eyebrows and agreed that it was unusual. He muttered something to Rajendra.

'My father says that you must not interfere in people's affairs or you will get a bad name.'

'But palmists have told me it's very good luck, that it means lots of money,' I protested. Both father and son gave me glazed looks and said nothing. This was not a matter for discussion. And the mole on the right side of my upper lip?

'You are a straightforward person but many people don't like your talk.'

'But I've been told that it means I'm social, sexy, fond of the opposite sex and have sweet speech.' More glazed looks.

We moved on to face-reading. Here again, Upadhyay did not enjoy reading westerners' faces.

'If you stay here you will get a different complexion, a sun-tan, and that makes a difference. Also the food you have been eating will have made a difference to the size of your cheeks.' I agreed that my face was a lot browner than it would have been back home and my cheeks were still sunken after my Ahmedabad stomach problems. Even so, we decided to give my face the once over. Upadhyay asked for my full name. He leaned back on his bolster and stared hard at me. Rajendra commented that there were few genuine face-readers left in India.

'Face-reading does not come naturally,' he said. 'My father has spent much time meditating by the Ganges to get his powers. He looks at the shape of the face, the complexion, the hair.'

The astrologer was reluctant to reveal his face-reading secrets to me. So I quote a few examples from some of the cheap fortune-telling booklets I picked up in India:

> If a man's eyebrows are joined, his wife dies early. If a girl's eyebrows are joined, the husband either dies or marries another wife. If the eyebrows are coarse and irregular, the person will find life a continuous struggle. Long, well-formed eyebrows mean a comfortable life, loved and admired by many.

Big and prominent teeth indicate learning.

Bald forehead indicates wealth.

Curly hair indicates good fortune.

If a man is seriously ill and his wife's face looks shining and bright he is sure to die.

A happy man will have a round, fleshy chin, broad and soft to touch. A thin, elongated chin indicates an unfortunate man.

A person with a small nose will be restless and hasty and will lead a 'common life'. If the interior of a person's nose is exposed to view, or flared, he will be uneducated, uncultured, stubborn and deceitful. If the nostrils are very wide and hairy the person will be avaricious and selfish. If the tip of your nose is like a lump it means you are oversexed.

Pity the Indian who is born without the standard head of black hair. It is said that brown hair denotes ill-luck (which writes off most westerners, including myself, before we've even started).

The trusty *Brihat Samhita* states that a person's character can be judged depending on what animal he resembles:

If the face be like that of a cow, the ox or the lion, he will defeat his enemies, be successful in fight, and will become a king; if the face be like that of a monkey, the buffalo, the hog or the goat, he will have sons, will be rich and will live in comfort; if the face be like that of the ass or the camel, the person will be poor and unhappy.[2]

Upadhyay spoke. Rajendra said, 'My father says your face is much governed by Saturn. You are unique but you don't adjust much with many people around you. The more you like someone, the more that

---

[2] There are also vedic rules of physiognomy for horses: much eating, great anger, are defects in women, but good qualities in horses; a horse having one colour in three legs and another colour in the fourth will reduce even a king to poverty; two hair circles on the forehead of a horse will bring the owner misfortune; a few white hairs on a horse's forehead which can be concealed by one finger make him objectionable.

person will pretend to like you but actually they don't like you much. You have an urgent need for knowledge but you will always be left unsatisfied.'

'And?'

'That is all.'

It was the shortest and gloomiest reading I had anywhere in India. If this was Vedic divination in its purest form then the sages of ancient India cannot have been a cheerful bunch. After another week in Varanasi I boarded a train for Calcutta. I continued on my journey with the hope of better news to come.

*****

Astrologically, Calcutta doesn't stand a chance. Indian astrologers claim that the city's geographical position means that it has for much of this century attracted the most negative rays that the planets can offer.

K.N. Rao and his Delhi associates believe that Calcutta has no future and that the city will be destroyed. They foretell bloodshed and upheaval.

'Calcutta occupies about the worst place in the zodiac of anywhere in the world,' Rao says. 'It means that whenever any important planetary transit takes place, disastrous things happen there and in the surrounding area of Bengal. The city is in for revolutionary changes and they won't be good.'

It was three years since my last visit to Calcutta and I noticed few changes in the City of Pot-Holes, although local people insisted with heavy irony that the place was in danger of becoming respectable. The new Hughli River bridge, which for years had been in a state of near completion, its spans never quite touching like the outstretched arms of lovers never destined to meet, was about to open. The underground railway was working smoothly – and almost all the holes in the road above it had been filled in – and it may have been their imagination, but someone said there was a day the previous week without a power cut. Even in the face of degenerate western influences like telephone sex, Calcuttans were proving that they were a moral band. A new dial-a-date service had just been introduced, with limited success. The organisers reported that it was used mostly by women, who called up other women to discuss domestic issues such as cooking and embroidery.

The traffic from Howrah Station to my hotel in the tourist ghetto of Sudder Street had certainly not changed. It was the usual clogged-up mess of cars, trucks, buses and rickshaws. Eighteen months earlier a party of Japanese road statisticians had arrived in Calcutta, promising the authorities a free blueprint to solve the traffic problem. They worked on it for a year before they threw in the towel. They were very sorry, but there was nothing they or anyone else could do to unravel the chaos.

There were more beggars than ever and the streets were strewn with the customary piles of rat-infested rubbish. Sure, there were plenty of rubbish skips, but as soon they were full they were emptied back on to the pavement by vagrants scavenging for recyclable glass, plastic bags and paper. The battered street signs requesting citizens to 'Help Keep Calcutta Clean' were like the sobs of a dying man.

But then the standards of behaviour and quality of life expected by Calcuttans are not what are expected in the rest of the world, or indeed the rest of India. Take the city's Durga Puja festival, for example. The annual festival dedicated to the mother goddess Durga was nearly over. Police commissioner Mr Tushar Talukdar was quoted in a newspaper as saying, 'Barring a few untoward incidents, the Pujas passed off peacefully this time.' The same newspaper article reported 1,102 arrests, three incidents of bomb-throwing between organisers and a riot in which the police fired teargas on a fifteen-hundred-strong stone-throwing mob. Untoward incidents? Anywhere else, and the army would have been called in.

Calcutta is so poverty stricken that it seems obscene for anyone even to consider spending money on jewellery but precious stones are one of the highest luxury expenditures for Calcutta's middle-classes. The city is home to hundreds of dealers specialising in astro-gems. Depending on your horoscope, an astro-gemologist will 'prescribe' stones to propitiate or reduce the effect of the planets in your chart. Hindus believe that God's most important symbol on earth is the rainbow, which forms the covenant between God and man. Its seven colours are recreated in the seven primary gem stones: ruby, pearl, coral, emerald, yellow sapphire, diamond and blue sapphire. Hindus say that each of these stones attracts cosmic rays that can be harnessed to enhance our well-being. The state of Bengal was once one of the richest gem-producing states in India until the British milked the mines dry. Today, astro-gems are still taken more seriously in Calcutta than in any other city in the country with both men and women wearing rings containing up to four different stones.

One of the oldest and largest dealers is M.P. Jewellers, which is patronised by film stars and government ministers. Like many of their competitors, the company employs consultant astrologers. I made an appointment to see their head astro-gemologist, a man called Mr Jataveda, who has been advising customers for nearly two decades.

The company's shop in the district of Ballygunge was an upmarket oasis surrounded by the usual Calcutta squalor. I stepped out of the cab into an overflowing drain. Muck clung to my ankles. Swearing under my breath, I fought my way through the crowds into a canvas alleyway of lean-to stalls up a flight of concrete steps. After stepping over a dozen snoozing workmen sprawled out on pieces of newspaper I found the showroom at the end of a balcony.

I walked through a smoked-glass door past a sleepy security guard who leaned nonchalantly on his shotgun, arms folded over the top of the barrels. Inside, it was if Calcutta's deprivation never existed. The shop was a picture of opulence with acres of mirrors, Italian-style black-tiled floor, recessed spotlights, potted plants and enormous crystal chandeliers. An air-conditioning unit emitted a soothing hum and Frank Sinatra's 'New York, New York' wafted from the piped-music system. There was not a beep of traffic to be heard in this hi-tech cocoon.

Smartly dressed young men presided over millions of rupees worth of gold and jewels nestling on velvet trays in glass display cases. A pair of middle-aged matrons wrapped in exquisite silk saris and with charge cards at the ready, greedily examined a collection of gold bracelets studded with rubies. A fawning assistant produced more and more lavish trinkets. The women fingered each one, noisily grunting their appreciation like truffle-hunting pigs.

At one end of the shop were three cubicles that contained the in-house astrologers. I was ushered into one of them where Mr Jataveda sat behind a tiny desk. The air-conditioning had not penetrated this far; a fan struggled against the fuggy heat.

Mr Jataveda rose to greet me. He was a distinguished-looking man with slicked-back grey hair, wearing the customary long white shirt and pyjama trousers. He started by telling me that he allotted each client thirty minutes' consultation – 'inadequate, but we are very busy' – in return for a nominal twenty rupee fee. He cheerfully admitted that he received a commission on gems purchased on his recommendation.

'Astrology is my passion,' he said, 'and I am glad to say that my employers are most generous to me. The best doctors in England are to be found in Harley Street, London. Here in Ballygunge you will find the best astro-gemologists in India.'

Astro-gems were enjoying a revival, he claimed. Although Bengal boasted a centuries-old tradition of astro-gemology, the science had become increasingly popular since Independence. As India's middle-classes became more prosperous, thus more people bought expensive stones.

'We take gems very seriously in Calcutta,' Mr Jataveda said. 'More and more people are putting their trust in astrology and the gems associated with the planets.' He added wryly, 'Perhaps it is because our country is becoming westernised. We need to hold on even tighter to our ancient beliefs if we are to remain sane.'

Mr Jataveda gave me his personal guide to the nine gems (seven primary plus two more) and the planets they represent. The sometimes eccentric recommendations that follow each stone come from the *Jatak Parijata*, which is considered to be the most authentic Sanskrit manuscript on the subject of astro-gems.

Ruby: the Sun, which controls the head and heart. Therefore the ruby gives protection against heart disease and headaches. The Sun is also responsible for fame and wealth. 'If your Sun is good in your horoscope you can become as famous as Mr Churchill,' Mr Jataveda remarked. The ruby is also known in India as the 'doctor's stone' because physicians wear them to enhance their reputation. Hindu mythology tells of a legendary ruby called the Samantak, which brought whoever owned it boundless prosperity and perfect health. Once owned by the god Krishna's father, this enormous gem disappeared centuries ago. The story goes that it remains hidden somewhere in India just waiting to be found. Rubies are also recommended for indigestion, anaemia and loss of appetite.

Pearl: the Moon, planet of emotions. Wear a pearl to avoid 'melancholic disposition or unnecessary worries'. A cheap substitute is the conch shell – Bengali brides traditionally wear conch bangles when they get married. The idea is that conch will protect a girl against emotional disturbances when she moves into her in-laws' home. Mr Jataveda pointed out, 'You do not get the full value with conch as you would with a pearl, but a little is better than nothing.' Pearls are recommended for: sexual weakness, impure conduct, fondness for undesirable company, drunkenness and insanity.

Red Coral: Mars, planet of bloodshed. A violent planet, Mars can nevertheless help people. Mars tries to help the human body, but the process can be painful. Thus red coral will sooth the after-effects of an operation or accident. The stone can also help stem a woman's menstrual flow and is frequently prescribed to new-born babies with physical problems. Red coral is recommended for: toothache, sexual diseases, idleness, depression and impatience.

Emerald: Mercury, planet of communication and collecting. Mercury collects both good and bad things such as poisonous elements in the mind and body. Emerald helps the intellect and concentration, and is suggested for schoolchildren. It is also recommended for stomach disorders, stammering, deafness, impotence and fondness for showing off.

Yellow Sapphire: Jupiter, the planet which controls the liver. Yellow sapphire is essential for good liver function and can help check epilepsy. It also brings wealth and is recommended for coughs, rheumatism, obesity, diarrhoea, talkativeness, self-importance, over-spending and fondness for law-suits.

Diamond: Venus. Wearing a diamond can only do you good. The effects are similar to those of pearl. Mr Jataveda noted wisely, 'A diamond may help your influence upon people because you are wearing a costly gem.' Diamonds are also recommended for sterility, hernia, fear of women, delusions and premature old age.

Blue Sapphire: Saturn, planet of delay and disappointment. Wearing a blue sapphire can deflect Saturn's harmful rays. Brides-to-be traditionally wear sapphire engagement rings so they will get married without delay. But be warned – worn by the wrong people, blue sapphire can be a dangerous stone.' If you begin feeling some sort of discontent, take it off immediately and consult an astrologer,' Mr Jataveda advised. 'It can lead to divorce.' It is also recommended for trembling of hands, feet and body, hysteria, foolishness and generally improper behaviour.

Gomet or Onyx: Rahu, the dragon's head, which is known for hindering progress. Excellent for preventing travel plans from going wrong. Also good for smallpox, constipation, disease of the brain, suicidal tendency and fear of goblins.

Cat's Eye: Ketu, the dragon's tail, which causes back-biting and gossip. Cat's eye will protect you from hidden enemies like business competitors. It is excellent for combating illness that cannot be diagnosed by doctors, and is also recommended for boils, skin diseases, itching, cancer, asthma and diseases caused by men of low caste.

I noticed that Mr Jataveda was wearing three rings, one each of yellow sapphire, catseye and pearl. Had the yellow sapphire brought him good fortune?

'But of course. Since I began wearing it I have become considerably more comfortably off and I now have my own car.'

'And would you approach blue sapphires with caution?'

'Oh yes. Extreme caution.' He sighed deeply. Prescribing blue sapphires was a heavy responsibility. 'Blue sapphire emits ultra-violet rays and excessive ultra-violet rays are very bad for a human being. Extra ultra-violet is only needed in special cases. I don't know what you do in England, but here if a tiny baby has growth problems, we massage it with oil and put it out in the early morning sun. The ultra-violet rays help the baby to grow. I will only prescribe a blue sapphire in order to provide a balance. If I prescribe a blue sapphire which is not needed, it will damage the body.'

'So you are in a responsible position.'

'Exactly. Like a doctor. Whenever I prescribe a blue sapphire I always put it on trial for between seven and ten days. Only if there are no adverse effects then only will I let a person wear one.'

The size and quality of the stone makes a difference. The better the quality, the more effective the gem. Settings are also important. Yellow sapphire must be set in gold – the metal of Jupiter – to increase the lustre of the stone; gomet should always be worn with silver. The other gems can be set in any metal.

'And to achieve maximum potency, I would suggest you wear them as rings,' Mr Jataveda added. I pointed out that most men in the West were unaccustomed to wearing jewel-encrusted rings. No problem. You can wear your gem on an armband under your shirt. Likewise, babies can wear their stones on a band around the waist.

'But never as a pendant. It swings and the power is dissipated.'

I showed Mr Jataveda the computer horoscope that Mr Rao had prepared for me.

'So what gem should I wear?' Mr Jataveda studied my chart.

'Your Moon is in Aries and there is a combination of Sun and Venus and that has got you into this profession of travelling and writing. But there is an aspect of Saturn, so there is some restraint on your achievements: you get a little less than what you deserve. Your Jupiter is retrograde so a pearl would do you good; also emerald. You could try blue sapphire to see if it helps your mental development but you would have to take it on trial.'

I resisted spending any money. On my way out of the shop, I stopped to talk to a young man who was buying an engagement ring for his fiancée. They had not bothered to consult an astrologer.

'What stone are you planning to have?' I asked.

'Blue sapphire.'

'I should watch out if I were you.' I waffled for a few minutes like an expert, ending with the words, 'and Mr Jataveda says it could lead to divorce'. The man frowned. The girl looked horrified. They agreed they should see the astrologer immediately.

8

The Mystery of the Nadi

I left the chaotic grasp of Calcutta and took the night train twelve hundred kilometres south to the city of Vijayawada in the state of Andhra Pradesh. My reason for coming to Vijayawada was to see an old friend, Dr Ramesh Singh Chouhan, whom I had met three years earlier while researching my Clive project. Ramesh is a cancer specialist, whose speciality is detection of the disease using the ancient holistic art of aura-reading. He has a keen interest in the occult sciences and had arranged for me to meet an astrologer friend who lived in a secluded town called Amalapuram on the east coast marshes of Andhra Pradesh. We were due to go there the next day.

Vijayawada was in a spiritually boisterous mood. Thousands of pilgrims were celebrating the end of the annual Hindu festival dedicated to Vijayawada's patron goddess Kanakdurga. Religious music blared from loudspeakers on every street corner and a twenty-four-hour stream of worshippers wound up the rocky path to Kanakdurga's temple, which sits on an escarpment above the town overlooking the Krishna River.

The Krishna is one of India's holiest waterways. It is said that the tongue of whoever drinks from the Krishna becomes so pliable that they can speak any language. This year's festival had special significance because the river was celebrating a rare astrological event. The rishis of ancient India decreed that each of the country's twelve most important rivers should come under a different constellation depending on their geographical position. The constellation changed every twelve years, and this year it was the turn of the Krishna's sign of Virgo. The river was said to be at its most astrologically potent and people from all over the subcontinent had come to purify themselves in the sacred waters. The ritual was supposed to cleanse them of their sins, granting them an unhindered passage to heaven.

My friend Ramesh was born in Vijayawada, but he now lived with his family in the former French colony of Pondicherry on the south-east coast of Tamil Nadu. He was back in his hometown to take part in the Kanakdurga festivities and to visit his mother, who still lived here. He was travelling with his wife Malla and daughters, Sunaina, aged five, and Vigita, three.

Ramesh's mother was one of the greatest characters I have met in India. She was an elegant woman in her sixties with glistening, dark skin and a fondness for green saris. She had a deep, rapid-fire voice and an easy laugh and she managed her family with a determined matriarchal force. Nothing escaped her and she would not tolerate bad manners from either her children or grandchildren.

The first time I had met this imposing lady had been a memorable occasion. I was staying with Ramesh in Pondicherry and Mrs Chouhan had come down from Vijayawada to see her grandchildren. It was a Monday and the next day the family were planning to move from their rented apartment in a Pondi suburb to a new, larger home up the street. Like most families in India, they had planned the move around the stars. Ramesh had decided that the position of the planets was perfect for moving on Tuesday. But that evening, disaster struck.

The drama began when Ramesh returned from a video hire shop with a film – *Other People's Money* starring Danny DeVito – to watch on the television. It turned out to be an appalling copy – no great surprise since virtually all videos in India are pirated and the quality often leaves much to be desired. After ten minutes of muddy sound and fuzzy pictures, it became obvious that the movie was unwatchable. Ramesh switched off the TV and we sat in morose silence registering our disappointment.

Ramesh's daughters amused themselves by playing with a pair of kittens that Daddy had brought home as a present a few days earlier. Unlike many Indians, Ramesh was not superstitious about having cats in the house. Far from considering them evil, he quite liked them. Indeed, the kittens were delightful little balls of orange fluff, and grown-ups and children alike spent much time oohing and aahing at their antics. I had become particularly attached to them during my short stay since they slept in a cardboard box under my bed in the guest-room.

I was stroking one of the tiny creatures when the quiet was suddenly shattered. We all gasped in horror as a fully grown, black cat charged through the front door with all the urgency of a pillaging Viking. With a terrifying roar, it grabbed one of the kittens by the throat, turned on its heels and tried to run out of the house. The children screamed. Ramesh lunged at the creature. The panicked cat dropped the kitten on the doorstep and bolted into the night. We rushed to the kitten's aid, but we were too late. The viciousness of the blow had severed its jugular vein. The mite writhed in pain, its little legs jerking spasmodically. A pool of blood gathered on the floor around the feebly kicking animal as it moved into its death throes.

No one spoke for several minutes. We were in shock and I could see now why Indians mistrusted cats so much. Malla comforted her sobbing daughters. The other women were wide-eyed with fright. The surviving kitten mewled pathetically. Ramesh and I went out on to the patio. We could see the killer cat on the wall of the house next door. It glared at us viciously. How dare we spoil its fun?

Ramesh gingerly picked up the bloodied corpse and disposed of it on a rubbish heap across the road. He returned to the apartment with a heavy face, took down a calendar from the wall and inspected the day's planetary positions. Most Indian calendars include the daily planetary positions as a matter of course.

'We will move tonight,' he announced.

It was nearly 10 p.m. I groaned inwardly. The thought of moving house in the dark was too much.

'What about the furniture?' I enquired evenly.

'We will carry it.'

Mrs Chouhan butted in.

'No, we will not move tonight.' I sighed with relief at this voice of common sense.

'I think your mother's right,' I told Ramesh. 'It's going to be awfully tricky moving in the dark.' Mrs Chouhan folded her arms and frowned at me. I had got completely the wrong end of the stick.

'It's got nothing to do with the dark,' she said brusquely. 'It's because the stars are not right.'

The conversation continued in Hindi between Ramesh and his mother. I did not understand it, but from the faintly hysterical voices, I could get the gist of what was going on. It went something like this:

Ramesh: 'The kitten being killed is a sign that we must move tonight.'

Mrs Chouhan: 'Nonsense. The kitten's got nothing to do with it. The stars are much better for moving tomorrow.'

Ramesh: 'Look mother, I understand more about these things than you do.'

Mrs Chouhan: 'That's the trouble with you young people today. You always think you know best.'

Ramesh: 'Damned right I know best.'

After a noisy argument, mother and son reached a compromise. We would move tonight, but it would be only a token move to appease the gods. A few items would go; the family and furniture could stay where they were until tomorrow. So for the next hour, Ramesh and I lugged the family's most prized possessions over to the new apartment. The statues of Ganesh and Shiva went first, closely followed by Ramesh's much-loved Sony hi-fi.

Back in Vijayawada, it was good to see Mrs Chouhan again. We reminisced about the kitten affair.

'What a distressing business,' I said.

'It was a very bad night,' she agreed.

If that had been a bad night, my morning in Vijayawada was not much better. Mrs Chouhan's home was a simple Indian bungalow overflowing with metal beds and cardboard boxes. Sun-bleached cane furniture cluttered the verandah and the front door was decorated with a dusty bunch of plastic roses. After putting my bags in the house, I explained that I needed to use the lavatory. Ramesh showed me to an outside privy at the corner of the front courtyard. Following my ablutions, I emerged from the tiny hut, stepping heavily on to an iron manhole cover on the ground outside. After surviving countless years of people walking over it, the cover chose this moment to collapse. The metal gave way with a loud crack and my right leg plunged into the drain below. Only my left leg, which remained on the manhole's concrete surround, stopped me from completely disappearing into the foul abyss. A horrible smell swirled up from the depths. I looked down to see blood seeping through my trousers.

The family heard my cries and Ramesh ran over and hauled me out of the filthy water. My injured leg was black with stinking effluent. I put an arm around my friend's shoulder and he helped me to a chair on the verandah. The others crowded around me jabbering in Hindi. I sat down and we all inspected the damage.

My knee was badly bruised and causing considerable pain, but I had been lucky. No bones were broken and I had suffered nothing more than a few surface cuts and hurt pride – falling down a drain does not do wonders for one's dignity. To be on the safe side, Ramesh gave his cousin some money and dispatched him to a drug kiosk to buy a syringe and a tetanus shot. You do not take chances with the germs that lurk in Indian sewers.

As the pain subsided, I managed a weak smile. Mrs Chouhan burst into riotous laughter. The fact that I was not seriously injured gave her permission to see the funny side.

'It is a gift from Andhra Pradesh,' she cried.

Ramesh tried to jolly me up.

'Maybe it was meant to be,' he suggested.

'Oh yes?'

'Well, you're researching into Indian astrology and the Krishna River is celebrating its planetary birthday this year. What better way of the Krishna making sure you meet it. Since you weren't planning to swim in the actual river, the Krishna must have thought that getting you to fall into a drain leading into it was better than nothing.'

I was not convinced.

'It tells me more about the reliability of Indian manhole covers,' I said.

'Maybe you're right.'

My visit to Ramesh's astrologer friend in Amalapuram had given the family an excuse for a weekend trip. They all decided to come. When we left later that afternoon on the train to Rajahmundry, the party included Ramesh, his wife, one of his wife's sisters, and his wife's cousin, a talkative man in his forties called Singh. Mrs Chouhan, resplendent in an olive sari with gold brocade, brought up the rear.

After a night in a Rajahmundry guest-house, we hired a cab to take us the sixty miles south to the home of Mr Ramajogeswara Rao, reputedly one of the finest 'nadi' readers in India.

The nadi is possibly the world's most baffling method of divination. You need to have great faith and open-mindedness to believe in it.

The reader produces a sheaf of palm-leaf manuscripts known as patras, each measuring about one foot long by two inches wide. Each patra is crammed with line after line of tiny Sanskrit text. The reader starts by asking you a few questions in order to find the leaf that refers to you. Nadi philosophers believe that there are certain basic patterns of destiny – three thousand six hundred in any one day – and one of these patterns will correspond to the client. Having found the appropriate patra, the reader proceeds to read directly from the Sanskrit. Using minimal interpretation, he claims to be able to tell you your past life, present life and future. The idea that there can be a leaf for every person in the world is a preposterous notion, but that is exactly what exponents of this ancient science claim. Of all the techniques of Indian fortune-telling, this is the one that seems most outrageous to westerners. Even mainstream Hindu astrologers are dubious about this system and

K.N. Rao warned me that I should be wary of frauds.

'Nadi readers can be either very genuine or very fake. I have known them to be fantastically accurate about people's pasts, but their long-range predictions can go hopelessly wrong. I would not trust nadi predictions of more than ten days ahead.'

Experts in this sacred science – often highly educated men with a leaning towards philosophy – strongly disagree. They swear that the nadi can tell you more about your inner self than any standard astrological reading. The nadi, they claim, delves into unknown worlds. I might use words like 'preposterous' and 'outrageous', but that is to be expected. Nadi readers claim the patras are the result of the forces of natural law that were discovered only after years of meditation on the highest plane of consciousness.

There are several collections of nadi manuscripts. The majority originated in South India and are believed to have been compiled by sages more than three thousand years ago. The versions you see today are likely to be copies rewritten during the past five hundred years.

The uncertain history of the manuscripts has led to a multitude of extravagant claims. For example, a series of patras, written long before Christ, is said to predict the rise of Christianity and describe Jesus and his disciples by name. The same manuscript also contains details about Islam and Soviet Russia with the names of Mohammed and Lenin written clearly in the spidery Sanskrit text. The scrolls are alleged to be in the possession of an unnamed nadi reader somewhere in India. Needless to say, their present whereabouts is unknown.

Just as bizarre are the stories concerning the actual writing of the nadi. For example, the collection of scrolls that I was about to see was worded in Sanskrit, but written in the script of Telegu, the language of Andhra Pradesh. This particular collection was said to have been compiled by a rishi in the fifth century BC. Yet Telegu is one of the newer languages of the subcontinent, having evolved no more than nine hundred years ago. So how was this possible? How can anyone write in a tongue that will not be spoken for another seven hundred years? Simple. The rishi had foresight. He knew that Sanskrit would become obsolete. Therefore he wrote his manuscripts in Telegu so that people in the future would understand them.

Nadi readers are famed for their neat arguments. Another man I saw later in Bangalore (whom I found after looking in the Yellow Pages under 'Astrologers', listed between 'Associations' and 'Audio and Hi-fi') regularly visited America where he had many clients. But how could he take a warehouseful of scrolls on the plane?

'Aha,' he replied. 'By my powers of intuition I am able to know which people in America will come and see me. Therefore I only have to take their leaves with me.'

I first discovered the nadi during my Clive trip. On a whim, I had gone for a reading at a small temple town in Tamil Nadu called Vaithishwaran Koil. The accuracy of the reader had impressed me, although I was shaken when he concluded the session with the precise details of my death. He specified the exact day and time that I would die . . . at the age of 73. I was horrified. It seemed so unethical to tell a person when he would die. Now, three years later, I was learning that death is a favourite subject for Indian soothsayers. So far I had been informed that I would live to a variety of ages ranging from 70 to 90 (86 was a popular figure). Predictions about my demise were becoming old hat. Far from worrying me, it was all going over my head.

The *Brihat Samhita* has clear rules on how to judge a person's lifespan from the number of lines on their forehead. This is a method of longevity divination still used widely in India. Three lines means you will live for 100 years; four lines, you will be a king and live for 95 years; no lines, 90 years; if the lines are near the hair, 80 years; five lines, 70 years; lines of the same length, 60 years; many lines, 50; bent lines, 40; lines in contact with the eyebrows, 30; bent on the left side, 20; very short lines, early death. Broken lines mean that the person will commit adultery.

After spending the morning shopping, we left Rajahmundry at midday. The dirt road to Amalapuram lay alongside a web of irrigation canals leading to the Krishna delta. This massive drainage system, built by the British in the last century, has been responsible for turning one of the poorest flood areas in India into an agricultural jewel. It was a pretty drive through a perfect tropical landscape of shiny coconut trees and rice fields sparkling in the sunshine.

Amalapuram is an unexciting, provincial town, the general attractiveness of which is not helped by endless derelict houses on the outskirts, victims of the terrible cyclones that periodically ravage the delta. We drove through the centre, dodging the customary mad mish-mash of cycle rickshaws and bullock carts apparently racing against each other, and turned off down a side street to the home of Mr Ramajogeswara Rao.

Away from his scrolls, Mr Rao was a zoology lecturer at a college in Amalapuram. As befitted a middle-class man of his profession, he lived in a spacious bungalow set in a leafy garden shaded by palm trees. The nadi reader greeted us on a verandah lined with potted plants. He was of medium build with thick black hair turning to grey. He wore a virgin white kurta; a meticulously tied dhoti hung low towards his ankles.

I was immediately struck by his immense presence. Our host was not any old run-of-the-mill soothsayer. With his distinguished Brahmin looks and commanding voice, he oozed enormous charm. Here was a local demi-god, an expert in his field, a man to be treated with reverence. Ramesh was gripped with devotion. He put his palms together, bowed, sank to his knees and kissed Mr Rao's feet. The rest of our party did the same. When it came to my turn, I opted for the western style of greeting and shook Mr Rao's hand. He seemed happy enough with this.

Mr Rao showed us across the blood-red terracotta floor of the terrace into his sitting-room. It was dark and cool. A ceiling fan creaked overhead. On one of the faded cream walls was a print of an elderly man with a flowing white beard. This was Mr Rao's guru from whom he had learned the art of reading the leaves.

We sat on fold-up garden chairs while Mr Rao settled himself into a type of metal deckchair that was known in Raj days as a 'planter's long-sleever'. This eccentric piece of furniture had wide and long wooden arms over which he draped his legs. He held court like a pasha and I got the impression that he was thoroughly enjoying the presence of a foreign guest. He lay back on a nest of well-plumped cushions, gave a sigh of extreme comfort and, after a pause of dignified silence, launched into the story of his life.

He had begun studying his craft aged 17 and was fully qualified by the age of 22 – exceptionally young for a nadi reader. He was now in his late-fifties and boasted a long list of clients who travelled from all over India to see him. Nadi reading was his public duty. He never charged for his services, although he accepted gifts. (In order to show our appreciation, we had brought him a large basket of custard apples bought that morning in Rajahmundry.)

'My nadi is priceless,' he declared with a theatrical swish of his arms. 'The cost of a reading would be the same as buying the whole of England.'

Mr Rao was the master of forty-eight thousand bundles of patras that formed a collection known as the Vharavwaja Nadi. They were stored in trunks all over the house where they would remain until it was time for them to be passed on.

The patras passed from one reader to another according to divine law. Outlandish though it may sound, the bundles are said to include a line of writing stating the name of the person who should inherit them. Mr

Rao had received his first bundle while a zoology graduate at Benares University. The leaves had been in the possession of his guru, who had been waiting for years to meet a man that fitted Rao's name and description. It was the will of God, rather than coincidence, that the 17-year-old student had turned up out of the blue in Benares. The moment that the guru met the teenaged Rao, the old man realised that this youth was destined to be the new master of the scrolls. Rao had amassed the rest of the Vharavwaja collection over the next thirty years as he had come into contact with other nadi readers who had handed over their bundles.

'Sometimes I find a leaf which indicates the whereabouts of other leaves in the collection,' he explained. 'I then visit the owner and he gives them to me.'

Likewise, the name of the man who would eventually inherit Rao's nadi was also written in the bundles.

'Do you know this person?' I asked.

'Well, it's not you,' he said with a laugh. 'No, I've never heard of him. One day he may visit me, or perhaps he will come after my death. Perhaps my children will have a curiosity to know about the leaves. Maybe they will take them to an astrologer and maybe that astrologer's name will be in the patras. Who knows?'

We were interrupted by a young man, who entered the room bearing a tray of glasses of water. This was Mr Rao's 16-year-old grandson. He was a studious-looking boy with round metal spectacles and a slightly startled look that reminded me of Woody Allen. He handed round the water. When the boy reached me, I refused the glass. Instead, I produced a plastic bottle of mineral water from my bag.

'You do not like my water?' Mr Rao boomed from his throne.

I explained that Indian tap water was likely to have a disastrous effect on my delicate western stomach. If it was all the same with him, I'd stick to the bottled variety. This did not satisfy Mr Rao.

'Love and adaptability is what is needed here,' he cried. 'I need the tolerance to accept you in my house and you should have the adaptability to live in India. When you are in India, you should live an Indian's life and drink Indian water.'

He explained that his drinking water came from a rain butt in the garden, and did I not realise that rain water was far healthier than bottled spring water? No I did not.

'Rain water is the only water you should drink if you want a long life. It gives you joy and elevation. If you drink only underground water your life will be shortened.'

I had been firmly put in my place. Mr Rao continued on a philosophical tangent. He talked about the purity of melted Himalayan snow before moving on to religion and nirvana. Words like 'cellular' and 'factorial' littered his sentences. I grasped little of what he was saying. It was then that I witnessed what was to be the eeriest moment of my journey. While Mr Rao was talking I had switched on the micro-cassette recorder that I use for recording interviews. Five minutes into Mr Rao's speech I glanced at the machine and noticed it was not working. I shook the thing and clicked it on and off several times. The tape refused to budge. Mr Rao suddenly stopped in mid-flow. He glared at me.

'You did not ask my permission,' he growled, a strange note in his voice.

'I don't understand . . . '

'You did not ask my permission,' he repeated, 'to use that.' He pointed at the tape recorder. 'Give it to me!'

I handed him the machine. He held it in his hands for a minute, blew on it, then passed it back to me.

'Try it now,' he ordered. I pushed the play button. It worked first time.

'Oh shit,' I muttered. 'That sort of thing really freaks me out.' I looked at Mr Rao. 'How the hell did you do that?'

'Transference of strength. You did not ask my permission to use that thing, so I stopped it.' I was speechless. I turned to Ramesh.

'Is he joking?'

'Certainly not,' Ramesh said. 'You saw what just happened. Has your tape recorder ever gone wrong before?'

'Never.'

'Well, there you are.' Mr Rao grinned wickedly. 'It's fun, isn't it? The last time a foreigner was here I did the same to his video camera.'

By now I was taking my host very seriously indeed.

'Is it okay to tape you now?' I asked quietly.

'Of course. Your machine will not go wrong again.'

Mr Rao made preparations for my reading. Before he was able to select the leaf that referred to me, he needed to cast my horoscope.

'What was your time of birth?' he asked. My heart sank. Here we go again. I explained that my mother wasn't sure. I trotted out that well-worn phrase: 'About 10 p.m.'

Mr Rao raised an eyebrow as if he expected no different from a heathen westerner.

'We shall see,' he said. He added that the birthtime must be precise.

An inaccurate time could change the patra and give a totally wrong reading.

The nadi reader called his female assistant into the room. She was a student of 19 who came to Rao's house each day after college to learn astrology. She was a pretty girl with a wheaten complexion and lavish, tombstone teeth. Rao gave her my birth details. She pulled up a chair, took a pen and paper and proceeded to draw up my chart. Her face contorted in worried concentration as she tried hard to impress her teacher. Five minutes later, she was still painstakingly thumbing her way through a tatty copy of the *Ephemeris*.

'Hurry up, girl,' Mr Rao huffed impatiently. He turned to me. 'I've taught her how to do these things quickly, but she never learns.' The girl put her head in her hands and giggled embarrassedly. She was used to being ticked off. She handed him my chart. Mr Rao put on a pair of reading glasses, leaned back on his cushions and studied it. He made some calculations in a notebook, then peered at me over his spectacles.

'You cannot have been born at 10 p.m.,' he said.

'I did say that my mother wasn't sure. I'll have to have words with her.'

'Yes, there does seem to have been a communication problem.' He went on in a firm voice, 'There was only one baby born in that part of southern England at precisely 10 p.m. on 21 January 1956, and that was a girl.' There was no trace of irony in his voice. He was stating a fact. Simple as that.

A low titter went around the room. Ramesh's mother seemed to find this claim particularly funny. The idea that I ought to be a girl was hilarious. Outside in the trees a squawking crow joined in the laughter.

'Well, as far as I am aware, I am not a girl,' I said. 'And anyway, how on earth did you work that out?'

'Astrological equations,' Mr Rao said simply as if this was the most obvious thing in the world. He returned to his notebook. After a few more minutes he concluded that I must have been born at 9.10 p.m., or rather 9.10 and forty-eight seconds which, whether my mother liked it or not, was nearly an hour earlier than she remembered.

'At that time,' Mr Rao concluded, 'a baby boy was born south of London and that boy was you.' He removed his glasses and gave a little bow of victory.

I listened in awed silence. Ramesh and the women burst into spontaneous applause. This was a moment for celebration. After forty years on the earth I was finally a complete human being. I had a precise birthtime at last. I wasn't sure what to make of it all, but I was surprised to find that I derived some strange comfort from this revelation. It was like being re-born.

Basking in the golden glow of discovery, Mr Rao now turned to the task of finding my patra. He wrote something on a piece of paper and handed it to his assistant, who left the room. The girl reappeared bearing a bundle of brittle, yellowing palm leaves. Mr Rao flicked through the bundle, his fingers working swiftly like a bank teller's. He stopped at one leaf and withdrew it, looked at it, shook his head and put it back. He repeated this process several times. Finally he reached the correct patra and held it up triumphantly. On this slender piece of palm were hidden the secrets of my destiny.

My patra was the twenty-fifth leaf in a section called the Sanketa. Mr Rao lay it gently on his lap and peered at the Sanskrit verses. Then he began to chant the words in a rich baritone. After singing each verse, he translated the lines into English. A hushed reverence came over the room. Ramesh and his family became silent as they prepared to listen to my reading. Everyone has a right to witness the nadi's revelations and I was intrigued that there was no question of confidentiality.

As well as revealing a person's past, present and future, the nadi includes a section about his or her native country, and this is where we began. The first verse disclosed that I came from a place known to the ancient Hindus as the 'Land of the Garundas'. This, according to Mr Rao, was an obscure Sanskrit description for ancient Britain.

'The rishi who wrote this nadi says that the Garundas have the appearance and head of a red monkey.' Mr Rao paused and gave me a sidelong glance. 'He means that you have reddish skin and hair.'

'But my hair's brown,' I cut in.

'That may be so, but to an Indian rishi of three thousand years ago who would have known only black hair, it would have looked most definitely red.'

He returned to the leaf and continued, 'The diet of these people is the diet of the lion and the tiger. You eat meat and many of you have blue eyes like the eyes of a cat.'

The rishi moved on to the future of my country. It did not look bright.

'In the first ninety-five days of the next century, England will have a lot of problems. Your country will be ruined, and Holland will be hit by tidal waves. England thought at one point that it had conquered the whole world and was master of the seas. But England will also be hit by these waters.'

'Do you really believe that?' I asked.

'Of course. I have heard that other nadis all predict the same thing.'

The patra trailed off into a complicated ramble. It talked about the five elements of nature – soil, solid, liquid, gases, heat – and how England could make itself at peace.

'Once your country felt very great and you thought that you understood the greatness and development of nature, but actually you do not care for nature.'

I nudged Ramesh.

'What's going on?'

'Maybe the rishi is talking about Charles Darwin and the origin of nature,' Ramesh said.

'In spite of all your so-called understanding of nature, you people in the West have failed to comply with nature. What with pollution and all your ecological problems, you are now beating your foreheads in frustration.' Mr Rao continued, 'But changes are coming. The leader of England is going to change his religious beliefs and make trouble.'

Which leader? The prime minister at that time was John Major. Was it him? 'The rishi does not say. Perhaps he is talking about the new King Charles. Whoever it is, there will be a change in the religious beliefs of England. At the beginning of the next century, England will turn towards nature once more and you will find new beliefs and a new spirituality. The land will be at peace, the animals will be at peace, the plants will be at peace and you will live in peace in the land of the Garundas.'

This was not the first time that I had heard this prediction. Several Indian soothsayers had told me that the West was heading for a great moral crusade. After the year 2000, Britain would lead Europe and America in a revolutionary non-political, non-denominational movement of pure spirituality. Mr Rao sighed happily.

'It sounds like England will become a nice place to live. So you see, Mr Holt, the Indian rishis could visualise the things to come as well as your own birth. They were gifted with great foresight. It was not a big battle for them.'

He then reached a section that I cannot fathom out to this day. Mr Rao said that the Garundas owed their freedom and liberty to a man called George Cornwall, who is said to have liberated England after decapitating two great people. The name of one of those people was similar to my father's. Mr Rao peered at me. He confessed that he hadn't a clue about what the patra was going on about. Did this George Cornwall mean anything to me? Absolutely nothing. (After returning from India, I thumbed through endless history books and encyclopedias searching for the elusive Mr Cornwall. Cromwell, yes, but he only decapitated one person. But Cornwall? Not a squeak.)

A bicycle bell tinkled outside. I looked through the window to see a man propping his bike against the garden wall. He hurried up the path, kicked off his shoes by the front door and rushed into the room in an anxious flurry. He dropped to his knees, kissed Mr Rao's feet and presented him with a bag of fruit, gabbling away in a burst of Telegu. The man, a local businessman, was one of Mr Rao's regular clients. He was in a terrible state having just received a two million rupee tax demand. He needed advice quickly. Could the nadi reader spare a few moments for an emergency consultation?

Mr Rao laid down my patra and stood up. This was a matter of great importance. His client needed urgent help. My reading would have to wait. He took the man into another room. While they were gone, I marvelled at the power Mr Rao wielded over the local community. Here was a small-town zoology lecturer, who, by virtue of a set of manuscripts of dubious origin, had set himself up as a great sage. Most of the astrologers I had met so far in India had been low-key and self-effacing, but this man was super confident. He truly believed that some sort of divinity had entrusted him with the secrets of the universe.

I had been so engrossed by Mr Rao's chanting and chatter that I had not noticed it getting dark outside. Someone flicked a switch and a neon strip spluttered into life, shedding its ruthless glare over the room – there is so much neon lighting in India that I sometimes wonder if fluorescent tubes were invented specially for the country.

I went out on to the verandah for a cigarette. The soothing stutter of crickets filled the night. An anarchic swarm of bugs buzzed around the street lights. The road echoed with the gentle slapping of plastic flip-flops as people walked home from work.

The master returned an hour later. He apologised for the delay and eased himself back into his deckchair. He lazily stretched his arms and picked up my patra again.

'The rishi says that when you were born, ice was falling on earth. The sun was not seen that day.' This was accurate. It was ferociously cold in Bognor on 21 January 1956. 'But the next day was very clear with much sun.' According to my mother's diary at the time, this was also true.

He vaulted to the present day. 'The patra says you must be careful of injuries to your leg.' This was alarmingly close to the truth. Since yesterday's encounter with the Vijayawada drain, the swelling in my knee had subsided and I was no longer limping, so Mr Rao could not have noticed that anything was wrong with my leg. What with this revelation and the incident with my tape recorder, I was beginning to feel a grudging respect for both the anonymous author of the scrolls and the nadi reader. I began to fret about what else I would learn. Would Mr Rao and his guide, the rishi, strip me down bit by bit? Would they tell me I was about to lose all my money and that I would die next year?

As it turned out, my future was good, with reasonable career prospects, a happy home life and no disasters to prepare for. We reached the inevitable subject of romance. Mr Rao read the leaf and smiled. He chose his words carefully.

'My dear boy, the rishi says you have had a lot of girlfriends.'

'True,' I agreed cautiously. Mrs Chouhan and the other women sniggered. This was more like it. They shifted in their seats in excited anticipation. The sexy bits of a nadi reading were always the best.

'The animals mate in a certain season and then they don't care about each other anymore,' Mr Rao went on. 'Man should not behave like that.'

'Is this a lecture?' I asked. Mr Rao ignored my interruption.

'But right now you are changing and you are trying to develop an intimacy with one girl.' Also true. My host seemed to be rather enjoying himself.

'And is she a nice girl?' he enquired politely.

'Very nice, thank you.'

'I look forward to meeting her.' The patra appeared to bore him. He swerved off on an impromptu discourse about the moon. Did I know that the moon ruled our sex lives?

'The moon activates us at night, which is why we are more likely to have sex at night than in the morning. And the reason you English have so much sex is because there's so little daylight in England.' He found this riotously funny. He almost choked with mirth and mopped his brow with a handkerchief. The moon also controlled our speech.

'The effect of lunar light changes your thoughts. Lunar light goes down to your stomach where it mixes with the gastric juices and then comes out as a sound. That is your voice. When you talk, your speech goes out as the alphabet. When the alphabet dies the sound continues through space. This sound is the result of your astorial desires.' In fact, everything we thought and said was a direct result of the moon. 'The moon produces action and sex,' Mr Rao concluded. 'That is why on a full moon the sea will be turbulent and all the animals in it will be breeding.' He returned to my patra.

'Ah, this is interesting. The leaf says the time of your birth is twenty-four minutes in advance of the time at this very moment that I am reading your patra. It is 8.50 now, so your birthtime is 9.14 p.m.' He read some more. 'And it says you should now add another four and a half minutes, which makes your birthtime 9.18 and thirty seconds exactly.' I had yet another birthtime. The excitement was becoming all too much for me.

The reading went on for another hour. Much of it was either inaccurate or downright puzzling with Mr Rao weaving from one subject to another. I began to feel sleepy and bored.

'Your father is connected with the literary world,' Mr Rao said.

'No, he's a retired farmer. Although he does read a lot.'

'You have two children?'

'None, to my knowledge.'

'The patra says you are a great man who can see things in the future like Nostradamus.'

'Well, I never . . .' I did not think that my elementary skills of palmistry qualified me for this accolade. All the same, I was quite flattered.

We ended on a gloomy forecast about my health. Within four years I would have trouble in my ligaments and shooting pains in my thighs.[1] I could prevent this by chanting mantras and wearing a blue sapphire. Mr Rao added that I would live to be more than 80. This cheered me up enormously.

The reading over, we stayed for another hour while the nadi reader's grandson brought us a light supper of samosas, sticky cakes and sweet tea. Mr Rao settled back into his role of lecturer. He insisted that none of what he had said was original. It had all been written down thousands of years ago by the great Hindu sages.

'I am not a copyist like Charles Darwin, who claimed his discoveries were his alone. In fact, they were written by our rishis centuries ago.' He added dramatically, 'If I ever falsely claim that a particular thought began with me, I hope I shall be thrown from the soil into the Bay of Bengal.'

It was midnight before we left for the five-hour drive back to Vijayawada. Ramesh telephoned for a taxi. It turned out to be an emaciated Ambassador with a gearbox that sounded like it was in pain. Ramesh and the three women squeezed into the back. Cousin Singh and I took the front bench seat with me wedged next to the driver.

A series of near misses and the blinding headlights of oncoming trucks made it a hair-raising journey. Our driver was a boy of no more

---

[1] As I write this seven months later, I am suffering from a foot sprain that refuses to go away . . .

than 18 and unscarred by education. His eyelids were heavy and I suspected that he had just smoked a large quantity of marijuana. He shouldn't have been in charge of a push-bike, let alone a car. I kept prodding him to stop him falling asleep. On several occasions I was forced to grab the steering wheel to prevent us crashing. He looked rather cross.

I spent much of the journey wrapped up in morbid thoughts about what would happen to my body if I died on this road. (Such was my terror that I had already forgotten Mr Rao's assurances of my longevity.) Did my travel insurance cover my remains being shipped back to England? Was my premium sufficient to pay for a coffin? Or would I have to make do with a body bag? Would the coffin have decorative brass handles? Or would we hit a petroleum truck resulting in my instant cremation? I favoured the latter. Death by inferno might mean that my eyes could no longer be left to medical research, but it sounded more convenient.

Cremation would also appeal to the sensibilities of Hindus like Mr Rao. Before I left Amalapuram, the nadi reader had treated me to his views on death. He claimed that the western practice of transplanting parts of the human body was little better than murder. What right had man to play God?

'We Hindus believe that a man is only dead when every part of his body is dead, when the spinal fluid is dead, when the cells are dead. So how can you westerners transplant parts of the body such as the heart? How can you have a clear understanding of human nature when you don't even understand death?'

Dawn was breaking by the time we arrived in Vijayawada. The pilgrims were still making their way up the hill to Kanakdurga's temple, their candles bobbing like fireflies.

We rumbled through the deserted streets looking for a hotel where I could sleep for a few hours. Most places were full, but Ramesh eventually found me one of the last rooms in town. It was a dismal, barred cell with peeling paint and a drip masquerading as a shower. I flopped on my bed, dirty and exhausted. Thanks to the stress of the drive – not helped by a hysterical Hindi cover version of Madonna's Greatest Hits, which the driver had played incessantly on the car stereo – a large spot had broken out on my nose. It was growing more hideous by the hour.

I am amazed at how the Indians can find good in the nastiest of things. The sage Varaha Mihira even has positive things to say about spots. According to the *Brihat Samhita*, a spot on the nose means that the person will get new cloth; on the cheek, you will get a son; on the lips, you will get food; on the forehead, you will become rich; on a man's genitalia, he will acquire a young woman and good sons; in the anus, wealth. It's difficult to believe, but eruptions on the testicles will also lead to good fortune. But a pimple on or between the eyebrows means bad luck; on the temples, the person will become a hermit; on both sides of the nose where the tears fall, great anxiety; on both wrists, imprisonment; on the back, grief and ruin.

Be extremely cautious of spots on the buttocks, heels or soles of the feet. They will lead respectively to loss of wealth, adultery or a troubled journey.

Before I fell asleep, I inspected my feet. They were thankfully free of zits. No more troubled journeys, I hoped. At the same time, I reflected that inspecting one's feet for bad luck signs was not necessarily the action of a sane man. That night I dreamt that the world had been conquered by a giant tortoise from outer space. Perhaps I was over-tired, but this astrology thing seemed to be going to my head.

9

The Sex Astrologer

When I began my travels I did not think that it would worry me if I allowed the soothsayers I met to tell me my fortune. Now, after two months of being told a variety of details about my past, present and future almost every day, I was beginning to have severe doubts. The past and present I could just about handle. The future was another matter altogether.

The whole business of prediction haunted me. More and more, I was worrying about what the future held, particularly on the subjects of health, money and romance. Matters were not helped by the fact that my girlfriend was back in England. What was going to happen? Would we stay together? I was plagued by insecurity; my obsessive thoughts were gathering like a dark cloud. What had started as a mild fascination was turning into a horrible compulsion. I was asking too many questions and the answers I was receiving, whether positive or negative, were doing me absolutely no good.

K.N. Rao had told me that the only way he survived as an astrologer – and as someone prone to compulsive tendencies whether it be bridge, chess or the planets – was to treat the science of divination as a psychoanalytical counselling service and to avoid all questions about the future.

'If people try to tell me what will happen to me, I tell them I am not interested,' he said. 'Personally I do not want to know what's going to happen.' I decided to take his advice. I vowed that the nadi reading would be the last time I would allow anyone to tell me how my life would turn out.

However, if other people wanted to know their futures I was happy to oblige. On the train from Vijayawada to Madras I was pounced upon by an elderly Sikh gentleman in a mauve turban.

'What are you doing in India?'

'Meeting fortune-tellers.' He did not fully understand me.

'You are a fortune-teller?'

'No, but I am learning to read palms.'

'Then you can read mine.' He stuck out his hand. There was a crush of people in our carriage. They crowded around us inquisitively as I studied the Sikh's palm. I told him that he was an impulsive man who had tried several careers. The Sikh had been a clerk and a salesman, and now in his twilight years he was training to be a private detective. I was right! The turban shook with delight. Suddenly everyone around me was jostling to have their palms read. Twenty pairs of hands were jammed under my nose. I looked at a few of them and made my predictions. No one seemed to understand my English. It mattered little what I said.

Top of my list of people to see in the sultry seaside city of Madras was a self-styled authority on the subject of sex and the stars. Forget about those niggling problems regarding money, and family matters such as whether granny will die next week. It is the subject of intimate relationships that always has been and always will be at the forefront of people's minds when they consult an astrologer. At least that was the view of Mr K. Parthasaarathy who was raking in the moolah as soothsayer to the rich and famous.

I had first heard about Mr Parthasaarathy from a female journalist friend in Delhi. She had once interviewed him for a magazine article and insisted that he was the most fashionable astrologer in Madras. He specialised in the subject of 'fatal attraction' and boasted a clientele that included tycoons and film stars and the inevitable government minister or two.

After settling into a guest-house, I made an appointment to visit Mr Parthasaarathy. His consulting rooms were in an early nineteenth-century bungalow in a narrow backstreet in Triplicane, one of the oldest areas of Madras. A middle-aged secretary dressed in a sari showed me into his air-conditioned office.

Mr Parthasaarathy was the first money-making astrologer I had met in India. He was unashamedly commercial with fees of twenty pounds a session and upwards – a substantial amount of money in India. He reaped yet more from his overseas clients and regularly travelled for special consultations in America, Singapore and the Arabian Gulf. In keeping with his upstanding position in the local community, he was also district chairman of Madras Lions Club.

Mr Parthasaarathy – motto 'Belief is relief' – was a short, dapper man who eschewed the traditional star-gazer's virgin white garb for a striped shirt and Permapress tan slacks. He displayed a silky, confidential manner that some people might have found patronising.

'Would you like me to give you a personal reading?' he asked. 'I can tell you all about your love life.'

'No thank you,' I said.

'Why not?'

'Because it does my head in.' I'm not sure that Mr Parthasaarathy fully understood my use of English idiom, but he seemed to get the gist of my reply. We settled for a chat about his career.

Before becoming a professional astrologer he had pursued various occupations including that of English teacher. He had also been a political attaché in the Japanese Consulate in Madras. But astrology had been his greatest love ever since he learned the science as a child from his grandfather. When he realised that his predictions were coming true he began charging for his services. To give Mr Parthasaarathy credit, he didn't flinch when I suggested that astrologers who charged large fees might lose their power. He looked me straight in the eye and said, 'Most people who consult me are millionaires. For them my charge is nothing. I am straightforward and blunt and brutally frank. By charging, I am in a better position to explain things in a dispassionate manner.' He leaned back in his executive-style swivel chair and added, 'If my charge was very low the riff-raff would come.'

'What's wrong with the riff-raff?' I asked. He gave me a superior look that implied I had asked an extremely dumb question.

'Hah! There are enough astrologers for them. Those who want a specialised study come to me. Highly educated people come to me. I am not interested in ordinary people's problems. They want to know about marriage and boring things like the height and weight of the bridegroom.' He lazily scratched an ear-lobe and sniffed with disdain. 'You must understand, Mr Peter, that those things are for ordinary astrologers. I would rather deal with more exciting things like extra-marital relationships.'

Eighty per cent of Mr Parthasaarathy's clients were film stars from the numerous studios in Madras. They came to him with all manner of problems relating to their sexual behaviour. If one of his clients was planning to marry it was important to study the horoscope of his or her partner to check that they matched in sexual enthusiasm. Otherwise there would be a clash because one would not be able to satisfy the other. He emphasised that it was important for me to realise that marriages in India broke down either in the bedroom or the kitchen.

'Each day I hear cases of married people having affairs,' he said.

'I thought adultery wasn't supposed to happen in India.' Mr Parthasaarathy laughed dryly. How naïve could a foreigner be?

'It certainly does amongst the rich. I frequently have to tell people that according to their planets it looks as if their wife or husband is going astray.' This sounded like dangerous stuff. Was he not fuelling his clients' paranoia?

'Perhaps I sometimes sail close to the wind,' he admitted casually. 'But in most cases it is reality.'

The changing times have brought astrologers like him much extra business. He explained that a growing mood of sexual freedom in India and 'women's lib' – it was a long time since I had heard *that* phrase – meant that wives were not prepared to sit quietly indoors while their husbands ran rampant. They wanted a slice of the action.

'Oh dear, ladies are always coming to me and asking whether their extra-marital relationships will continue. I even know of ladies who give more importance to their extra-marital relationship than their marriage.'

'You sound a little shocked by this,' I pointed out.

'And why not? Please remember this is India, not Britain or America.'

The life of a sex astrologer was worse than a doctor's. Sometimes Mr Parthasaarathy was woken by frantic knocking on his door in the early hours by people requesting an emergency consultation.

'Oh dear, I need to have patience in this job. The other night I was visited by a husband and wife. They had been beating each other all evening. Just before they were about to kill each other' – he stifled a tiny giggle – 'they decided to come to see me to find out if they would get divorced. They were most irritating. The man was drunk and the woman was screaming.' It sounded like a gripping tale.

'And what happened?' I enquired.

'Frankly, Mr Peter, I did not need to look at their charts because if they were going to divorce they wouldn't have bothered to see me in the first place. I pretended to study their horoscopes and told them that they would not divorce. So you see, sometimes I do the work of a psychotherapist.' Then there was the case of the prostitute.

'One day a woman came here. I could see from her horoscope that she was a prostitute, but she did not know that I knew. She asked my advice on what business she should get into. I was quite tactful and said she would be good in any business associated with ladies. She started weeping and said that God had made her so bad that she was a prostitute. When she could see that I was not judging her she suddenly stopped crying and asked me how long she would continue in her profession because she felt she was doing a great service to humanity. I like frank people, so I told her that she would be very good at her job for a long time. She left me looking very pleased. As far as I know she is still a prostitute.'

Mr Parthasaarathy concluded that his predictions were so accurate that he could foretell whether a married woman was going to have affairs.

'That is why I don't do marriage matching. I am too good at my job. For if an engaged couple come for marriage matching, how can I tell the man that the girl is not all right? If I say that a girl is immoral, who will want to marry her?'

I stayed a few days in Madras where I spent much of the time sitting in chai shops talking to people about their thoughts on astrology, sex and marriage. In one restaurant I met a part-time astrologer who was also a devotee of the Ischon organisation, better known as the Hare Krishnas. He was a smiling man in his thirties with a narrow face and a traditional Hare Krishna pigtail balanced on the crown of his head. He told me little about my future, but delivered a lengthy sermon about why I should not eat meat, especially beef. The cow is a mother figure in Hindu mythology.

'You should not eat the cow in the same way that you would not eat your mother,' he argued. He also had firm views on sex, which the Hare Krishnas believe should be for procreation only. 'Parents should choose an auspicious moment in the stars to have sex. Then they will have good contact with God and good children.' He added that a woman must never close her eyes at the time of conception; otherwise her child will be born stupid, or at worst, blind. He muttered darkly, 'Sex is not a time for enjoyment – that is how animals do it. Take the male gorilla. He can have sex sixty times a day because that is what nature has given him. Likewise, a pigeon can have sex thirty times a day. But men are not that strong. If you display that sort of desire, you will be reincarnated as either a gorilla or a pigeon in order to fulfil your carnal desires.' I had said little during this lecture.

'Isn't it difficult to have sex on a normal basis without enjoying it just a little bit?' I jumped in.

'Absolutely not. That is why we have AIDS. The brain has to be controlled.'

The Hare Krishna related the story of how an Indian philosopher compared man to a bumble bee and woman to a lotus flower.

'The bumble bee has enough strength to drill through wood. But when it goes into the lotus it is suffocated. The bumble bee enjoys itself so much that it would prefer to die rather than drill through the lotus.' He gave me a caring look that oozed manipulative cunning. 'At Ischon we train people how to have sex,' he said.

'Oh really.'

'Yes, it is a very nice course.'

'And I suppose you're going to say that you can train me.'

'You would be most welcome.'

The idea of joining the Hare Krishnas on their celibacy drive was not greatly appealing. To the contrary, I rather liked the idea of becoming a bumble bee. We eventually parted company after he tried unsuccessfully to sell me a pamphlet titled *The Joy Of No Sex*.

On another morning I ended up in conversation with a couple of middle-aged men called Ravi and Joseph whom I met in a café in one of the roads leading to Marina Beach. We sat at a table stained by tea and talked about the thriving business of astral marriage matching.

Since ancient times Indian families have demanded to see their prospective son or daughter-in-law's charts. Even today, most marriages on the subcontinent go ahead only after astrologers from each family have examined the couple's birth charts. But the practice has long been the subject of much debate. Janardan Joshi, a civil servant turned social historian, enraged India's astrologers when he published a savage exposé on astral arranged marriages in his 1906 book *Oriental Astrology, Degeneration and Darwinism*. Joshi declared:

> Marriage by consulting horoscopes is the work of persons whose brains have run riot. Is it not a singular instance of perverted judgement that a people may defy all dangers and roll in plague microbes on the theory of Fate, and yet be veritable cowards to lay such importance on auspicious and inauspicious marriages? Is death from the former more pleasant than death from the latter? . . . the sacred marriage institution is converted into a sort of lottery office, all prizes, no blanks, conducted by somewhat unscrupulous office-bearers, the astrologers.

Joshi presented a scenario that he claimed was typical in turn-of-the-century India:

> Because of her horoscope, a beautiful girl has to marry an ugly looking swarthy villager. She and her parents curse her Kismet all their lives,

while the rustic praises the astrologer and is congratulated for his good
luck. A hideous girl is united to a good-looking boy, and in a few
months his parents are full of anxiety because his behaviour is totally
changed. He is morose and perverse. They think that the girl's stars are
bad and are in search of another to make their son happy. Then these
two girls quarrel and one of them goes in search of the village sorcerer
to alienate her husband's affection for the second. In this materialistic
age the sorcerer's charms fail, and she takes a large quantity of opium
and goes to bed to rise no more.

The final ghastly turn to this tragedy? 'The next day there is a report of
her death from dysentery.' He concludes that if his book 'saves the
misery of even one Hindu girl, I am sufficiently rewarded'.

My teatime companions Ravi and Joseph had been friends since
childhood. They shared several similarities. They were the same age –
58 – and lived a few streets from each other in a Madras suburb. They
were both professional men. Ravi held a senior post in a finance
company while Joseph was an agricultural engineer. They differed only
in religion and size. Joseph was a Catholic who attended a born-again
Charismatic church. Ravi was a devout Hindu who prayed twice a day
at his local temple. Joseph was a short man with large, black-rimmed
spectacles and a weighty biblical beard. He had a soft voice and was the
quieter of the two. Ravi was well over six foot tall and built like a
cuddly giant.

Ravi said, 'I am a Brahmin and, according to old customs, if I touch
Joseph I must take a bath and wash all my clothes before I enter my
house. But all that has changed now.' To emphasise this, he put his arm
around Joseph's shoulder and gently hugged his friend. They asked
what I was doing in their country and I told them about my astrological
researches. They exchanged glances and leaned forward with interest.
Like so many Indians, they found astrology a source of endless
fascination.

The men shared another important similarity. Each of them had a
daughter who had married the previous year. In keeping with tradition,
Ravi had demanded to know his future son-in-law's horoscope. It was
only after his personal astrologer decided that the boy would make a
suitable husband that he allowed the marriage to go ahead. Likewise,
the boy's parents also instructed their family seer to study Ravi's
daughter's chart before they gave their blessing to the match. I
remarked that the astrologers sounded more like solicitors getting
together over a divorce. Ravi laughed.

'It is more than that,' he said. 'It is a council of war! If a girl is destined to marry a boy then the horoscopes will automatically be okay. This is a route worked out by God.'

'So it means putting a lot of trust in your astrologer,' I said.

'Definitely, but I had do it because I don't understand astrology.'

'But you might get an astrologer who is wrong.'

'That is why each side has their own man. My astrologer may be wrong, but I have to accept everything he says.'

I turned to Joseph. As a Christian, and an evangelical Christian at that, what did he think about all this?

'I don't agree with astrology,' he said gruffly. 'I often argue about it with him.' He waved a dismissive hand at his friend. 'According to my faith, anybody who goes to an astrologer, a soothsayer or a fortune-teller is cursed. I would never dream of doing it.'

His radical views had caused severe problems when he began searching for a suitable husband for his eldest daughter. He looked wistful for a moment. Then he said quietly, 'To be quite frank, Mr Peter, she is not that beautiful and I was having difficulty sending her off. She had umpteen proposals by letter, but as soon as the men saw her they changed their minds. I was desperate to see her married, so I was delighted when this lecturer turned up and wanted to marry her. He was well educated with good qualifications.'

The fact that the man was a Hindu did not deter Joseph. What did concern him was that the man's father demanded to see his future daughter-in-law's time and date of birth so that his astrologer could draw up a chart.

'At first I gave it,' Joseph continued. 'You see, Mr Peter, I was literally craving a son-in-law and I did not want anything to stand in the way of my daughter's happiness. But then a sort of guilty feeling came over me. I said to myself, "Joseph, you are a Christian, this astrology business is nonsense." So I went back to the father and said that if he wanted such a thing I did not want such an alliance. He refused to back down, so the marriage never took place.'

However, there was a happy ending. A few months later, another man turned up and offered his hand.

'My daughter is now married,' Joseph added happily. 'To a Christian.'

Ravi had been listening with amusement to our conversation. He slapped his friend on the back.

'I appreciate Joseph's views because no horoscope can be a hundred per cent correct.' He added, 'And, of course, if you want your son to marry a rich girl because she'll bring a good dowry, you can always bribe your astrologer to produce a good horoscope.'

'Does that happen much these days?' I asked.

'Oh yes. All over India.' Forged horoscopes were becoming increasingly common. There were plenty of unscrupulous astrologers with underworld contacts able to produce forged birth certificates. The cost of fabricating your child's destiny? The equivalent of around a thousand pounds.[1] I detected a note of cynicism in Ravi's voice. Did he truly believe that compatible horoscopes would guarantee a successful marriage? He put his elbows on the table and his head in his hands.

'If I am being honest, I have to say that the main reason we follow this tradition is to satisfy the community.'

'So you're saying that you do this to make a good impression on your family and neighbours?'

'I suppose so. But it seems to lead to mental satisfaction. The most important thing is that the boy and girl are happy. Let them put on garlands, let them embrace each other, and if the planets have something do with it, so much the better.'

A waiter brought tea in a battered, black kettle. He filled our chipped glasses with the treacly liquid. Joseph had been deep in thought. He blew ripples into his tea to cool it down and announced suddenly, 'The trouble is that most Indians believe that if a couple who do not match astrologically get married, there will be many calamities in the house. It is the same as believing that a black cat will bring you bad luck. Both are just silly superstitions.' I remembered my talk with Mr Chataiwala and Mohammed back in Ahmedabad. Why did these conversations always revert to the subject of cats?

'Actually, we British believe black cats are very good luck,' I said. Ravi was astounded.

'If a black cat crosses the road in front of me when I am going to the office it means the start of a terrible day.'

Joseph chipped in, 'Do you walk under ladders, Mr Peter?'

'Never.'

'You see, Ravi, he wouldn't walk under a ladder.'

'I'd walk into the traffic rather than walk under a ladder,' I added. Joseph laughed.

....

[1] A horoscope by a reputable astrologer was often held as the equivalent of a birth certificate in rural India until as late as the 1940s. Horoscopes were even accepted by insurance companies as proof of birth.

'You are almost Indian. And would you stay in room number 13?'

'Yes, probably. But I'd feel very uncomfortable sitting thirteen around a table.'

'You will not find a room 13 in a hospital in India,' Ravi said. Joseph shook his head.

'Oh dear. We are funny people, human beings.'

But both Hindu and Christian agreed that some of the old Indian superstitions should be followed. For example, the process of washing. Showers were not good for the health.

'It is very bad for water to touch your head first,' Ravi said. 'You should follow the Brahmin custom of first pouring water from a bucket over your feet, then your body and finally your head. I cannot explain why but within a week you will feel fitter.

'And have you noticed in Hindu temples how first thing in the morning people put wet towels around their tummies and walk around a banyan tree? The wet towel helps circulate the blood through the spinal cord and does wonders for the health. The banyan is known for producing much ozone and breathing in ozone in the morning makes us happy.'

More obscure was the belief that you should never place anything on a book or written material of any kind. You must never even stand on a newspaper.

'I have heard that in the West you might put newspaper down to protect the floor when you are painting your house,' Ravi said.

'We would never do that. The written word is knowledge and we have great respect for knowledge. If you abuse the written word you will offend Saraswati, goddess of scholarship.'

I turned to Joseph. Did he also believe this?

'Of course. I may be a Christian, but I have no desire to offend Saraswati.'

*****

After a week in Madras I met up again with Ramesh and his family and we took the bus south to their home in Pondicherry.

The old French quarter of Pondicherry is beautifully kept by Indian standards. The streets are clean, the traffic minimal and bougainvillaea climbs gloriously over the whitewashed walls of nineteenth-century seafront villas. The town tends to be popular with dreamy-eyed, middle-aged western women who come during the cool winter months to practise yoga at the many ashrams. Unfortunately, these expensive retreats of peace, love and spiritual learning appear to have a rather different effect on the local populace. A recent police survey revealed that Pondicherry had the highest crime level in India, well ahead of places like Delhi and Calcutta – perhaps something to do with the rich pickings that come with so many foreign visitors.

Ramesh was keen to introduce me to an old friend of his, Dr Swami Gitananda Giri, an octogenarian yoga guru, who owned an ashram on the outskirts of Pondi. Swamiji, as Ramesh called him (and as I was expected to call him given his venerable position in the community), was famous for his forthright views on the tricky business of life. He was also an expert in the ancient science of foot-reading and could predict a person's future through the lines on the feet in the same way that a palmist reads the hand.

His ashram was a large, concrete building on the coconut-fringed beach to the south of Pondi. You reached it down a rutted track that wound past an encampment of peasant huts, the homes of Tamil refugees from Sri Lanka. To the side of the ashram was a line of stable-like cells that housed Swamiji's students, mostly foreigners paying large quantities of dollars for six-month courses at what was regarded as the South India Oxford of yoga.

Swamiji had a reputation for being a tough disciplinarian. He ran a harsh regime in which his word was only marginally less final than that of God. His ashram was not a retreat for indolent hippies who had come to India with the idea of dropping out in a marijuana haze with a bit of meditation on the side. The students' day began at 4.30 a.m. and ended at 10 p.m. There was one half-day off a week for shopping in town. Those who objected to the hectic round of lectures and yogic exercise were, quite simply, expelled.

Ramesh and I arrived at 6 p.m. A young man, one of the ashram staff, showed us in. We walked through the meditation hall, a cavernous concrete room resembling a squash court, and into a waiting room where we signed our names in the visitors' book. With more than a touch of Edwardian formality, the minion took the book and went to ask Swamiji whether he was receiving visitors. The man returned five minutes later. We were in luck. His honoured master had agreed to a private audience. We climbed a flight of stairs to his office.

Swamiji was an enigma. He was Indian in all areas of his life except for the colour of his skin. He was white, having been born a British subject in Pakistan of Canadian parents. His Canadian accent remained surprisingly strong for someone who had spent most of his life surrounded by Indians; but a passer-by would have found it difficult to spot his caucasian features. His skin was deeply tanned and his face was all but covered by an enormous white, Father Christmas beard. Long ivory hair fell about his shoulders. Only if you looked carefully would you find a clue to his origins in the form of two dimpled, rosy cheeks. Little was known about Swamiji's background. He would only divulge that he had spent a short time in the British Army and was minus one kidney having been shot during the Second World War. In his mid-twenties he had quit the services for a spiritual life of yoga and Vedic study. He claimed to be 86 years old.

The guru greeted us from a heavy carved wooden throne. He was swathed in orange robes and a chain of rudraksha beads hung down to his lap. His room was large and airy with an abundance of potted plants. Tall windows overlooked the beach, their shutters thrown open to let in the cool sea breezes.

Swamiji's exuberance belied his age. It was obvious from the glossy twinkle in his eyes that he was thoroughly enjoying his position as Pondicherry's senior sage. Far from being a humble wise yogi cosily enjoying his dotage at the peak of his spiritual maturity, I was to discover that he was judgemental, moralistic and candid to the point of rudeness. Cast him in a film as a hellfire man of God and critics would say he was over-acting. I found him enormously entertaining.

Ramesh fell to his knees and kissed Swamiji's feet. I managed my usual handshake. Ramesh introduced me as a writer from England. On a table was a newspaper article about Bill Clinton. For want of something to say I asked the guru what he thought of America's president. Swamiji growled. I could almost see his hackles rising.

'Clinton?' he said steadily in a tone that suggested he was nurturing a long-standing resentment. 'America has the power to be the moral and ethical leader of the world. But what can we hope for with a wife-cheater, pot-smoker and congenital liar as president?' Ramesh stifled a laugh. The old boy was on his usual sparkling form.

A Shih Tzu lay sprawled out like a hearth rug at the guru's feet. Sensing its master's anger, it raised its head and eyed me nervously through a furry fringe.

'Are you always so outspoken?' I asked Swamiji.

'Why should I hide what I am?'

The Shih Tzu gave a muffled snarl. I treated the dog with caution. Ramesh had warned me that it was famous for its tricky temper and had been known to shatter the serenity of ashram visitors by biting their ankles.

'So you don't think much of the West?' I went on. Swamiji adjusted his robes and settled into a master-pupil routine.

'The white skin dominance has always been such that westerners claim to know more than anybody else whether they know anything or not.' He paused to let the insult sink in. 'All the West has given us is drug addicts, AIDS and condoms.' And that was Swamiji's bugbear – condoms. He could not stay off the subject of condoms. They were his mania. The world's miseries could all be blamed on condoms. If he could destroy every last condom in the world – both used and unused – he would have achieved his life's work. He pointed out of the window towards the sea.

'Let me tell you, young man, you cannot walk on that beach without stepping on a condom.' This prophylactic proliferation was entirely the fault of foreigners who lived in Auroville, the so-called Utopian city that was established in the countryside outside Pondi in the sixties. 'Auroville is full of cheats, liars, prostitutes and dopers. They come on to the beach, they suck and they fuck, and they leave their condoms behind.'

Our fun was interrupted by the arrival of Swamiji's wife, an elegant, long-necked American woman in a pink sari. She was about thirty years younger than her husband. With her was their son, a quiet, studious man in his early twenties. The pair had caught the tailend of Swamiji's condom assault and looked embarrassed as if they had heard it all before. Oh no, Dad was off on one of his tirades. Mrs Swamiji patted her husband's hand and gently reminded him that it was time to join his students. Since it was a full moon, tonight's programme featured a moonbeam gazing session followed by supper around a campfire on the beach.

'Last week it was star-gazing,' the guru explained. 'We lie on the roof and stare at our constellations. Everybody should know their constellation. By actually seeing your stars you add wisdom to knowledge. Otherwise, it is like saying there are things called radio waves and then not turning on the radio.'

Ramesh and I accepted an invitation to join the ashramites for the evening. We left the ashram and followed the guru and his family on to the sand. Swamiji led us in a brisk march. Two servants trotted behind carrying his throne. I looked hard for condoms in the sand but could see none. We met up with his students at the water's edge. They were of assorted European nationalities and wore local clothes. Their faces were fixed with the sort of toothy, distant grins that you find on students in Indian yoga ashrams.

Panting heavily, the bearers dropped the bulky throne on the sand. A

French girl in voluminous pantaloons helped the old man into his seat. He pulled his hair back from his face, smoothed his beard and hauled his robes around him. Like King Canute, he sat bolt upright facing the sloshing ripples of the Bay of Bengal. We arranged ourselves in an arc around him, sitting on the sand with our backs to the dying sun.

'Stare at the moon!' Swamiji commanded. We raised our eyes and squinted at the shiny disc above the sea. It was snowy white – a good sign, according to the *Brihat Samhita*: a white moon brings prosperity. But beware if the moon is ashy or red black. This forebodes war, disease and famine.

'Now flicker your eyelids and move your heads from side to side keeping your eyes on the moon.' We followed his orders. As darkness fell he repeated the words again and again. I gradually succumbed to his hypnotic monotone. He spoke more softly. 'Imagine a track of light coming down from the moon into the sea. Imagine it curling like a ribbon off the sea and entering the centre of your brains.'

A motorway of light shot across the sea towards me. The more I flickered my eyes and rocked my head, the more intense the light became, until all I could see was darting sheets of silvery moonbeams. It was an extraordinary sensation.

The meditation over, we moved to a fire that some of the students had built from driftwood a few yards from the shore. They had dug a bowl in the sand like a tiny amphitheatre. We sat on the ridge and ate baked sweet potatoes and drank soup from metal canteens.

Swamiji directed me to sit next to him. I asked him to tell me about his experiences in the world of prediction. He had learned basic palmistry from his grandfather. It was not until his mid-forties that he became interested in the yet more ancient science of foot-reading, known in Sanskrit as *pada sastra*.

The lines on the soles are said to produce a more reliable picture of a person's character and destiny than you will find on the hand. Connoisseurs of the Indian occult sciences, including the most devout Brahmins, would rather have their feet read than their palms. The feet have special metaphysical significance because of the prints they leave upon the soil of Mother Earth, and temples in India sell souvenir pictures of the footprints of Hindu deities such as Vishnu and Shiva.

'I was 43 when I first had my feet read,' Swamiji said. 'It was done by a priest at a temple south of here and I could hardly credit the forecast. He said that I would be literally installed as a spiritual Maharajah.' He pointed proudly across the sand towards his headquarters. 'And how true that was! He also said that the lifeline on my right foot was very long and that I would live to a great age. I was puzzled because the lifelines on each of my palms are extremely short.' He thrust his hands at me in order to prove his point. I studied his palms in the flickering firelight.

'You should have died in your mid-twenties,' I said.

'Between 27 and 30, actually. Perhaps I am living by some sort of divine grace. Many palmists are astonished when they see my hands. I tell them immediately to look at my feet.'

He was expert at reading the feet to detect diseases such as diabetes. He even claimed that the feet provided the only sign on the body that a person would become diabetic in the future.

'I look for swelling, shortened blood vessels, toenail changes . . .'

I asked innocently whether *pada sastra* was similar to the system of reflexology that is so popular in the West.

'Reflexology?' A warning growl. I steadied myself for his next onslaught. 'Reflexology, young man, is western robbery! Modern bullshit! Another example of you people dabbling in something you don't properly understand. A mere reflexologist won't be able to predict something like diabetes.' He relaxed slightly and nudged me cheekily. 'You foreigners need to accept that you haven't invented anything in the West but murder and political cheating.'

He surveyed his students. They had been listening intently. A German boy gave a little nod as if to acknowledge his teacher's greatness. Swamiji looked like a cat with a lifetime's supply of cream. With a delicate flick of his fingers he removed a few grains of sand from his robes and turned to the important subject of caring for one's feet.

'If you look after your feet, you are less likely to get illnesses. You should wash them in an oil bath whenever you come in from outside and coat them with turmeric to kill the germs. A salt bath once in a while is very good.

'By not caring for your feet you block the energy flow leaving them. It backs up into the body and you end up in trouble.'

Hindus have known for centuries that keeping your feet bare will give you greater energy. This explains why tribals in India and elsewhere can dance continuously hour after hour without getting tired. Their bare feet connect directly with the ground and any excess energy is earthed, thereby providing a balance between man's exertions and the forces of nature. Translating this into a western sense, it means that if you want to dance all night, simply kick off your shoes. Furthermore, the Hindus believe that pleasure generates energy and they say that excess energy is best released and it must come out in rhythm. Thus the person who derives pleasure from rhythm is energising himself, which is the basis of dance.

According to Swamiji, the feet provided the clue to harmony on earth, and the West's troubles, mental and physical, were entirely due to the fact that we wore shoes.

'Shoes are killing you,' he declared. 'They stop all the natural energy from leaving your body. Sandals are okay, but bare feet are best of all. That is why westerners should go and walk in places like Hyde Park or Central Park without shoes.'

'Surely that's not very hygienic,' I said.

'No, you're right, what with all those broken beer bottles and condoms . . .'

And so the conversation returned to the subject closest to the guru's heart. From across the ruby embers of the fire I could see Swamiji's wife. She rested her head in her hands in tired resignation. The old man was off again.

*****

The state of Kerala is rich by Indian standards. It also claims a hundred per cent literacy and has one of the best health services in the country. Left-wingers argue that this bounty is due to the local communist government. In 1957, Kerala became the first place in the world to democratically elect a communist government. Kerala, they claim, is a marvellous example of how the doctrines of Marx and Lenin *have* worked. More entrepreneurial citizens disagree. They credit their wealth to the number of Keralans who have found lucrative employment in the Arabian Gulf countries. The state accounts for over half the total Indian emigration to the Gulf.

Whatever the answer, Keralans take great pride in their land almost to the point of assuming an edge of superiority over the rest of India. The change becomes obvious the moment your bus crosses the state border from Tamil Nadu. Within a mile, the road surface has improved and the housing is better. The villages vibrate with fresh coats of whitewash. The people seem to be happier and more energetic than their Tamil neighbours.

I left Pondicherry for a dusty journey across South India. A day later I was in Trivandrum, capital of Kerala. I changed buses and headed ten miles south to the village of Kovalam which was to be my base for the next week.

In barely fifteen years, the crescent-shaped beach at Kovalam has grown from a tiny fishing settlement into one of India's most popular seaside resorts for foreign tourists. In high season the numerous, cheap boarding houses are crammed with backpackers of all nationalities. Surrounded by their own kind, they can escape the pressures of the real India and build up their suntans. Dope smokers consider the place to be less hassled than Goa where police only drop their constant war against drugs in return for large bribes – and there are fewer heroin junkies down here. Even so, commercialisation is on the increase and visitors are likely to be pestered by young men offering either timeshare apartments or 'homo sex' behind the rocks.

Of course, there is the resident fortune-teller in the form of Mr Shenkar and his parrot, Cara. Prediction by parrot is one of the cheapest types of divination in India. You will find itinerant parrot men all over the south. The idea is that you lay several cards in front of the parrot's cage. The bird then steps out and picks up a card in its beak. Your fortune depends on which card is selected. Some hawkers employ specially trained white rats to do the same job, but parrots are more common. With the small wooden cage containing his livelihood in his hand, Mr Shenkar would spend each day lolloping along Kovalam beach ensnaring tourists with the cry, 'Parrot read fortune.' He cornered me one morning as I was going for a post-breakfast stroll. We sat down on the warm sand and negotiated his fee.

'I must tell you, sir, that I am a very fine expert at prediction,' he said. To prove his point, he produced a letter, purportedly from another satisfied English client saying what an outstanding chap he was. I wondered whether the letter, like so much else in India, was in fact a forgery. I had a vision of a street-corner scribe churning out fake letters of recommendation from foreigners.

After a long and pointless haggle, we eventually settled at a ridiculously high fifty rupees. I justified my extravagance with the thought that I was supporting a local cottage industry. Mr Shenkar was beside himself with joy and he gaily slapped some cards face down in front of Cara.

The bird was trained to perform upon the production of hard cash. The moment I placed my money on the sand, Cara shot out of her cage and plucked out a card. She waved it aggressively in her beak before returning to her box. Mr Shenkar rewarded her with a pinch of bird seed.

My card featured a picture of Shiva and Pavroti and their son Ganesh.

'Very good luck, sir,' Mr Shenkar said. 'The family card. It means you will have a good family life.'

'And . . . ?' I waited for more. Mr Shenkar smiled innocently. 'That is all, sir.'

I hardly thought this snippet was worth fifty rupees. Mr Shenkar noticed my disappointment and tried to compensate with a palm reading. He started off by tracing my life line from the wrist upwards – the wrong way round.

'You were very ill aged 20,' he said.

'Actually, I'm going to be very ill aged 70.'

'No, sir.'

'Yes, sir.'

Mr Shenkar looked distinctly uncomfortable when he realised I knew more about palmistry than he did. He made a valiant effort at studying my other lines – none of which he got right – and it soon became evident that he couldn't wait to leave me. I took the fifty rupee note and stuffed it through the bars of his partner's cage.

'For the parrot,' I said. 'Buy it some more bird seed.' Cara had been a lot of more interesting than him.

10

A Cosmic Inquest

Keralans cheerfully admit that their state is the most superstitious in India – ironic when you consider that twenty-one per cent of the population is Christian and the first question that a foreigner is likely to be asked is, 'What is your faith?'

Kerala takes the power of the planets more seriously than anywhere else in India. Here you will find the most in-depth astrological ceremony of them all: the asta mangela. This is best described as a cosmic inquest into why certain evil events have happened. If there have been a series of disasters either in your family or at your temple, you conduct a special astral investigation into what has gone wrong and to find the remedies to put things right. Asta mangela is a Sanskrit phrase meaning 'eight auspicious happenings'. The 'eight' refers to a collection of items that was traditionally studied by astrologers in ancient times: a lamp, mirror, book, gold, dhobi cloth, betel nut, betel leaf and a piece of gold. The practice has been amended over the years so that not all these items are used today.

The rules of the asta mangela are described in a book, the *Prasna Marga*, which roughly translates from Sanskrit as 'seeking the answer to questions'. Authorship of this lengthy volume is attributed to an unnamed seventeenth-century Nambudri Brahmin of Calicut, Kerala. The Nambudris were the holiest of Brahmins, who were believed to possess incredible psychic powers. Keralans tell stories about Nambudri Brahmins, who were able to pinpoint the position of an object that had been buried forty foot under the ground. Like works such as the *Brihat Samhita*, the *Prasna Marga* is a collection of event-based predictive astrology and basic superstition that covers almost every aspect of human existence. It includes everything from the causes of food poisoning and advice to rulers 'regarding the capture of elephants' ('if at the time of query Jupiter occupies the 1st, 7th, 9th, or 5th house . . . elephants will be secured by the querying kings') to the type of mantras that should be said to cure schizophrenia, catatonia and paranoia.

The asta mangela originated as a method for sorting out problems in families and temples. For example, if everything is going wrong in your household – dad's lost his job, no one wants to marry his daughters, the son's a drunk and mum's threatening to walk out – you hire a specially qualified asta mangela astrologer to find out what is going wrong. Are the family's spiritual forefathers displeased? Have they landed their descendants with a curse? Has the accumulated effect of hundreds of years of evil resulted in turning your brood into what the Americans term a 'dysfunctional family'?

The *Prasna Marga* further claims that diseases are the result of the actions of a person's past life. For example, if you suffer from piles, it means that you stole food and had sex on prohibited religious days.

If acne's your problem, you talked ill of elderly persons and were a compulsive liar; eye diseases mean you cast 'wily glances' at women; rheumatism means you criticised respectable people and hated your parents; ulcers mean that you stole vegetables, destroyed trees and had 'immoral relationships with undesirable women', chronic indigestion means that you had sex with virgins, widows and assorted farmyard animals. All these are remedied through various mantras or by making gifts to the gods.

In ancient times wealthy households would employ a panel of seers for up to three weeks, but these days family asta mangelas are rare, mainly for reasons of cost. Curses or not, few people can afford to hire an astrologer – and maybe two or more assistants – for several days' work. Temple asta mangelas are still common in Kerala. If a temple is falling into disrepair or, worse still, there is a disaster such as someone being burned during a fire ceremony, you call in an astrologer to discover why the gods are unhappy. Once he has been hired, the astrologer takes total control of the temple's future.

Possibly the world's greatest expert in the asta mangela is Mr Kochinaryan, an astrologer who lives near Trivandrum. His surname is Naryan, but the suffix Kochi – meaning small in the Kerala language of Malayalam – was given to him as a child because of his diminutive stature. In thirty years as a professional astrologer Kochinaryan has established a formidable reputation as a cosmic troubleshooter. Despite encroaching westernisation in India, Vedic traditions like the asta mangela show no signs of dying. Indeed, Kochinaryan is busier than ever. He undertakes more than fifty asta mangelas a year, as well as individual astrological consultations, and spends most of his time travelling all over the state. He is booked up at least two months in advance and is estimated to earn the equivalent of ten thousand pounds annually, a very comfortable living in India.

The day after my arrival in Kovalam, I went to meet Kochinaryan at his surgery on the outskirts of Trivandrum. He was in his fifties, a tiny man, no more than five feet tall. His youthful looks were accentuated by his badly cut grey hair that stuck up in tufts like a shoolboy's. He spoke only Malayalam but we managed to converse with the help of one of his waiting customers who understood a smattering of English. I told him that I had heard he was the top asta mangela man in Kerala. Could I join him on his next assignment?

Kochinaryan was delighted that a foreigner was showing interest in his work. Later that week he was due to conduct an asta mangela on a temple at a village called Alathirakkal near the town of Neyyattinkara. The local people were complaining that their prayers were not being answered and the temple committee had hired Kochinaryan to discover what was going wrong. He would be honoured if I would accompany him. We arranged to meet at his house in a couple of days time.

That night disaster struck Kerala, and this was to have an eerie significance for Alathirakkal temple. With little warning, a cyclone moving up from Sri Lanka bombarded the south-west Indian coast. Devastation followed. It rained for twenty-four hours resulting in widespread flooding. Sixty people drowned and thousands more were made homeless as 100 m.p.h. winds ripped apart their flimsy homes. An elephant left chained to a tree drowned in the torrent.

The gales whipped the sea at Kovalam into a terrifying frenzy. The waves turned brown from the churning sand. Several of the beachfront bars were swept away and debris littered the shore. The palm trees on the headland by the lighthouse doubled up as if in agony, crackling in the wind. Tourists huddled miserably inside restaurants over tea and backgammon. Fishermen under makeshift awnings stared gloomily at the frothing breakers and mourned their lost earnings. Only the stray dogs, their coats sleek from a salty mixture of rain and spray, showed any sign of happiness. They trotted through the sandy puddles, pleased to have the beach to themselves.

I spotted Mr Shenkar, the parrot man. He refused to let nature ruin his day and was going from restaurant to restaurant touting for business. He wore a little plastic cape and a black sou'wester tied tightly around his face like an executioner's mask.

I spent the morning in a café where water dripped through the canvas sun-awning, thumbing through my battered copy of the *Brihat Samhita*. The sage Varaha Mihira has much to say on the weather and devotes no less than four chapters of his book to rain. For example, it will rain if a cat is seen scratching the ground with its claws; if cows raise up their heads and look at the sun; if sheep are reluctant to go out, and shake their ears or kick their legs; if dogs look at the sky all round; if snakes are seen to copulate. I pondered on how snakes copulated and whether they enjoyed it. I read on.

> If at the time of sunrise or sunset the sky should be of the colour of the wings of the partridge, or if there should be heard the sound of birds at play, there will be immediate rain that will continue through the day and night . . . If the sky should be the colour of the cow's eye or if salt should turn into water or if the colour of the sky should be that of the crow's egg, or if fish should be found to jump from water on the bank or if the frog should be heard to croak incessantly, there will be immediate rain. . .

The weather showed no sign of improving and the sea was in such torment that it would have taken a Superman of the fish world to jump out of the water. Despite a rural English childhood, I found it difficult to recall the exact colour of either a cow's eye or a patridge's wing; milky brown and mottled russet, perhaps.

In the afternoon I sat over several coffees improving my German with an enormous backpacker called Harry. He was a bookseller from the Bavarian town of Wurzburg and moaned about the 'shit weather' which was about the only English he spoke. He was recovering from an ear infection which he had cured by pouring vodka into his aural canal, a remedy highly recommended by German travellers.

Harry was keen to tell me about the torture chamber at some castle near his home. We spent the morning discussing thumbscrews and a complicated punishment that involved sitting the wrongdoer on a pointed piece of wood with stones tied to his ankles. I managed to understand about fifty per cent of what he said. It sounded extremely unpleasant.

The storm abated late in the afternoon. With great effort, the sun appeared to reveal a messy evening sky. Smudged grey clouds hung over daubs of orange, like smoke over an oil fire. Raindrops clung to the palm trees like stars.

The next morning I took an auto-rickshaw to Kochinaryan's home in a village on the outskirts of Trivandrum. I was joined by my interpreter for the day, a young student called Peter, whom I had met after asking around in the restaurants along Kovalam Beach for someone who spoke good English. Peter was an English graduate at Trivandrum University. He paid for his studies with a part-time job at one of the souvenir shops at Kovalam. The son of a tailor, he was a good Catholic boy of 22, who attended mass regularly. He was quite shy with a calm, if slightly fragile, manner.

It was 8.30 a.m. when we arrived at Kochinaryan's house, a comfortable suburban villa lying in a colourful garden with a beautifully kept herbaceous border. An air-conditioned Ambassador sat in the driveway. A chauffeur was carefully polishing the pinky-brown bodywork. We walked on to the verandah and rang the bell. A small man came to the door, peered through the flyscreen and said something to Peter. Then he was gone again.

'What was that all about?' I asked.

'That was Mr Kochinaryan. He says he cannot leave the house until 9 a.m. today because the stars are not favourable.'

'Really?'

Peter nodded.

'It is bad luck for him to leave before then. Even members of his family will not leave the house. His children won't even go to school. They would rather miss exams than go out.'

'But if they miss their exams they'll fail them anyway and that can't be good luck.' Peter shrugged. I got the impression that my translator thought the Kochinaryan family were verging on the insane.

'You wouldn't do a thing like that as a Catholic?' I asked.

'No.'

'Do you believe the Pope when he says that astrology is Satan's work?' Peter shrugged again.

'No one around here takes any notice of the Pope.'

'Will your family ask for the girl's horoscope when you get married?'

'Definitely.'

Kochinaryan emerged on the dot of 9 a.m. carrying a briefcase and a little red raffia basket containing a thermos flask. He glowed from the after effects of a bath. From the way he was dressed in simple dhoti and mauve shirt you would not have guessed he was the richest astrologer in Kerala. We climbed into his Ambassador. The astrologer sat next to his driver. Peter and I sat in the back. As we left the gates, Peter whispered, 'He may look simple, but he has a lot of money.'

'I can see that.'

'Good money. All in cash. Nice house. Nice car. The income tax officer has not found him yet.'

The destruction from the storm became evident as we drove south. The walls of mud huts had been cracked open like eggs. Rivers had breached their banks and spilled their mud into rice fields. We crossed bridges where crowds of people gazed blankly at their waterlogged homes. A government helicopter flew overhead inspecting the damage. All along the road were telegraph poles blown down by the wind. They lay at jagged angles, their wires a mess of matted tangles in the trees.

But at least the rain had gone. A swift breeze had swept away the clouds to reveal a fresh blue sky. The sunshine highlighted the brilliant green of the jungle foliage. It is this green that Kerala is famous for. Keralans say that their green is unlike the green anywhere else in India. It is a dazzling green, brighter than the clearest emerald, a colour of extraordinary density, proof of the purity of Mother Nature.

The millions of glossy green coconut palms that support much of Kerala's population play a large part in the local mysticism. For Keralans will tell you that a coconut will never fall on a person's head unless they are seen by the gods as a sinner. If you want bad luck for the rest of your life, cut down a coconut tree.

A coconut palm is like a child. It is a sensitive soul and will bear fruit only if there are people to keep it company. A friend of mine from Madras, who owns a smallholding in Kerala, told me that no fruit appeared on the coconut trees during the two years that his property was empty. The moment his retired father went to live there permanently, the coconuts began to sprout again.

A few miles before Alathirakkal, we stopped to pick up the temple priest, Mr Krishnyer, at his home. He was an untidy man in his fifties with a pot-belly and a shirt unbuttoned to the navel. He appeared to have made only a half-hearted attempt at shaving that morning and his face was gritty with stubble. His unkempt moustache was more suited to a cashiered colonel than a servant of the Almighty.

Mr Krishnyer was crestfallen. He explained that we would be unable to conduct the asta mangela in the temple because part of the building was under water a metre deep. The ceremony had been moved to the house of the temple committee chairman. Kochinaryan greeted the news with a wry smile. He spoke rapidly to the priest.

'He says the cyclone was an omen,' Peter translated. 'He could see from the position of the planets a month ago that this disaster would happen.'

'What? The flooded temple?'

'Yes. He says it is no coincidence that the asta mangela was planned for today. The gods are angry. But the stars are beneficial today. It is a good day for looking into the temple's problems.'

'Do you believe that Kochinaryan foresaw the rains?'

'No I do not,' Peter sniffed. 'It is a coincidence.'

The temple wasn't having much luck. It had been plagued with problems for years and had been flooded once before, back in 1978, when another asta mangela had been performed. The position of the gods had been changed and there had been no further problems until recently. Today's ceremony was a final desperate attempt to sort things out.

Mr Krishnyer squeezed into the back seat of the Ambassador and we continued on our way to Alathirakkal. We passed fields of budding pink pineapples where banks of steamy vapour rose from the drying earth. A mile before the village, the tarmac abruptly tailed off into a lake. We left the car and walked. Local people gawked at us as we strolled along a maze of paths past huts decorated with crudely painted hammers and sickles. The villagers looked tired and depressed. I learned that the deluge had left more than a hundred homeless. The state government had set up a special camp in the local school. No one had died, but hundreds of thousands of rupees worth of tapioca and rice had been ruined. Acute financial problems were forecast. I asked Peter why the village thought God had abandoned them.

'The people are worried, they are saying that God is no good. They say their prayers are not being answered and there are a lot of sinners here.'

'What sort of sins? Wife-swapping?' Peter smiled at my western interpretation of sinning.

'Maybe. But perhaps they are just working against God. There are little problems within families and people are arguing. The crops are failing and there has been a lot of illness. The people want Kochinaryan to tell them what the answer is. Maybe they will have to rebuild the temple.'

'You don't think that a couple of Christians will bring them even more bad luck?' Peter laughed awkwardly.

'Maybe.' I was gaining the impression that my Catholic interpreter was not keen on spending the day at what he saw as a pagan rite. He seemed exceptionally uneasy.

We reached the centre of the village. There was a smell of woodsmoke. Chickens scattered in our path. A rag-taggle of children with runny noses stared at me before scampering away in fits of giggles to hide shyly behind lines of washing. The sun flashed through the palm trees as if in welcome. A cockerel crowed a raucous salute. People came out of their homes to greet us. Smiles gradually replaced the sadness as they saw Kochinaryan. The great astrologer had come! Here was a saviour who offered hope on a day of misery.

We were welcomed by the six members of the temple committee. The committee chairman, a brawny man in his mid-thirties, led us along a path to his house. It was a simple brick-built bungalow surrounded by hibiscus plants. A sign above the front door announced in English that 'God Is Love'.

We sat on the verandah and discussed the day ahead. There was much gossip about the gods to whom Alathirakkal temple was dedicated – the goddess Durga and the snake king Naga Raja. It was not so much that the pair were angry, but rather they had become distant. They had not responded to a heavy dose of prayer and the villagers wanted to know why.

Kochinaryan listened carefully to the chatter. Then he turned to Peter and me. For a moment, worry replaced his usual cool. He had taken on a tough job; a lot was riding on his reputation. He said the temple had so many problems that in an ideal world he would recommend a panel of six or seven astrologers working on the asta mangela over two weeks. But the village was poor. They had managed to raise only three thousand rupees (around fifty pounds) with door-to-door collections. They would have to make do with a one-man, two-day show. Kochinaryan hoped to tackle the main problems in that time. The finer details would be left to the mercy of the gods. He stressed that no personal questions must be asked. He had come only to sort out the temple. The asta mangela was for the good of the community, not for individuals. Anyway, he added with a meaningful look, if he started dealing with family problems, he would be here all week.

Kochinaryan began his preparations. He went behind the wall of a latrine to change his clothes. He reappeared wearing a brand new cream dhoti. Around his neck was a shawl edged with gold braid. We followed him into the house. The chairman's wife was hastily brushing the wooden floor of the living-room in readiness for the ceremony. She glanced at us timidly and retreated into the kitchen. The room was bare of furniture. A few pictures were nailed to the walls. There was Mahatma Gandhi, dangling at a jaunty angle, as well as posters of Shiva and Ganesh. A faded print of Lenin reminded us of Kerala's communist ties. The beloved Vladimir Ilich, with goatee beard and funereal black tie, hung next to a scuffed 1971 promotional calendar for Exide TVs featuring a sexy model in a sari.

Two fold-up metal chairs were produced for Peter and me. The priest and the committee arranged themselves in a line on the floor at the other end of the room. Kochinaryan sat at the side like a tennis umpire. He opened his briefcase and brought out a gold-plated notebook and pen. He was now ready for business.

The astrologer took on a powerful new personality as he began to direct operations. Many years of dealing with people in difficult situations had given him an assertiveness that he cleverly combined with his natural charm. He may have been short with a *Just William* haircut and bandy legs, but he flaunted the magnetism of a Hollywood star. His voice was deep, his cheekbones high, and he beamed a smile of perfect dentistry. I should imagine that he held a certain sex appeal for women.

Two small boys brought in the puja offerings – flowers, banana palm leaves, incense, betel nuts, grain and a couple of coconuts. The priest assembled them around a copper oil lamp as an offering to Ganesh.

Kochinaryan took a small sack from his briefcase. He shook out a pile of cowrie shells and washed them in a bowl of milk. They rattled against the metal sides of the bowl as he swished them around. He rinsed them in water and dried them in a cloth. Meanwhile, Krishnyer the priest drew a swastika – sign of the Sun-god Surya and used throughout India as a symbol of prosperity – on the floor in incense ash taken from the temple. Then he stood up, clasped his hands in front of his bulging tummy, and formally related the temple's problems to the astrologer. Kochinaryan nodded politely throughout the priest's speech. He removed the lid of his gold fountain pen and took some notes. The asta mangela had begun.

A boy of 12 was called into the room. This was Abhilash, the son of one of the committee members. He stood to attention in the presence of his elders, proud to be taking part in such an important village event. Kochinaryan ordered the boy to draw a twelve squares representing the signs of the zodiac on the floor in ash. The size of the squares would be significant. This is an important part of the ritual, which demands the participation of a pre-pubescent boy or girl. While Abhilash drew, the priest piled incense on the lamp and muttered prayers over the smoke. The room was filled with a sweet musky perfume.

Outside the house, a scrum of villagers was pressed against the open windows. They stared at Kochinaryan. They had come to see the star in action.

Kochinaryan asked the priest for some more rice, which caused the first hiccough of the day. The priest looked shifty. Unfortunately, he had put all the rice around the lamp as a gift to Shiva. Having given it to the god, he certainly couldn't take it back. He murmured an apology. The temple committee giggled at the priest's mistake. Kochinaryan barked an order towards the kitchen. The wife of the committee chairman appeared with a small bag of rice.

'Very special, good quality rice,' Peter remarked. 'Very scarce in the village at the moment.'

The woman handed the bag to Kochinaryan. He mixed the grain with sandalwood incense and laboriously pounded it into a paste, adding a tiny gold nugget that the temple committee had given him earlier. Having completed his task, he handed the mixture to the Abhilash, who placed small piles on each of the squares. Finally, the boy put a coconut at the centre of the design. None of us knew it at the time, but the coconut was to have a far bigger significance than any of us could have imagined.

The priest sat cross-legged and began to chant mantras to invoke the power of the gods. Another member of the temple committee sauntered into the room. He loudly apologised for being late.

I nudged Peter.

'You don't look happy.'

'I am frightened.' He pointed with mild disgust at the puja offerings. 'I do not like all this. We pray in silence and stand up when the priest comes in. And if you're late for church you're in trouble.' My friend was not enjoying himself. Everything was becoming just a touch too heathen for him.

Kochinaryan commanded Abhilash to walk around the square three times and look to the east. Having done this, the boy's job was now over. He seemed relieved. He gave a clumsy, embarrassed bow and retreated to a corner of the room.

Kochinaryan ordered the priest to search through the piles of paste for the gold. With creaking limbs the priest got down on his hands and knees and sifted through the rice. The astrologer tut-tutted. Could the priest be more careful not to disturb the rice? He added curtly that the puja offerings were incorrect – the banana should have been offered to Ganesh peeled, and not with its skin on.

The priest pulled his face into what was to become one of many grimaces of the day. His fingers searched for the nugget. He could not find it. Amid laughter from the others, the committee chairman handed over his spectacles. The priest put them on and continued to search. He gave a grunt as he found the gold. Kochinaryan noted the square on which the nugget lay and scribbled some notes in neat, tiny handwriting.

Next, the oil lamp. Kochinaryan checked the wick. It turned out to have nine threads, four leaning east and five leaning west. The smoke from the flame was blowing to the north.

Even the match that had lit the lamp was examined.

There was a brief argument over the level of the oil. The priest said it was full. His committee insisted that it was half-full. Kochinaryan invited me to have a look.

'Definitely half-full,' I said.

'No. Lamp full,' the priest said in his limited English.

'The priest has eye problems, I think,' Peter said.

This prompted more mickey-taking. The chairman offered his glasses again. The priest looked hurt and harassed. Everyone laughed at his discomfort. This was his first time at an asta mangela and he didn't have a clue what was going on.

We moved on to the most important part of the morning – the betel leaves. The astrologer took a bundle of leaves and picked out twelve at random. He held up the first leaf. It was ragged at one end suggesting that it had been munched upon by an insect. The laughter quickly subsided and the committee waited anxiously to hear Kochinaryan's verdict. The astrologer carefully examined the leaf and spoke. Considering the disastrous news he was about to deliver his voice had a surprisingly matter-of-fact quality.

'It is very bad,' Peter whispered. 'He is saying that there is decay in the leaf. This means that God is not present in the temple.' A frisson of fear went around the room. The priest wiped the sweat from his brow. The committee chairman gently drummed his fingers on the floor. Peter went on, 'He is saying that they must build a new temple.'

The committee looked at each other in horror. Build a new temple? But that would cost a fortune.

'He is saying that this is the only answer. Particularly after the flooding.'

Kochinaryan took the second leaf. This one had also had bites taken out of it.

'It shows that the people don't care about the temple,' Peter said.

The third leaf was similarly decayed, on the left side.

'The left means the moon and the moon's god is Durga. It means that they are not giving enough importance to Durga.'

The fourth leaf indicated the position of the temple. The left side was likewise damaged. This meant more problems with Durga; worse, the temple was not even in the right place. The committee was appalled. It looked like turning into an expensive day. The fifth leaf dealt with the positions of the statues. It was much smaller than the others meaning that more statues were needed. The sixth leaf had a scar running across it. People were stealing things from the temple. The committee chairman nodded dourly. Yes, the astrologer was right. Several statues had disappeared recently. The seventh leaf curled towards the left. The committee should consider swapping Durga for one of the other gods such as Ganesh.

All this talk about the different gods was getting complicated. Peter looked as baffled as I was. I was reminded of the story about the Christian and the Hindu. The Hindu asked the Christian, 'What is the difference between Hinduism and Christianity?' The Christian said, 'Well, we only have one god.' Whereupon the Hindu thought for a moment and replied, 'Which one?'

We reached the eighth leaf. The committee chattered excitedly. This leaf indicated any problems with the deities' food, or puja offerings – the direct responsibility of the priest. Krishnyer looked horribly uncomfortable. He did nervous things with his hands.

Kochinaryan held up the leaf. It was decayed on the left side. There was silence in the room as we waited for his pronouncement. The astrologer was blunt.

'He says that the priest is not right,' Peter said. 'He is not offering the right pujas to the gods and he is not saying the right mantras.'

Krishnyer was a man in pain. He opened his mouth to say something but thought better of it. He fretfully scratched his stomach instead.

We were witnessing the absolute authority of an astrologer at an asta mangela. I marvelled that the village elders were prepared to allow a complete stranger to tell them how to conduct their affairs. He held even more power than the priest. By dragging the temple's problems out into the open, Kochinaryan had assumed total charge over the religious life of the village.

The ninth leaf was equally dismal. It showed that the old people of the village did not care about the temple. The tenth leaf referred directly to the priest. Peter said, 'If there are any problems with this leaf they will replace him.' Kochinaryan beamed his dazzling smile and playfully dangled the leaf in the direction of Krishnyer. The committee laughed. Krishnyer put on a brave face and pretended to join in the fun. I could not see what they found so funny.

Krishnyer heaved his bulk off the floor. He crept forward and peered closely at the leaf. He may not have known much about an asta mangela, but one thing he did know was that his livelihood depended on this slender strip of vegetation. One miserable betel leaf and he could lose his job. He turned round, spread his arms beseechingly and said something to the committee.

'The priest is telling them there is no problem with the leaf,' Peter said. Kochinaryan shook his head. The priest was wrong. There was definitely a problem with the leaf. It was curled at one end.

Krishnyer was stunned. We waited for the bad news. Kochinaryan smiled again. A curled leaf was not the end of the world, he said. It simply meant that the priest was not conducting the right type of puja. But more important, God was not angry with him. There was no need to sack him. Deep relief spread over Krishnyer's face. He sank to the floor exhausted. It had been the tensest moment in his career.

But he was not going to give in that easily. He argued that he'd been doing the same pujas for years and no one had complained until now. Sorry chum, said Kochinaryan. Unless you change your pujas there's going to be big trouble in the temple. To rub this in, the astrologer launched into a long lecture about which pujas and mantras should be used. Krishnyer was thoroughly humiliated. He tapped his foot and chewed his lip in anger. How dare this intruder tell him how to do his job? And in front of his flock.

The eleventh leaf referred to the temple funds. Again the left side was decayed. If more prominence was given to Durga, the temple would make more money. The twelfth leaf symbolised the temple's previous priest. It was even more decayed than the others. This meant that Krishnyer's predecessor had not done his job properly either.

At this point we stopped for lunch. We strolled up the road to another house for a meal of rice and vegetables. I was surrounded by children who thought I was the funniest-looking thing they had ever seen. I spent ten minutes teaching them the English word for 'ant'.

Various committee members confided to me that Kochinaryan was startlingly accurate so far. After lunch I was taken to the flooded lake on the edge of the village and shown the temple. I could just about make out the pillars through the trees. One of the committee pointed out that, asta mangela or no asta mangela, the water had damaged the foundations so badly that it probably would fall down anyway.

'And they seem to think it's all the priest's fault,' I remarked to Peter.

'Poor man. At least Catholic priests only have one God to say prayers to.'

We returned to the chairman's house where the chairman's wife was chasing a couple of chickens out of the room in case they ate the sacred rice. Kochinaryan emerged from an afternoon nap in a back room, yawning. Asta mangelas always took it out of him.

From the betel leaves, Kochinaryan moved on to the cowrie shells. This is another system of divination that is much used in South India. He counted the pile on the floor in front of him. There were three hundred and eighty-one shells. He scribbled some calculations on his notepad and declared that this figure meant that the temple was ruled by the planet Jupiter.

The presence of Jupiter showed that a previous temple on the site had once been famous all over Kerala. If the village built a new temple, it would become even more famous. The committee exchanged satisfied looks. The idea that Alathirakkal might become a respected spiritual centre was appealing. As Peter pointed out, 'A famous temple makes more money.'

Kochinaryan shifted to an analysis of the people he had met from the village. When he had been first asked to conduct the asta mangela, three members of the committee had visited him at his office. The number three was important. It meant that the village must start worshipping three gods. Thus Ganesh should be given prominence alongside Durga and the Snake King. Furthermore, the men had got lost on the way to his office. This meant that they were ignorant. Therefore the temple worshippers were ignorant.

The three committee members laughed at Kochinaryan's undisguised rudeness. Yes, one of them admitted, they were an ignorant bunch. Their humility was touching. They were prepared to go to any lengths to make their peace with God.

Kochinaryan reminded the men that on the day of their visit another client had been waiting to see him. The three committee members had told the man that they had the first appointment of the morning and had barged in front of him. Kochinaryan explained that their act of discourtesy signified a problem on the former temple committee. Was he right in saying that everyone had been sacked and the village had started a new committee? The men looked at each other in astonishment. Yes, the chairman nodded. The astrologer was absolutely correct.

Likewise, Kochinaryan noted the first letter of the first word that the first committee member had spoken on that day. It had been 'Neyyattinkara', the name of the largest nearby town. The letter 'N' is a consonant. This indicated that the temple was very poor, that the priest didn't know how to pray and needed to devote more time to his duties.

But worst of all had been the moment earlier in the day when Kochinaryan met the priest at his house. One of the strictest rules of Hindu superstition is that you must never pick up one Brahmin – it must always be a pair. The fact that Krishnyer had been on his own was exceptionally bad luck. Krishnyer chewed his lip in despair. He must have regretted ever getting up this morning.

Kochinaryan rambled off on a long astrological exploration. We seemed to be covering a lot of old ground – the gods were hungry; they wanted better offerings; new mantras must be learned; and so on. The repetition was typical of Indian astrologers. Having started well, they tended to become rather dull. I felt hot and fidgety. Eventually I dozed off.

Raised voices woke me twenty minutes later. The chairman of the committee was waving his arms and shouting at the astrologer. I asked Peter what was going on. He explained that an argument had started over the boy Abhilash. The astrologer had told the child to pick up any object in the room. He had lifted a flower from the floor.

'Very bad,' Peter said. 'A flower means sadness in this room. If he had chosen the lamp it would have been very good.' Moreover, the boy had drawn the squares on the floor in a clockwise direction. This meant that the temple had severe financial problems.

More ominously, the astrologer had noted that Abhilash was wearing trousers the colour of ash. Ash was a bad colour. It meant that an evil spirit haunted the house where we were holding the asta mangela. This is what prompted the row.

Our host, the chairman, was outraged. Nonsense, he cried. There was no way his house was haunted. I could understand his distress. No one living in a small, fearful Indian village wants the reputation that his house is possessed.

The chairman's wife appeared at the kitchen door. She, too, was distraught at hearing this alarming news. The chairman swore that Kochinaryan had got it all wrong. An angry murmur rose from the rest of the committee as they sided with their friend. The astrologer's placid expression did not budge. He was sorry, but the house was definitely haunted. What's more, the ghost was so powerful that the family would have to do some special pujas before the temple was rebuilt.

The chairman's wife stifled a sob and fled into the kitchen. The chairman threw Kochinaryan a murderous look. He stood up, stormed past the astrologer and went to console his spouse. A smile of utter serenity had settled on the astrologer's face as if to say 'don't worry, he'll simmer down soon'.

The show was further enlivened by the arrival of the oldest man in the village, who, blind and crippled with arthritis, chose this untimely moment to stumble into the room. He wore only a dhoti into which was stuck a battered toothbrush. The man shouted in the direction of Kochinaryan. Peter translated, 'He is saying that he may be blind, but the village is even more blind. He is telling the astrologer to open their eyes because the temple has had problems for a long time.' With that, his dhoti dangling down like an elephant's trunk, the old boy groped his way back to the door and staggered out.

There was a hush while we digested all that had happened. Someone shooed away a dog that had stuck its nose in the doorway. The committee muttered amongst themselves. The sound of a quarrel came from the kitchen. The floods and the uncertainty of the village's future had produced an enormous amount of tension. Perhaps this had not been the best day for an outsider to tell the people of Alathirakkal how to run their lives.

The chairman returned. He had calmed down. He nodded curtly to Kochinaryan as if to acknowledge the astrologer's seniority. With as much dignity as he could muster, he returned to his place on the floor next to his committee.

Kochinaryan was unmoved by this passionate display and continued as if nothing had happened. His job was not to make people feel better. There was no room for tact on a matter of such importance. Everything he had said was in the stars – and therefore the word of God – and that was the end of it. Putting it mildly, the temple was a disaster and the gods were a hundred per cent unhappy. The structure needed to be razed to the ground and rebuilt.

I wondered how the village could afford such an expense, particularly after the destruction of their crops.

'They will get money from collections,' Peter said.

'But that could take years.'

Peter shrugged. The problems of superstitious Hindus were not his concern.

Kochinaryan rounded off the afternoon with another lecture about 'correct' mantras. Krishnyer the priest sat quietly in a corner nodding glumly. Having had all day to reflect, he agreed reluctantly that he had not been doing his job properly. This was difficult for him to admit and I felt sorry for him. His pride had collapsed and his bravado had been stripped away to reveal a humble man. He admitted that he knew he must change his ways; that he must spend more time in the temple.

Kochinaryan was like a dog with a particularly fascinating bone. He would not let go. Why had the priest spent so little time in the temple? Krishnyer's face paled. His voice went quiet. Perhaps, he stammered, it had something to do with his part-time job.

Part-time job? The committee sniggered. This was the moment they had been waiting for.

Yes. Part-time job. For the Kerala Transport Corporation.

Kerala Transport Corporation? Kochinaryan looked interested. Could the priest be a little more specific.

Well, yes, actually, it was a job in the ticket office at Trivandrum bus depot. He added that he'd only been able to attend today's asta mangela because he'd asked for the day off. Bus depot? Tickets? Kochinaryan could hardly contain his astonishment. He'd encountered some pretty strange experiences in his career as a travelling soothsayer, but this was the first time he'd met a priest on the buses.

From where I sat, this startling fact was beginning to make the asta mangela seem pretty pointless. The priest's moonlighting was a fairly good reason to suspect why the temple was on the disorganised side. A part-time job selling bus tickets would neither offer succour to one's congregation nor please the gods, one thinks.

Krishnyer was on the verge of tears. He was a poor man. The priesthood paid very little. He had been forced to take this job to feed his family. He stared back boldly at Kochinaryan and swore that he would do anything to keep his job and save the temple. Show him a new mantra and he would learn it; give him new statues and he would worship them. One of the committee members patted him gently on the back. There was no need for him to fret. His position as priest was secure. The committee might even consider a wage increase.

The surprises were not over yet. The humble coconut at the centre of the ashen zodiac still had to be examined in the final judgement of the day. The astrologer retrieved the coconut from the pile of puja offerings. He brandished it in the air so we could all see it.

Look! He was exultant. Look! The coconut was cracked down the middle. He handed it around. When the day started it had been a perfect specimen. But now, for some unfathomable reason, the husk had split. I could see the white flesh through a gash in the side. Kochinaryan declared that this could mean only one thing – the temple had a serious structural problem, probably a crack in the stonework.

The priest looked baffled. He knew of no such problem. Then the committee chairman spoke. Yes, there was a crack in the temple. It was in the upper portion of the main building. He had noticed it a few weeks ago. He hadn't mentioned it because he didn't want to cause the village yet more worry. The committee gasped. Peter, ever the good Christian boy, murmured, 'It's a miracle.'

Krishnyer the priest took the coconut and studied it. He rolled it over and over in his hand with an expression of deep wonderment. In an attempt to lighten the atmosphere, one of the committee asked him whether it was a male or female coconut. Krishnyer shook his head, puzzled. He confessed he had no idea. The committee burst into gales of laughter. Their priest had done nothing right that day. For if you are capable of nothing else in the palm tree state of Kerala, the one thing you should know is how to sex a coconut.

******

Kochinaryan was in a buoyant mood as we drove back towards Trivandrum. Before he dropped off Peter and me at Kovalam, he confided that he was certain that Alathirakkal temple would sort out its problems. He needed to return the following day for a thorough examination of the planets, but he had every hope that Alathirakkal would become one of Kerala's most popular places of worship.

'What about the priest?' I asked.

Oh, the priest would be okay. He'd learn his new mantras and would tackle his work with renewed enthusiasm, especially after his drubbing. Kochinaryan grinned broadly. That was the trouble with Brahmin priests. After too long in the job they became lazy. There was nothing like an asta mangela for knocking some life into a weary Brahmin.

11

Astrology and the Brain

Nearly fifty years after Independence, Bangalore retains a feel of the Raj. The capital of Karnataka state was one of the most important administration centres of nineteenth-century British India and the architecture is unshakeable colonial of the grandest kind. Lying on a cool plateau a thousand metres above sea level, the city is an elegant sprawl of parks and tree-lined boulevards. It is renowned for its excellent schools and health service and people come here from all over India looking for work opportunities.

With its brisk, businesslike atmosphere, Bangalore is not the sort of place that you associate with cosmic vibrations. Yet living here in a cosy suburban house on an acacia-shaded avenue, is B.V. Raman, India's most famous astrologer this century and astral guru to the thousands of readers of his immensely popular *Astrological Magazine*. The *AM* is an in-depth journal that includes complicated lessons in different branches of Hindu astrology. You need a basic grounding in the science before you can comprehend many of the articles – further proof of how seriously the Indian public take astrology.

Before I visited 'The Wizard', as so many of the astrologers I had met had described Raman, I wanted some questions answered. Why do people visit astrologers? What is it in a person's psychological make-up that makes him or her desperate to know the future? Why are Indians so obsessed by prediction? The man whom I thought could provide the answers was Dr R.M. Verma.

Dr Verma is India's top neurosurgeon. After working for several years at a hospital in Bristol, England, he returned to his native Bangalore to become director of the National Institute of Mental Health and Neurosurgery, the foremost psychiatric hospital in India. He spent ten years heading the institute until 1979 when he went into private practice.

I arranged to meet the doctor at his favourite watering-hole, the Bangalore Club, a dusty nineteenth-century relic of the Raj set in jungly grounds near the city centre. The place was all pillars and verandahs and Wedgwood blue paint, although the colonial effect was rather spoiled by a large yellow banner at the entrance advertising a forthcoming teenage disco on the lawns.

Inside, moth-eaten hunting trophies and pairs of crossed battle-axes hung from walls of faded cream. A few members were sunk into worn leather armchairs while bearers dressed in whites brought them pre-lunch cocktails on silver salvers. A notice on a green baize board invited participation in something called an 'open slosh tournament'. The atmosphere was solid and traditional. It was a strange place to be discussing an esoteric subject such as divination.

Dr Verma arrived soon after me. With him was a friend called Hari, who introduced himself as a counsellor working with mentally retarded children. Dr Verma led us through the hall to the coffee room. We settled around a table overlooked by the glassy eyes of a stuffed leopard.

The doctor was a man of medium stature with a large rectangular moustache plonked across his upper lip like a clothes brush. He wore a grey tweed jacket and on one finger sported a huge emerald ring. I had heard that his skills of oratory were much in demand on the conference circuit where he had a reputation for doing little jigs around the microphone. He was an energetic man, expressive and noisy, and once he got talking there was no stopping him. He reminded me of the exuberant Grandpa Munster in the 1960s US television show.

I secretly hoped that Dr Verma would come up with a scathing attack on astrologers and all so-called experts in prediction. Maybe it was my western conditioning, but I had imagined that such a big name in the psychiatric field would be especially damning of people who dabbled in the whimsical world of horoscopes. But nothing is straightforward in India. As I was to discover, my host was an impassioned disciple of astrology, even though he had known patients who had developed severe mental problems as a result of taking their stars too seriously. What's more, he regularly visited astrologers himself.

Dr Verma began by describing the different categories of people who visit astrologers. I sat back and listened as he took over the conversation. The first group of people are terrified of astrologers.

'Whether it is good or bad they are frightened of what they might be told. We will not waste time on this group. They are not important.'

The second group desperately need guidance to solve their problems. Of these people, some are positive and hear only the good things the astrologer says while the others hear only the bad.

'This is the type with the psychological disorder. They are doomsday people, often of inadequate intelligence, seeking astrology like seeking drugs or alcohol. They are obsessed by wanting to know the future.'

The third group visit astrologers out of curiosity and for mild entertainment.

'They derive considerable benefit out of astrology. It is an attraction to the unknown and they only listen to the good things. If a person in this group likes something, he remembers it. If he doesn't like it, he forgets it.'

'I suppose I'm in the third group,' I said, although I was beginning to doubt it. I had a nasty suspicion that I was one of Dr Verma's second group obsessives.

As for the astrologers themselves, the first type is the exploiter. He is wildly inaccurate and terrifies his clients.

'The problem is that if he is the first astrologer you go to, you will think that maybe everyone is like that.'

Astrologers of the second type was what Dr Verma described as a 'left-brain person'.

'Do you know the difference between the brains?' he asked me.

''Fraid not.'

'The right brain is creative and can see across time and space. The left brain is linear, applying only to logical reasoning. These left-brain astrologers are purely expert calculators. They work within the system they have learned and they communicate their predictions irrespective of your sensitivity. They may produce undesirable effects on a person because you may hear a truth that you don't want to be told. For example, what disease you will die from.'

The doctor temporarily suspended his lecture to click his fingers at a bearer. We had been sitting for fifteen minutes during which time the servant had been hovering by the door and had made no attempt to approach us. Because we had not asked him to bring us tea, he had not asked if we wanted any. Highly significant stuff, according to the doctor.

The bearer sauntered over at Dr Verma's command. After taking our order, he wandered off to the kitchen. The doctor's eyes followed the man's back. He talked about his specimen like a Victorian anthropologist.

'Now that fellow is a left-brain person. Because we didn't ask for tea he didn't bring us any. But we are sitting in a club at 11.30 in the morning and any creative person might expect we would want something to drink.'

The other group of astrologers uses an holistic approach. They are transpiritual, finding strength from God and combining their calculations with intuitive perception.

'They are the most pleasant astrologers to go to,' Dr Verma said. 'They are authentic because they know the science but they feel at the same time. After seeing one you are left on a high. They think of astrology as a process and not as a state. They will tell you bad things might happen but that you can avoid them by taking precautions.'

'And they always ask if you want tea?'

'Exactly. They are what I call creative psychotherapists.'

Dr Verma paused to smooth his moustache. The bearer returned, and arranged the tea things on the table barely acknowledging us, noiselessly returning to his station by the kitchen door.

'Not a creative fellow,' Dr Verma tut-tutted. 'A creative person would have poured for us.' Instead, it was given to the doctor to play mother. He briskly filled our cups from a silver-plated teapot decorated with the club crest. He took a gulp of tea and moved on to his personal experiences.

'I have consulted astrologers many times and it has never disturbed me.'

'So it's a bit of fun for you,' I said.

'Exactly. Curiosity. Like exploration in science.'

I made the point that a senior medical man of his position in Britain or America was unlikely to have ever visited an astrologer. Indeed, they would probably regard astrology with the utmost suspicion. Why was India so different?

Dr Verma was suddenly on his guard. He had little time for narrow-minded western attitudes.

'Doctors in the West conform to a fixed framework and moving out of that framework will get them the sack. I would lose my credibility if I talked about astrology in a hi-tech hospital in England. As a neurosurgeon I am expected to conform to the scientific and to reject everything else.'

'But why is everyone in India so obsessed by astrology?'

Dr Verma looked at me sharply.

'That is a statement made from a closed mind.'

'Fair enough. But I come from that sort of society.'

'The simple answer is that in the East we are more open than you.' He talked at great speed.' It is not a question of belief or disbelief. There are tremendous advantages in being open and not closed. One of my favourite sayings is, "Attitudes harden earlier than arteries". In an open system you may end up with inaccuracy, but at least you do not become biased. You have the freedom to utilise all these parameters to come to a judgement.'

Our conversation was developing a competitive edge with the doctor's skills in argument proving superior to mine. He would have made a good defence brief for a man on a murder charge. I asked if some Indian psychiatrists might disagree with him.

'You will always find people like that,' he sniffed. And what about those people with intense neurosis from believing their horoscopes too much?

'They would be prone to mental problems anyway,' came the swift reply. Quite simply, the benefits of astrology could be enormous.

'Suppose a man has a brain tumour and I have to operate. If the astrologer tells him the day before his operation he will live for twenty years, the man will come to me quite happily.'

'But he might die two days later.'

'He might. But when I do the operation he is perfectly peaceful, and that is good, is it not?'

But what about the astrologer who tells his client that there's nothing wrong with him when actually he is seriously ill?

'Then he doesn't consult me and he dies of a brain tumour.'

'But that's not very healthy, is it?'

'No, it is terrible. But it doesn't degrade the positive point of astrology.'

Until now, Dr Verma's friend Hari had said little except for occasional words of praise like 'wonderful, beautiful' whenever Dr Verma uttered something particularly pithy. Hari seemed to regard the garrulous doctor as sort of guru. Now he piped up, 'My mother goes to an astrologer. When she comes back looking most cheerful I am happy, but when she has heard something that doesn't make her happy then it worries me slightly.'

I looked at Dr Verma. 'And do you think that is healthy?'

'Life is like that. Is every day always bright for you?'

I played devil's advocate.

'Bearing in mind that there is little proof about whether astrology works, surely it would be better if people didn't go to astrologers at all.'

'Pah! No one complains about lotteries. I have seen people not believing in astrology tossing a coin to decide whether they should come for an operation.' Hari and I laughed. Dr Verma protested that he was being totally serious. 'And anyway, if you are not happy with your astrologer, you can go to another one and get a second opinion. The answer is to be open-minded and then you won't become obsessed about anything.'

'That's beautiful,' Hari murmured.

Our conversation took a downward turn, a case of East versus West with neither prepared to budge. I have to admit that my opinion was being coloured by my own doubts about how healthy it was for me to hear about the future. The trouble began when the doctor began telling a story about a late sage from Madurai who could tell everything about a person's background and personality by doing nothing more than feel their pulse. I had heard this sort of thing before in India. Numerous people claimed to know of psychics who could tell you your name and your father's name, even what you had for breakfast that day. The problem was they had never actually met these people themselves. It was always 'a friend of mine' who was told. I wondered how much was truth and how much urban myth.

I told Dr Verma this, and how the great Mauni-Baba, for example, had been so reluctant to tell me anything about myself. My attitude annoyed him.

'Do not judge by example,' he scolded.

'I'm just looking forward to meeting someone who will tell me what my name is, where I come from and all the rest.'

'You have not seen the right person,' Dr Verma snapped.

'Well, I'd love to meet the right one. Just give me a name and I'll be genuinely impressed.'

'I know of several people. But if you have a powerful bias against this sort of thing it won't work.'

'So you mean that because I have a bit of reasonable doubt . . .'

'If I go to someone with a sceptical mind, he will be ineffective even if he is a god.'

'So if I don't believe the man in the first place, he will not be able to tell me anything? That's a spurious argument. Very neat.'

Hari interrupted. He was angry that I dared contradict his champion.

'If I go to a doctor who I believe cannot cure me, he will never cure me,' he said. 'If I go with an open mind, he might be able to cure me.'

'All I want,' I sighed, 'is to meet someone who knows nothing about me and who can tell everything about me.'

'This can happen,' Dr Verma said.

'But has it ever happened to you?'

'I have never gone to such a person.'

'Neither have I,' Hari joined.

'But I know of people who have,' Dr Verma said.

'So do I,' Hari said.

I was exasperated.

'That's exactly what I'm saying. Everyone in this country seems to know someone who is supposed to have gone to a person like this, but when it comes to the crunch no one is prepared to come up with a name.'

The atmosphere was turning grim. In an attempt to switch to a less controversial subject, I made a admiring remark about Dr Verma's emerald ring. Bad move.

'That's a lovely emerald,' I said. 'Do you wear it for astrological reasons? To attract the power of the planets?'

'No.'

Dr Verma suddenly went quiet. He did not want to talk about his ring. I pressed him. Surely he could tell me something about it?

'It was a present,' he said flatly.

'A present?'

Dr Verma explained that a few years earlier he had attended a symposium at the ashram of a certain Sai Baba, one of the most famous yoga gurus in India and probably the richest with a worldwide empire worth around three hundred million pounds. The shock-headed Sai Baba, who boasts a fifty-million-strong following of Indians and westerners, claims to possess magical powers. There has been much debate about him. His disciples argue that 'he is God because he acts like God'. They are convinced he is a genuine holy man of the highest standing. Critics denounce him as a fraud and reject his 'miracles', such as materialising apples from mango trees, as nothing more than competent conjuring tricks. They cite a July 1993 assassination attempt on the guru by four disgruntled devotees, saying that if he truly possessed supernormal powers he would have foreseen the attack and made himself scarce that day.

'And are you a devotee of Sai Baba?' I asked the doctor. Dr Verma reacted defensively.

'You are asking a wrong question,' he chided. 'I am open to anyone.'

'I would have thought it's a perfectly reasonable question.'

'No it is not. Don't ask that question.'

I felt like a child whose wrist had been slapped. Dr Verma composed himself and went on to say that at the end of the symposium Sai Baba called him and his wife over for a chat.

'He took my hand and materialised this ring. That was eight years ago. It remains on my finger. I don't know where it came from.'

So that was it. This brilliant man, one of the top neurosurgeons in India and the former head of the country's number one psychiatric hospital was telling me that a baba had materialised an emerald ring onto his finger. My open-mindedness was stretched to its limits. The culture gap between West and East was turning into a vast, gaping chasm.

'How do you mean, materialised?' I said.

'He just put his palm over my hand,' the doctor mimicked the action, 'and it appeared. He does this to many people. It was given with great love.'

'I'm sure it was. But it's the materialising aspect I'm not so certain about. It sounds like a magic trick to me.'

'I don't care whether it was magic or not. The point is that it was given with love.'

'Well, if I was given a gold ring with a large emerald in it, I wouldn't care where it came from either.'

'In the context of love, there is no difference between magic and miracles.'

'I suppose not if you take the line that it's the thought that counts.'

My interview with the doctor had degenerated into a battle of wills with neither of us prepared to concede ground. My western conditioning made it almost impossible for me to see his point of view. I eventually left after Dr Verma and Hari promised to find that elusive expert in divination who could tell me everything about myself by merely looking at me. I left this challenge with several other people in India. I have not heard a thing since.

*****

B.V. Raman's large house was to be found in a leafy enclave of Bangalore. I walked up a short flight of steps and through a side door into the cramped offices of the *Astrological Magazine*. A couple of girls in saris pounded ancient manual typewriters. On the wall above them a poster advertised a recent issue: 'Will there be a World War in 2000 AD? Buy your copy from your newsagent today!'

One of the girls looked up from her work. She was busy and bothered, with little time to deal with visitors. She was startled when I announced that I had come to see her boss. He saw few visitors these days and I imagined that he was constantly plagued by fans arriving at his house unannounced.

'And do you have an appointment?' she asked with a tilt of her nose. 'As a matter of fact, I do.'

She eyed me cautiously, gathered the folds of her sari and got up. She went into the next room, and returned looking surprised. Yes, I did have an appointment. A few minutes later she showed me into the great man's office.

At first glance, B.V. Raman was rather a disappointment, small and extremely ordinary looking. I had expected someone more formidable, perhaps a larger than life guru with a twirly Gallic moustache and ruffled silk shirt. But here was a modest little man in polyester-cotton and grey flannel. With his horn-rimmed glasses he looked more like a bank manager than the father of twentieth-century Indian astrology.

He was fit for a man of 81, with a boyish face.

'I practise yoga every day,' he explained with a gentle smile. 'So I do not have any of the diseases of civilisation. Like age.'

B.V. Raman's extraordinary talent for astrology was first noticed by his grandfather, himself a well-known astrologer. By the age of 13 the schoolboy Raman had already memorised the entire *Jataka Chandrica*, the foremost Hindu astrological teaching manual, and was practising his skills on the citizens of his home city of Mysore in South India.

Divination was beginning to rule his life. In his autobiography he reveals a simple and ancient method of Hindu divination that he learned as a teenager. Use it to discover whether a task, meeting, date etc will be successful. Think of any three-figure number. Then add the numbers together until you reach a single figure, e.g. 248 = 2 + 4 + 8 = 14 = 1 + 4 = 5. (If your total is 9, try again.) Your final number represents a planet and may be interpreted as follows:

1 The Sun. Your task will be partly successful, your ambition realised.

2 Mars. Will result in quarrels; beware of accidents and enemies.

3 Jupiter. Success guaranteed. Access to wealth, realisation of desires, smooth sailing in all affairs.

4 Mercury. Much effort necessary. Skin problems, trouble from domestic animals, loss of business unless you work hard.

5 Venus. Success and pleasant happenings. Good sexual enjoyment, happiness with your partner; excellent time for making money.

6 Saturn. Much effort necessary. Indigestion, emotional pain, misunderstandings and bad results in general.

7 The Moon. Not bad. Mental peace, domestic happiness and acquisition of desired object.

8 Rahu. Not successful. Misunderstandings.

At the age of 14 the precocious Raman made his first major

prediction. He declared that the stars foretold that both he and his grandfather were about to die.

'The adage "a little learning is a dangerous thing" applied to me in its entirety,' he recalls. 'My grandfather scolded me for my impertinence and pretensions. Of course, I had got it all wrong and we both remained very much alive. Grandfather warned me that longevity should not be predicted without a very careful examination of the horoscope. It is something I have never forgotten.'

The *Astrological Magazine* was originally started early this century by Raman's grandfather, who closed it down in 1924 due to lack of funds. In 1936 it was relaunched with the 25-year-old Raman as editor. He was on his way to becoming known as the world's foremost authority on Hindu astrology.

The magazine gained a reputation for unnerving accuracy. The October 1937 issue included an article which analysed the birth charts of Mussolini and Hitler. Raman claimed that a European war was certain in 1939, but he declared that the position of Mercury in Hitler's chart would eventually 'pull him down as speedily as he rose to power'.

He continued to publish his predictions throughout the war, but he had to tread carefully. The British realised that his magazine could be a powerful propaganda tool. He was frequently visited by military personnel, who issued veiled threats that predictions not favourable to the Allies could land him in trouble. Ironically, the same officers often sought his advice about their own futures.

Raman's rise to fame continued. He became well known outside India and the highpoint of his career came in 1970 when he delivered an astrological lecture to the United Nations. When I met him, he had recently returned from one of his regular lecture tours of America. Back home, he was in the process of redesigning his magazine. The latest issue featured the first full-colour cover. He proudly showed me a copy. It was headlined 'Future Of The British Monarchy' and was illustrated with possibly the most unflattering snapshot of the Queen ever taken. Her face was screwed up in torment, her mouth hanging open in pain.

'Where on earth did you find that picture?' I asked.

'I don't know, probably a library somewhere.' Raman was delighted that he had impressed his English guest. He added cheerfully, 'Her Majesty looks unhappy, doesn't she?' As well she should, if the predictions in the *Astrological Magazine* were anything to go by. The article claimed that the sovereign was in for a tough time until the end of this decade. 'Saturn . . . presages a period of great tension, anxiety, personal unhappiness as well as physical danger.'

'Will it be that bad for her?' I asked.

'It will be a period of tremendous change.'[1]

The Wizard sat behind a blockhouse of a desk in a room lined with bookcases stuffed with leatherbound books and ledgers. A big old green metal fan blew a brisk breeze. Raman directed me to a chair opposite him and we shook hands. His fingers were pencil thin and finely formed; his palms bore deep, firm lines denoting a strong character and sense of purpose. I wanted to ask if I could take a closer look at his hands but I did not have the courage. Somehow you just don't do that sort of thing with India's greatest living astrologer. Raman began by describing the qualities of a good astrologer.

'He should have no hatred, no jealousy, no vengeance and no bitterness. He should be spiritually inclined, a contented man.'

'Are you a contented man?' I asked.

'I am a contented man.'

He never charged for his services, and lived off the profits of his magazine and more than forty books. He retired from doing personal consultations ten years earlier and only saw people privately today in special circumstances.

'I will see someone who is in distress. A man may come to me and says his wife is seriously ill and the doctors may say that she won't live. I will give him some relief and tell him that his wife will not die.'

'Do you ever lie?' I asked.

'When I see the horoscope of a person I first find out his mental make-up. If a person is thinking of committing suicide I will not tell him he will do it. Instead, I will ask his close friends or relatives to come and meet me and then I will hear about his tendencies.

'One of the most important things to know is that astrology is a science of tendencies. We are living in a world of relativity, there is nothing absolute. What is happiness unless you have experienced misery? When you have developed your spiritual powers to such an extent that you are not bothered with this world, you need not show your horoscope to anybody. But so long as we are part and parcel of this universe, and we have families and so on, the horoscope guides us.'

....

[1] India's astrologers feel there is some kind of mystical link between India and the British Royal Family. Prince Charles was born on 14 November, which happened to be the birthday of the late, great Pandit Jawaharlal Nehru. Princess Anne was born on 15 August, which is also Indian Independence Day. Coincidence, or strange forces at work?

Without exception, all the Indian astrologers I had met claimed that the planets affected us because of the their special energy, whether it be magnetic, gravitational or light. Raman dismissed this as a romantic notion.

There was no proof whatsoever that the planets had any effect on us. Instead, he believed that astrology was empirical having evolved over the years through observation. He rested the tips of his fingers gently on the edge of his desk.

'We simply don't know whether the planets influence mankind. Scientists all over the world are desperately trying to prove that the planets give out some sort of force but they are groping in the dark. Astrology has developed by example and not because of any scientific reason. Over the centuries people noticed that certain things happened depending on certain combinations of the planets. For example, Mars in the second house always tended to result in a death. Astrologers today continue to observe these things and so it goes on.' For this reason he had little time for the use of astro-gems.

'It is a practice that is abused,' he sniffed. 'Yoga or the saying of mantras is better than wearing an expensive stone. You must work in order to change yourself.' Likewise, he dismissed the daily 'stars' in newspapers. To divide humanity into twelve groups and predict on the basis of sun signs alone was illogical. 'But then commercialisation is the bane of astrology whether in India or elsewhere.'

I admired his honesty. Bearing in mind the lack of proof of planetary power, did he accept that astrology had its shortcomings?

'Any science has shortcomings,' came the blunt reply. 'That's why we can't find a cure for AIDS.'

After all these years, Raman has remained passionate about his subject. He has consistently championed the theory that all astrology – and indeed all types of occult prediction – began in India and was taken up later by the Chaldeans and Babylonians.

Raman insists that Indian astrology has an important part to play in the world. Like his Hindu colleagues, he believes that the spiritually blind West could learn much from the technologically lame East. A greater understanding of the Vedic sciences would benefit countries like Britain and America. Okay, many people in India were so mystical that they had become lazy. God was controlling their fate, they said, so why should they work hard? But, conversely, the West was too obsessed by material comforts.

'The problem is that western science equates a human being with matter,' he added. 'To us a human being is matter *and* spirit. You spend your time in the West trying to right the body. We can offer the spirit back as well. Indian social life is so hard that we are forced to undertake certain religious practices to see that our minds are kept clean. That is yoga. Likewise astrology keeps our minds clean.'

Despite being trumpeted as a twentieth-century phenomenon, western psychology, Raman insisted, was as old as the Himalayas.

'Our greatest psychologist was Lord Krishna. He said that tensions arise because of our hatred, jealousy and all that, and when tensions arise the mind is affected. Supposing a man gets a telegram that he has won a hundred thousand dollars in a lottery. He becomes so happy he might even die. If he learns that he has lost a hundred thousand dollars, he collapses. Extremes. Lord Krishna said take things easy; let there be no extremes.'

During the 1950s Raman corresponded with the Swiss psychiatrist Karl Jung.

'Jung told me that in all complicated cases of psychological analysis he always studied the horoscope. He said that astrological data elucidated certain points which he would have otherwise been unable to understand.'

The old man's eyes were bright with happiness. He was proud of his relationship with such a master of the mind. He was proud that a westerner of such stature had officially acknowledged his beloved science. But, of course, the Indian sages had known the power of astrology over man for centuries.

'An experienced astrologer can find out the mental structure of an individual far quicker than a psychologist. The horoscope is a blueprint for the future. For example, if the Moon is with Venus, the man will be sensual and thinking only of this world. Your British poet Lytton had Venus with the Moon and he never touched philosophy. But Emerson had the Moon with Jupiter so he wrote on philosophical works. Then, if the Moon is with Mars, the man will be a distressed personality. With Saturn, he will be schizophrenic.

'Abraham Lincoln and Charles Darwin were born on the same day and we find similar combinations. Lincoln became great in politics and Darwin became great as a naturalist. But their ascendants were different. Therefore, Lincoln was assassinated and Darwin lived to old age.'

Raman chuckled softly. 'And to think that in the West they describe this sort of thinking as New Age. To us Hindus it is very old age.'

What about today's India? Was it not becoming increasingly materialistic? Had not the chance to own a colour TV become the most important goal of many Indians? Raman sighed. This was the fault of the West. 'The urban population in India is becoming more materialistic because they have been exposed to the West by the media. But even though they may superficially show that they are materialistic, their belief in God and their acceptance of our culture and the values of life have not changed. This consumerism does not appeal to us. If you want comfort, the mind must be controlled. It should not be exposed to too many sensual things.'

I asked Raman for his view of the future. Did the planets point to big changes in the next millennium?

'There will be a change after the year 2000, a spiritual change for the better.' Another light chuckle. 'It will be a big change and India will be taking care of the rest of the world.'

Epilogue: The Future of the World

Make a note in your diary for 20 May 2000 – 'Stay in bed.' For that is the day that the world begins its big change. It is the day that Saturn moves into conjunction with Jupiter. The last time that happened was in 1939.

Virtually every seer I spoke to on my travels claimed that we were heading for the Third World War, or at least a similar cataclysmic event. The astrological forecast is made even more doomladen by the fact that Saturn enters the star of Rohini (known in English as Aldebaran) in 2002. Saturn in Rohini is known for causing war, devastation and famine. So it comes as little surprise to hear that the conjunction first occurred this century during 1914–18.

Quite how things will turn out in the next millennium is uncertain. K.N. Rao believes it can only be bad. During one of our teatime chats in Delhi he told me that Europe and America would suffer until 2002. Before we reached the exciting subject of Armageddon, Rao asked me how much I believed in astrology. It is a question friends have posed many times since I returned home. Bearing in mind how many events from my past had been accurately pinpointed, I told Rao that I believed about fifty fifty.

'You are open-minded for someone with so little experience in the science,' he laughed. 'At the most I, with all my knowledge of the subject, would say that only seventy per cent of what I hear or say is true.'

'And, anyway,' I added, 'I forget most of the disturbing things I hear.'

'That is good. Then you will not worry about the year 2000.'

Rao's view of the future was particularly gloomy for Europe. He predicted the collapse of the European Union and economic turmoil. Of all the western countries, Britain would face the toughest time.

'I don't see the end of the world, but I definitely predict that world culture will undergo a total change and the superpowers will vanish. England will suffer greatly. I don't see much future for England beyond the year 2000.'

'So it's time for me to move countries?'

'A good idea . . . will you have some more tea?'

Was it possible to change our destiny?

'Yes, through leading good moral lives. But most people in the West aren't interested in leading moral lives.'

And the future of India?

'We will give up our present habit of aping and not emulating the West. Aping implies taking the worst characteristics of a society. The West has some good things to offer like deep scientific investigation, but that is where we should leave it.'

Later in Bangalore, B.V. Raman was evasive when I asked him for his view of the future. (Despite my vow not to ask personal questions, a decision that had brought me untold relief, I had made an exception regarding more global matters.) The senior sage stared at his feet and looked uncharacteristically restless. I mentioned the much-quoted French medieval prophet Nostradamus who talked about China fighting the West in 1999 with Russia joining the side of America and Europe. Raman winced and gritted his teeth.

If you want to make an Indian astrologer really cross, just mention the name of Nostradamus. K.N. Rao reckons Nostradamus is 'the biggest menace to the growth of honest, intellectual and scientific astrology that the world has ever known'. He says that so many politically volatile predictions have been made in the name of the Gallic seer that an international espionage agency could be behind the Nostradamus industry.

And Raman? 'To put any credence to Nostradamus is absurd,' he said. He conceded that Nostradamus was a great astrologer, but unscrupulous publishers have rewritten his verses to make them sound more controversial than originally intended. 'These translators came across a word like Hister and say it is Hitler, which is nonsense. Hister is plainly not Hitler. There is no scientific logic to it. The Nostradamus paperbacks published before the Second World War said hostilities would cease in 1942. Now they have all been changed to say it ended in 1945. Nostradamus's name has been exploited so much for commercial purposes that I don't give any importance to his so-called forecasts.'

I pushed Raman for *his* predictions for 2000. He reluctantly gave me his views. He did not agree with Rao that we could expect the worst. Things would not be so bad after all.

'There is no immediate threat to the world.' He allowed a slight smile. 'You can be sure that it will continue for another four hundred thousand years at least.' This was more like it.

'And human life?' I asked.

'Oh, human life will continue. I know some people are terrified of environmental pollution, but nature always has its safety valves.'

What about the next world war that his magazine was so fond of discussing?

'There may be some sort of world war,' he said cagily.

I pointed out that this was not the first time this century that the world's future has been in doubt. On 5 February 1962, holy men throughout India sat up all night waiting for the big nuclear bang which was expected to be the result of a conjunction of the main planets in Capricorn. On the other side of the world, twenty-two members of an American society called 'Understanding Inc.' retreated to a small town in the Arizona mountains which they considered, for some reason, to be the one place to survive the catastrophe.

'No it is not the first time,' Raman agreed. 'But on 20 May 2000, you can expect events of a very great magnitude to take place.'

'What will happen?' Raman trod cautiously.

'So far as the future is concerned, I have not made any deep studies, but probably the fight will be between Europe and the Arab powers. Probably a fight between the West and Islam. After this war there may be a change in the attitudes of many of these nations, especially in Arabia where they will become more sensible. There will be a new world order, a new spirituality.'

The question was burning my tongue. 'Who will win?'

The old astrologer leaned back in his chair, arms folded. He carefully prepared his answer. Would it be sugar-coated to keep his customer happy? Or did a matter of this importance demand a straight reply?

The Wizard spoke quietly.

'The western democracies will win. You need not worry about that.'

I cannot be sure he was telling the truth.

Bibliography

Abbott, J., *The Keys of Power: A Study of Indian Ritual and Belief*, University Books Inc., New Jersey, 1974

Ayer, V. A. K., *Judging People at First Sight*, Raj's Astro Research Centre, Bangalore, 1991

Bhattacharyya, Benoytosh, *Gem Therapy*, Firma KLM Private, Calcutta, 1957

Chophel, Norbu, *Folk Culture of Tibet*, The Library of Tibetan Works and Archives, Dharamsala, 1983

Curry, Patrick, *A Confusion of Prophets*, Collins and Brown, London, 1992

David-Neel, Alexandra, *With Mystics and Magicians in Tibet*, The Bodley Head, London, 1931

Defouw, Hart, and Svoboda, Robert, *Light On Life: An Introduction To The Astrology Of India*, Penguin Arkana, London, 1996

Dreyer, Ronnie Gale, *Indian Astrology*, The Aquarian Press, London, 1990

Dubois, Abbe J. A. , *Hindu Manners, Customs and Ceremonies*, Oxford Clarendon Press, 1906

Iyer, N. C., *The Brihat Samhita* (English Translation), Sri Satguru Publications, Delhi, 1987

Joshi, Janardan, *Oriental Astrology, Darwinism and Degeneration*, Pioneer Press, Allahabad, 1906

Knappert, Jan, *An Encyclopaedia of Myth and Legend: Indian Mythology*, Indus, London, 1992

MacNeice, Louis, *Astrology*, Aldus Books, London, 1964

Majumder, Harihar, *Hindu Science of the Future*, Chhatra Siksha Nikitan, Calcutta, 1983

Mookerjee, Ajit, *Khanna, Madhu, The Tantric Way*, Thames and Hudson, London, 1977

Nathan, R. S., *Symbolism in Hinduism*, The Central Chinmaya Mission Trust, Bombay, 1989

Parker, Derek, *Astrology In the Modern World*, Tapliger, New York, 1970

Parker, Derek, *The Question of Astrology*, Eyre and Spottiswoode, London, 1970

Raman, B. V. *Hindu Astrology and the West*, Raman Publications, Bangalore, 1991

Raman, B. V., *A Manual of Hindu Astrology*, IBH Prakashana, Bangalore, 1988

Raman, B. V., *Planetary Influences on Human Affairs*, Raman Publications, 1991

Raman, B.V. *Prasna Marga Parts l and ll* (English Translation), Motilal Banarsidars Publishers, Delhi, 1991.

Rao, R. G., *Your Face Mirrors Fortune*, Ranjan Publications, New Delhi.

Sen, K. C., *The Indian Science of Hand Reading*, Treasure House of Books, Bombay,

Singh, Prahlad, *Jantar-Mantars of India*, Holiday Publications, Jaipur, 1986.

Tester, Jim, *A History of Western Astrology*, Boydell Press, 1987

Vasudev, Gayatri Devi, *Astrology and the Hoax of 'Scientific Temper'*, Dr B. V. Raman and Mrs Rajeswari Raman Foundation, Bangalore, 1989

Vasudev, Gayatri Devi, *Practical Horary Astrology*, Raman Publications, Bangalore, 1991

Index